CONCEPT OF LAW
IN
ENGLISH-SPEAKING
AFRICA
By

C. OGWURIKE, LL.M.; Ph.D. (Lond)
Of Gray's Inn Barrister-at-Law;
Barrister and Solicitor of the Supreme Court of Nigeria;
Formerly Professor and Dean, Faculty of Law,
Makerere University, Kampala

NOK Publishers International
New York • London • Lagos

Published in the United States of America
    by NOK Publishers International Ltd.

and simultaneously
    by NOK Publishers (Nigeria) Ltd.

Library of Congress Catalog Card Number 78-64622
International Standard Book Number 0-88357067-X

Printed in the United States of America

CONCEPT OF LAW
IN
ENGLISH-SPEAKING
AFRICA

NOK LEGAL STUDIES SERIES

Already published
INTERNATIONAL LAW PERSPECTIVES
OF THE DEVELOPING COUNTRIES:
The Relationship of Law and Economic Development to Basic Human Rights
by Charles C. Okolie, *formerly Legal Research Scholar, Harvard Law School.*

To Jim and Peggy Gower

CONTENTS

PART I
THE SCIENCE OF JURISPRUDENCE

PART II
THE CORPUS JURIS

PART III
THEORIES OF LAW

Acknowledgments

My thanks are due to my colleagues in the University of Lagos, Nigeria, and the University of Ghana, Legon. I am particularly grateful to Professor R.B. Seidman for helpful discussions, criticisms and stimulation at the initial stages of the work, and for his assistance with references to some works cited. I am much indebted to my colleagues of Makerere University, Kampala, and to the librarian who made most of the reference books available to me. Thanks also to Mrs. Chinwe Amechi of the College of Management and Technology, Enugu, who proofread the typed scripts and checked the references.

NOK Publishers have given me both encouragement and help in most generous measures that I will always remember.

Finally, it is a pleasure to be able to acknowledge the great debt I owe my friend and colleague, Professor J.S. Read of the School of Oriental and African Studies, University of London. Without his guidance and encouragement, this book would never have been written.

The responsibility for the opinions expressed or any errors or omissions remains mine.

Chijioke Ogwurike

Owerri
September, 1978

Preface

Concept of Law in English-speaking Africa is a book on jurisprudence written with a practical approach to the philosophy of law for African students. It is divided into ten chapters and has an introduction.

The whole work is made up of four parts. Part 1 (Introduction) deals with the Science of Jurisprudence. It gives the student a general idea of the subject. Part 2 (Chapters 1-2) deals with the sources of Law in English-speaking Africa, the hierarchy of the courts, and the technique adopted by the courts in dealing with the various sources when administering the law. Part 3 of the book (Chapters 3-8) gives a general short survey of various theories of law in a rather historical sequence pointing out, where necessary, the problems of the periods of the writers and the possible factors that might have influenced their legal thinking. This part of the work is intended to give the student just enough working knowledge of the various legal theories to be used by him as a working tool to analyze laws within his own system and in the light of the socio-economic and political background of his country. Part 4 (Chapters 9-10) deals with law and society, and ends with a general evaluation of laws in English-speaking Africa.

The author has had the opportunity of studying the legal systems of several countries *in situ* in both Western and Eastern Africa and has taught law in some of the universities in those areas.

Table of Cases:

Table of Laws and Statutes:

PART I
THE SCIENCE
OF JURISPRUDENCE

Introduction

To adopt the view of Holmes, as was elaborated by Friedmann, "Law is not a brooding omnipotence in the sky." It is "a flexible instrument of social order," based on the political, economic and social values of the society which it is meant to serve. The legal conditions of any society have therefore to be constantly reassessed and readjusted to meet the ever-changing social needs and requirements of the time.

Jurisprudence as a legal philosophy which deals with law, its scope, function and principles as opposed to actual legal rules, cannot have a specifically limited and technical meaning for all time, even in a given society. All legal philosophers that we know of have been the products of their respective times. Their conception of law cannot be fully divorced from their social, economic and political experiences in life. To try to fit all or some of their various legal expositions into the African situation in our period is apt to bring contradictory and inadequate results. It is on this score that we have undertaken to reexamine legal notions and the scope and province of jurisprudence in the light of the African situation.

Meaning of "Jurisprudence"

The story of jurisprudence has been "one of movements of thought and ever changing ideas."[1] This is so because "law," the subject matter of jurisprudence is, unlike the natural sciences, a social fact, and no society ever remains static.[2] Secondly, societies differ in history and culture, among other things, and the political philosophy of one community is often at variance with that of another community. Even where two independent communities adopt the same political ideology, its interpretation by them differ more often than not. There are no universal rules of law, and jurisprudence is not concerned with the study of actual rules of law. In a fundamental and general sense, it includes an overall study of the doctrine of law. Paton describes jurisprudence as "a particular method of study, not of the law of one country, but of the general notion of law itself."[3]

From the inception of jurisprudence as a method of study, however, the word has acquired various limited meanings. Literally, the word taken from the Latin word *iurisprudentia* means "knowledge of law." Ulpian, in the Digest, defines it as "divinarum humanorumque rerum notitia iusti vel iniusti scientia"[4] (the concept of things human and divine, the science of the just or the unjust). The first part of his definition is too wide and could include the concept of religion. The reference to divinity is a reflection of ancient times when the knowledge of law and its practical application was a privilege and a monopoly of the board of the patrician pontiffs.

The second is a definition of jurisprudence of a later Roman period when legal knowledge became secular. During this period the XII Tables[5] and the Ius Civile Flavianum[6] were published. Both documents and public teaching of law helped to secularize knowledge of law. Roman jurists at this time were very active and their extensive activities included the drafting of legal forms for legal transactions, the drafting of wills, assisting litigants in questions of procedure and forms, and the giving of opinions (responsa) on questions of law addressed to them by private individuals, magistrates, or judges. Responsa were given in writing or orally. From the time of Augustus the practice acquired an official character: it could be practiced by jurists authorized by the Emperor (ius respondendi). At this stage responsa delivered ex auctoritate principis, in writing and sealed, had a decisive authority in the trial for which they were issued. Under Hadrian, responsa received binding force even though they had been issued in similar cases by now defunct jurists. Only if different opinions were produced did the judge have a free hand in deciding a case.

Such was the way the Romans promoted the evolution of legal science. Being members of the Consilia of magistrates, jurisprudents, as the Roman teachers and legal writers were known, had a wide influence on legal development. It has been suggested that the Roman jurists "never developed any such subject as 'jurisprudentia,'" and that Ulpian's definition is a "whole sweeping assertion" which should "be treated as no more than a florid piece of rhetoric not pursued by the Romans themselves."[7] There is no doubt, however, that during the Roman period "jurisprudence" acquired the limited meaning of "skill in the law," the study of which remained a vocation of the nobility in Rome.[8]

In English and modern European languages the word came to be used in various senses, such as "Equity Jurisprudence," "medical jurisprudence" and "Honours School of Jurisprudence." The first sense was a title given to a text book on equity,[9] the second is used as the title for books on forensic medicine,[10] while the third is used to describe the examination which at Oxford is the equivalent of the LL.B. degree. We are not concerned with the meaning of "jurisprudence" in any of these senses. The tendency has been to reject the use of such terms as "Equity Jurisprudence," "Medical Jurisprudence" or other similar terms.[11]

In French, *jurisprudence* is the term used to describe a course of decisions made by the court. In English (as in French law), the word had been used in a more limited sense. Holland defines it as "the formal science of positive law."[12] To him it is a "formal science" because unlike the "material science" of English law, jurisprudence does not supply the facts nor does it tell us what are the rules of any substantive law. It deals with general conceptions of positive law. The next point in Holland's definition is that jurisprudence is concerned with positive law, i. e., that it deals with law as it is and not with the objects of law, nor with law as it ought to be.

The definition of jurisprudence as a formal analysis of the concepts of positive law dominated English legal thought till the end of the 19th Century. John Austin, in his *The Province of Jurisprudence Determined,* which was published in 1832, maintains that "positive law" is the "appropriate matter" of jurisprudence.[13] The discussion about law, he maintains, should deal with law as it is and should not be confounded with law as it ought to be. Law in action might be good or bad, but this can be seen only from the ethical point of view. Jurisprudence is not concerned with ethical evaluations of law, and the fact that law is bad, Austin insists, is irrelevant to its being the subject matter of jurisprudence.

Like Austin, Salmond, another eminent English jurist of the late 19th Century, saw jurisprudence as a formal analysis of the concepts of positive law. He defines jurisprudence as "the science of civil law in general and of the first principles of the civil law."[14] The object of jurisprudence is the analysis of the first principles of civil law. By "civil law" Salmond meant almost the same thing as Austin's "positive law."[15] He maintains that neither the historical origin or development of law, nor its "ethical significance or validity," should be the concern of Jurisprudence. Allen, modifying this view, is of the opinion that jurisprudence is concerned with the "examination of legal rules without reference to their goodness and badness" because it is empirical in its approach. It aims at building up principles from the examination of observable facts. It does not aim at deriving truth by a deduction from "principles conceived immediately by our reason without the aid of experience."[16]

Such were the orthodox views of English writers on the meaning of jurisprudence. Since the 20th Century we have witnessed increased social problems, most of which are due to conflicts in ideologies and the struggle for economic power and control. The need for law as an instrument for the control of life in society has been felt perhaps more than before. Consequently, legal thinking is departing from the orthodox views about law. Jurisprudence is seen now in a broader sense, and its definition is being brought within a broader social context.

Jurisprudence as a "general theoretical discussion about law and its principles, as opposed to the study of actual rules of law,"[17] is ceasing to have a specifically limited and technical meaning. Its meaning is no more confined to the narrow limits imposed on it by legal positivism. Jurisprudence has, in Stone's words, become "the lawyer's extraversion. It is the lawyer's examination of the precepts, ideals, and techniques of the law in the light derived from present knowledge in disciplines other than the law."[18]

If law is going to fulfill its functions in society, jurisprudence, as a particular mode of study of the general notion of law, must have a wide even though cumbersome scope. The big question is, however, what should be the ideal function of law in society which shall be the concern of jurisprudence? In other words, will our study of jurisprudence be confined to the notion of law as a superstructure arising out of values that exist in society? Or will it deal with the values that ought to underlie the law? The problems raised are fully dealt with here in the chapter evaluating laws in Africa.[19] Furthermore, these problems pose other questions for our consideration: What relevance, in Africa, have the various theories developed in Europe? What contribution can legal thinking in Africa make to the development of Jurisprudence?

The Scope Of Jurisprudence in Africa

One might in another sense ask what relevance Jurisprudence has in legal training and legal development in Africa? In all democracies judges and lawyers are known to be the sentinels of the individual's freedom and fundamental rights. They are the guardians of social justice. In developing countries their task is even more challenging and onerous.[20] Consequently, all those in Africa upon whom these tasks devolve must not only acquire the techniques, skill and knowledge of the principles and rules of the substantive laws in action, they must also be able to know the scope and functions of the law which they may in future be called upon to interpret and administer. No subject is better equipped to give them the latter knowledge than jurisprudence. Jurisprudence, as was the view of Professor Laski, is "the eye of the law." It should give lawyers their insight into the environment of which it is the expression, and relate the law to the spirit of the time.[21]

Our main problem is to determine the province of jurisprudence in Africa, or the kind of jurisprudence that will be most appropriate for the spirit of our time. To find a solution to this problem is not easy, as much of it depends on the type of community we have, the political ideology, the social values, and the social changes that obtain or are to be envisaged in the community. As Friedmann has said, "the major assumptions are, first, that law is not a brooding omnipotence in the sky," but a flexible instrument of social order, dependent on the political values of the society which it purports to regulate.[22] For any adequate answer to be given to this question of the province of jurisprudence in Africa, attention ought to be firstly directed toward both the past and the present history of the communities in question. Secondly, a full consideration ought to be given to the successes and failures of the various theories developed in Europe, and the problems of the societies in which those theories were expounded.

Before the advent of the colonial era Africa was purely a traditional continent. Its political machinery and legal institutions were indigenous to its people, and the prevalent law which regulated life in its various communities was the customary law[23] operating in the various local areas. During the period of colonization of its various states by the British, the French, the Germans, the Italians and the Portuguese, new political institutions known to the European world were introduced and new legal machineries were developed by the colonizing powers to work, side by side sometimes, and where necessary with the local institutions. "The wind of change" which blew across the continent of Africa and which gathered momentum in the 1950s ushered in an era of self-determination and independence for the new States. The process of change is still continuing. Western values have been accepted through the process of education and closer contact with the western world.

Of late other influences, from the USSR, and from Asian countries, are being felt. The new African States are now greatly dichotomous and more complex. Consequently, it has become obvious that a new instrument of social order is necessary if what is good of the past is to be retained and the acquired new values and new standards welded in to build up modern States suitable for the temperament of the people. This is the task of law and it is within this sphere that the province of jurisprudence is to be redetermined.[24] As Friedmann once observed, the law must, especially in contemporary conditions of articulate law-making by legislators, courts and others, respond to social change if it is to fulfill its function as a paramount instrument of social order.[25]

Analytical Positivism offers too narrow a scope for this purpose. It is also meaningless, to some extent, to apply it to Africa. It offers no adequate explanation of the operative laws, as we shall see from an examination (in the next chapter) of the sources of law in Africa. Furthermore, since it is concerned with the impartial analysis of the law as it is and not with efforts for its improvement or alteration, it is most doubtful if it will accommodate and enhance the upsurge of industrialization and other social changes. The positivists' attitude has been seen to be indifferent to the justice or injustice of existing conditions of life. Its adoption will mean perpetuation of the status quo and a negation of the march toward a more liberal development, for an improved standard of living for all.

If we may learn from the English experience, as from the time of Austin, legal positivism dominated the field of jurisprudence, we shall recall the 20th Century attitude toward the limited scope which Austin's philosophy gave to Jurisprudence. There is today in England a change from analytical positivism and this change is being determined by the social, economic and political conditions which now prevail in that country. Buckland describes this change thus: "The analysis of legal concepts is what jurisprudence meant for the student in the days of my youth. In fact it meant Austin. He was a religion; today he seems to be regarded as a disease. He cannot be replaced on his pedestal; the intensely individualistic habit of mind of his day is out of fashion."[26] If legal positivism is out of fashion in England of today, it is out of place in 20th Century Africa. The new African States are fluid and tremendously dichotomous, and all are striving toward rapid development in all spheres of life. Worse still, analytical or legal positivism will bring a great deal of confusion to the meaning of law in these states, some of whose prevalent laws cannot pass the test of the Austinian definition of law.[27]

Economically, modern African States, unlike the traditional African communities, are pluralistic. Economic life in each new state can be divided into two major sectors. There is a subsistence sector, where economic life and the standard of living are more traditional than modern. And, there is the modernizing sector, which looks toward modern economy, industrialization, mechanized agriculture, and a rising standard of living. Economic principle governs social phenomena, and material and economic forces are the major factors that determine human behavior in society. In the circumstance, if law is to be a superstructure on the existing economic system there will be a widening gap between the two sections. The Haves, who for the present constitute the minority and who hold political power in the States, would seek to protect their property and their improved standard of living against the Have-nots. The result would be a vindication of Karl Marx's theory that law and state in capitalist societies together form an instrument of compulsion used by the wealthy minority to oppress and exploit the working class majority.[28]

On the other hand, if the gigantic scheme of modernization and industrialization is going to go forward in Africa, there must be state intervention through law. The main problem is the degree of intervention which will bring about the kind of changes needed. To avoid turning the law into an instrument of domination, human values and the individual's rights and freedom ought to be the guiding principles. The State ought not to be objectified as an "abstract and mystical entity moving and acting with a mind and soul of its own"[29] to the utter disregard of human values.

The problem confronting the African student of jurisprudence is very exciting, but he is not in an enviable position. The basic law of the new African States today is either English law or French law, depending on the colonial history of each State.[30] All the former British colonies accept English law as the basic law. Their local statutes enjoin the courts to apply "the common law of England and the doctrines of equity together with English statutes of general application"[31] of a specified date. The customary law, which is viewed as law *par excellence* and as an expression of the "Volksgeist" in the Savignyan sense, runs parallel to the received law. Its scope is limited to the subsistence sector, which we have mentioned earlier, and its application is subject to a test. Customary law is applied only if it is not "repugnant to natural justice, equity and good conscience,"[32] and this criterion is in no way limited to any African conception of the phrase. The formula was introduced to Africa from India by the British Colonial Administrators.[33] At one time it appeared to mean the application of the rules of English Law.[34] Earlier on, in 1868, the Privy Council gave a more acceptable interpretation of the phrase (in *Degumbaree Dabee v. Eshan Chunder Sein*) in the following words:

> Now, having to adminster equity, justice and good conscience where are we to look for the principles which are to guide us? *We must go to other countries where equity and justice are administered upon principles which have been the growth of ages,* and see how the courts act under similar circumstances; and if we find that the rules which they have laid down are in accordance with the true principles of equity, we cannot do wrong in following them.[35]

The purpose of the above illustration is simply to show that foreign systems of law provide the operative legal machineries today in Africa. Even customary law, the law regarded as par excellence and a reflection of the common consciousness of the people, is of no avail if its rules are against a basic principle of law acceptable by countries other than Africa. The task of the law reformer in Africa is therefore onerous. If, as is Dicey's view,[36] the opinion of yesterday underlies the law reform of today, the African jurist of today would seek in vain for that African opinion. The scope of jurisprudence cannot be confined to methods which would merely bring the law into slow and grudging accord with changes already accomplished in public opinion. There are factors to determine the scope of our law reform. These factors include the dynamic urge for progress felt by many in the new Africa, plus the international encouragement and aid for modernizing social and economic life, the swift expansion of educational facilities, the solidarity aroused by popular nationalist philosophies, and the disproportionate influence of the small elites of the countries.[37] These factors combine to speed considerably, and influence, the process of reform of the law.

The inescapable attitude would seem to be to regard law as a determinant agent in the creation of new norms in society, and not that law should follow the clearly formulated social sentiment in society. Unfortunately, however, with some aspects of the law, such as property and family law, there is bound to be a disparity and an ensuing struggle between what Eugene Erlich, the Austrian jurist, terms the "formal law" and the "living law" of the people. The people (and there are instances of such a trend)[38] will react unfavorably to some abrupt change to norms which do not reflect their "Volkgeist."

The Kind of Jurisprudence

The choice of a kind of Jurisprudence for Africa undoubtedly will not favor the orthodox European theories of law. The various theories developed in Europe grew out of the social facts and socioeconomic problems of Europe. "The first call of a theory of law," said Justice Holmes, "is that it should fit the facts,"[39] and an adequate theory of law in Africa is one that should fit the facts in Africa. An empirical or constructive method, as opposed to the prior or demonstrative method, seems to be a more appropriate method for us. The view that law should follow and not lead the clearly formulated social sentiment in society will do no justice to the emerging new African states. Consequently, Von Savigny's Historical Jurisprudence, though quite attractive, would be out of tune. The present social, historical and economic facts would support the opposing view, that law should be a determining agent in the creation of new norms in society. Therefore, legal Teleology or Teleological Jurisprudence appears to be a more appropriate philosophy to adopt and follow. This study, though broadly functional, differs from other functional approaches in that it deals with the values that ought to underlie the law and not with the values that exist.

The main problem, as we see it in Africa today is: if law is to bring about values which ought to govern life in society, who determines such values? Our first answer is: the State, through its legislators. The first task of Jurisprudence, therefore, is to train the mind of the lawyer who may become the legislator of tomorrow to acquire the true knowledge that would help him determine the right values. Our approach to Jurisprudence must be one that is suitable for this purpose. Without a disciplined mind which has acquired the right values, the tendency would be for the legislator to objectify the State and regard law as an abstract concept consisting of rules that are divorced from the social values. Such a tendency would lead to fascism. Secondly, it is the province and function of the court to interpret the law. Law, as Professor Marshall once observed, is "a choice between alternatives,"[40] and only the judge has the legal right to make and pronounce that choice. His disciplined legal mind, and the acquired true social values through the study of Jurisprudence, are good assets for this task.

The function of a judge in the legal process lies mainly in this sphere of choosing between alternatives. His power to make law ought not be over-emphasized, as the American Realists have done. A concentration on the Realist Approach would lead to a diversion from the real social values which ought to underlie the law. The judge, like any other individual, is part of the society. Like the legislator who is to make laws to bring about the required social values, the judge ought to interpret the law so as to accord with those values. The judge's state of mind, the condition of his stomach at the time of making a decision, his prejudices, and his psychology, are to be regarded only as some of those factors which may militate against society in its struggle to create and achieve the desired values. Such factors cannot rightly be regarded as true determinant factors in the law-making process. The judge's duty and function is to interpret the law in accordance with the accepted theories of social justice and social values, and only the perverted judge will, after acquiring the necessary discipline and knowledge, fail to keep to the underlying principles.

Lawyers, on the other hand, have been likened to craftsmen, and the analysis of legal concepts to a dissection of the tools of their trade. As the craftsman improves his skill in the use of his tools with his knowledge of their nature and functioning, so does the knowledge and functioning of the law and legal concepts enhance the lawyer's (and the judge's) prowess in the interpretation and administration of the law. "To be a good craftsman of the law," said Professor Rheinstein, involves both knowledge of the law and proficiency in the use of its tools. "These tools are concepts, logic and language."[41] An analysis and knowledge of the law based on the African social milieu will be more profitable to the African than ordinary abstractions of concepts and the acceptance of orthodox legal theories.

The Essence of Law

Other problems which confront students of Jurisprudence are the true nature and the basis of law. We shall here try to determine and formulate the main basis of law.

The various schools of Jurisprudence, which we shall discuss later, have all dealt with the essence of law. In their quest they have found more grounds for disagreement than for agreement. The main views which have been put forward can be summarized as follows:

(1) that the essence of law lies in its imposition upon society by a sovereign will;

(2) that the essence of law consists in the evolution of its own vitality from within the society; and,

(3) that the essence of law consists in its divine or ethical character and origin.[42]

1. The Sovereign Will:

According to Analytical Positivism, otherwise known as the Imperative Theory, law is a command of the sovereign backed up by sanction. The existence of law, therefore, is preceded by the existence of a sovereign who, in the Austinian sense, may be a person or a body of persons. In other words, law can only exist within a monarchy or in a bureaucracy. Furthermore, the binding force of law lies with the sanction. Any rule imposed upon society in these circumstances is law and is valid. No moral or ethical values are necessary to justify the existence of law, and its function in society is not a necessary consideration for its existence.

The Imperative Theorists are not alone in advocating the expurgation of morals or ethics from law. Hans Kelsen puts forward the view that a theory of law must remain "pure," i. e., that it must be free from ethics, political, sociological, and historical considerations. The essence of law, therefore, does not, in Kelsen's view, lie within any moral or social factors. It is found in the Basic Norm, which he terms the *"Grundnorm,"* according to his native German language. "The basic norm of a legal order," he said, "is the postulated ultimate rule according to which the norms of this order are established and annulled, receive and lose their validity.... The quest for the reason of validity of a norm is not—like the quest for the cause of an effect—a regressus ad infinitum; it is terminated by a highest norm which is the last ground of validity within the normative system."[43] Unlike the Imperative Theorists, the advocates of the Pure Science of Law do not attach much importance to the idea of sovereignty. The determination of the basic norm "implies no categorical statement as to the value of the method of law-making or of the person functioning as the positive legal authority; this value is a hypothetical assumption."[44]

The expurgation of morals or ethics from law, as advocated by the analytical school, overlooks the fundamental fact that the legal and the moral are closely related. "Legality is an aspect of moral experience which extends far beyond the legal field proper.... Such conceptions, said d'Entreves, "can still enrich our minds."[45] The idea that morals or ethics are involved in the essence of law should not be ignored by the African legal philosopher. This idea has been recognized, for example, in Tanganyika (Tanzania) where the Constitution, the Basic Law, is being framed to have as its *mainstay* what is termed (by President Mwalimu Julius Nyerere) the "National Ethic."[46]

A final analysis of the validity of law as deriving from the *Grundnorm* still reveals ethics as a necessary factor in determining the essence of law. If law consists of a hierarchy of norms, and if all the norms derive their validity from the basic norm, the *Grundnorm,* the question left unanswered is: From where does the Grundnorm derive its validity? Such a source would obviously lie outside the law. It could be found in ethics.

2. The Volksgeist:

The next view, that the essence of law consists in the evolution of its own vitality from within the society, is a product of the historical school led by Von Savigny, a German jurist (1779–1861). To this school, law is a matter of unconscious growth, a reflection of the common consciousness (der Volksgeist) of the people. Any law, therefore which does not conform to this common consciousness is pernicious and doomed to failure. Consequently, the essence of law is to be sought in direct relationship with the life of the people. It is manifest in the spirit of the people.

The theory of the Volksgeist is rather akin to the doctrine of the "General Will" put forward by Rousseau about two decades earlier. The doctrine of the "General Will," according to Rousseau, supplies the answer to the question "whose business it is to make laws, since they are acts of the General Will." It can no longer be asked, Rousseau went on, "whether a prince is above the law, since he is a member of the State; nor how we can be both free and subject to the laws, since they are but registers of our wills."[47] The doctrine of the "General Will" was known in Italy as early as the 14th Century. Marsilius of Padua, in his *Defensor Pacis* written in 1324, adduced the same doctrine. To him, laws are not only the expression of the will of the people, but it is because they are the expression of the will of the people that laws are good and just.

Both the doctrine of the "General Will" and the theory of the "Volks-geist" have one thing in common, i. e., that the essence of law lies beyond the law itself and is a matter that is directly connected with the people and their common aspirations. They differ, however, in that, while the theory of the Volksgeist adheres to the historical aspect of the peoples' common consciousness as the basis of law, the doctrine of the "General Will" makes no distinction as to time. The validity of law, according to the doctrine of the "General Will," depends on its general acceptance by the people. Received laws would, for example, be valid and binding not because they are imposed on the society by a sovereign, but because the Local Act enabling their reception is of the people. Provided, of course, the Act reflects the "General Will." Where there is unanimity the problem of the doctrine of the "General Will" is solved, but the fact remains that unani-mity has never been possible in any society.

3. The Divine or Ethical Character of Law:

Those who advocate that the essence of law consists in its divine or ethical character and origin, look for a permanent underlying basis of law. They find the essence of law in unchangeable moral principles. Hu-man actions, according to Socrates (c. 470 B. C.), are not governed solely by inclinations and desires, as the Sophists once held. The faculty of in-sight into the nature of conduct is man's heritage. This insight is the knowledge of goodness and badness possessed by man, and it forms the criterion by which all human conduct must be examined. It offers a more adequate and acceptable reason for obedience to law than mere force. To command obedience, positive law must therefore conform with these principles, which are the dictates of natural law.

Notwithstanding, the Greek philosophers such as Aristotle, who be-longed to the School of Socrates and Plato (429–348 B. C.) believed that natural law demands that Positive Law should be obeyed even when it falls short of the basic principles. Where positive law is bad and imper-fect, the citizen should aim at reforming it rather than breaking it. This ambivalent attitude of the Greek writers was the result of the social facts and requirements of their period, and it was calculated to take care of the much needed social security and stability of their era.[48] In ancient Greece the main motive for observing positive law and the reason be-hind the punishment given to one who committed a public delict re-mained nevertheless superstitious.

The association of law with a belief in the supernatural was by no means peculiar to Greek law and Greek philosophers. The Romans, as we have seen earlier, at one time regarded jurisprudence as *the concept of things human and divine,* and they confined the knowledge of law to a religious board of the patrician pontiffs.

The most primitive code, the Hittite Code, contains some additions of a religious character, and other primitive codes, like the Hebrew Pentateuch, the Hindoo Code of Manu, and the Roman XII Tables, though secular in nature, contain religious sanctions. It is true that, according to Diamond,[49] these codes have no religious origin, but the comixture with religious writing or religious sanctions showed man's strong attachment to the Divine and to Ethics as essential factors of social order.

In traditional Africa the customary law appeared and operated at stages of development much the same as those of the Greek and the Roman periods we have discussed. The times are not the same, but the relative progress is similar. Like their Roman and Greek counterparts, the traditional African developed a similar notion of law. The essence of customary law (and especially those aspects of it known as public wrong) lies in its character as a command handed down by the departed ancestors who act as liaison between the deity and the living. The individual who commits a public wrong is confronted with a strong public opinion which in extreme cases excommunicates him from the community. But behind this social sanction lie religious or superstitious fears.

Man, especially in early society, held religion and ethics as fundamental to law. Eminent jurists, among whom are Sir Henry Maine and Diamond whose views we have noted earlier confirm this. Writing about the four stages of legal development in an early society, Maine describes law in the first stage as a personal command of divine inspiration.[50] Even Hegel, a great critic of the traditional natural law, identifies the life of a nation in terms of ethics. Calling for a positive approach to the problem of natural law in 1802, he found that the real task of ethics is to understand and assert the totality of ethical life. And "the absolute ethical totality is nothing but *ein Volk*—a people or nation.[51] By implication, law, therefore, is an aspect of ethics, deriving its validity from what in Tanganyika is referred to as the "National Ethic."

Conclusion

The collective life of man in society is the balancing of interests, and the main objective is to advance the social purpose and progress. In early society, the function of law

> was to compel certain acts and to prevent others; its function was to maintain the established order. The function of much contemporary law has come to be to make possible the achievement of new goals.[52]

and to forward the social purpose and progress. Law in modern society, therefore, concerns itself with the establishment of new paths of social action and the creation of new values. In Africa today these functions are made necessary by the influence of modern civilization and scientific technology.

The problem of the authority of law does not become an issue in any society like those in traditional Africa where law is concerned merely with maintaining the basic structure of society. The authority claimed may be divine or moral or based merely upon tradition, and as Thompson said, "no real alternative is in sight."[53] The problem becomes different and acute when law concerns itself, as in our time, with what is good and desirable to fulfil the social purpose. The question of what standards or what values to go by then becomes an issue. The Africa of today is a society where the old mingles with the new, a society where customary law, the received foreign law, case law, and local legislation together form the laws of the community. To determine the appropriate essence of law in such circumstances a medium should be found between the orthodox and the modern claims of authority of law.

Customary law, no matter what changes it has undergone as a result of legislation, still owes its authority, not to the will of any sovereign, but to the general consensus of the people. This consensus or "general will" is founded upon a doctrine similar to that of natural law. Legislation, on the other hand, derives its binding force from the authority of the legislature, and this sometimes results in legislative action being a method by which the desires of a few are imposed on all. The legislature however, should act within an underlying principle. This principle is that upon which the society itself rests. It is the social life and the social purpose of the community, and it differs from the principle which governed traditional African society only to the extent that modernization has affected it. We should find here the medium for the authority of law in our time.

Law, as the structure of human relationships and functions which constitute a society, is binding because it is the dictate of the social order and an expression of the collective power and purpose of society. The totality of values in society determined by social facts and social requirements is molded into the peoples' ethics and beliefs to bring about an orderly state. Any law which is not a reflection of this social sentiment may be enforceable, but it is not naturally binding. For example, an Act of Parliament which conforms with the legislative process may be enforceable, but inasmuch as it operates against the social sentiment, it is inauspicious to its very foundation and it ought not to be binding. Such an Act, however, can be enforced, unless in the meantime there is a successful rebellion against it. For just as the lion pounces upon its prey for no just cause except that it has the power to overwhelm its victim and assuage its hunger, in the same manner does the upholder of a law that is divorced from its social purpose and sentiment fall upon the so-called violator, because of the former's possession of sheer brutal force.

A rule of conduct is not necessarily law because it is imposed by a superior authority and backed up by sanction, which is largely applied through force. In order not to be arbitrary, force should be exercised in conformity with the social order. Jurisprudence in Africa should avoid the use of legislative enactment to meet the desires of those who prevail in the struggles for power between conflicting interest groups.

Notes to Introduction

1. Dias R. W. M., and Hughes G. B. J., *Jurisprudence* (London: Butterworth and Co. Ltd., 1957), p. 1.
2. See however Sir Henry Maine's idea on the development of law in "static" and "progressive" societies. *Ancient Law* (London: John Murray, 1920), p. 27.
3. Paton, G. W., *A Textbook of Jurisprudence* (Oxford: Clarendon Press, 2nd Edition), p. 2.
   4. D.1.1.10.2; this passage is also quoted in Justinian's Institutes ,1.1.1.
5. This is the earliest Roman Code of Law drawn up by a special commission of Decemviri Legibus Scribundis in 451–450 B.C. Enacted by the Comitia Centuriata as a Statute it became the starting point in the development of Roman Law. The object of the Code was to collect the most important rules of the existing customary law, the knowledge of which till then was confined to the pontifices. It also sought to level the existing legal customs by abolishing patrician privileges. The XII Tables contain rules from all spheres of law, including private and criminal law, procedure, public, and sacral law.
6. This legal document, commonly known as Ius Flavianum, was published by Flavious Gnaeus, a son of a libertus. Flavius was a jurist and author. One of his works is a dissertation, De usurpationibus (on interruption of the usucapio). The Ius Flavianum was the first publication containing the legis actiones. It gave the people knowledge of the civil law and of the forms of procedure which had been the monopoly of the pontiffs. In spite of his humble origin, but apparently due to his work, Flavius became tribunis plebis.
7. Dias and Hughes, *op. cit.* p. 2.
8. The Republican jurists belonged to the senatorial families and occupied the highest offices as pontiffs, consuls and praetors; and under the Principate the prominent offices in the administration of Rome and her provinces were often occupied by jurists who always enjoyed high authority in public life.
9. Ames, *Equity Jurisprudence.*
10. Such books contain mere extractions from the law of those aspects which a medical practitioner ought to know.
11. See Stone, J. *The Province and Function of Law* (Sydney: Maitland Publication Pty. Ltd., 1961), p. 26.
12. Holland, T. E. *Jurisprudence* (Oxford: Clarendon Press, 1916), p. 13.
13. Austin, J. *The Province of Jurisprudence Determined* (New York: Noonday Press, 1832), pp. 79–80. For his meaning of "positive law" see Chapter 4 of *Concept of Law in English Speaking Africa.*

14. Salmond, Sir John *Jurisprudence*, 8th edition by Manning, C.A.W. (London: Sweet and Maxwell Ltd., 1930), p. 2.
15. See Salmond, Sir John *Jurisprudence* by Williams Glanville (11th edition, 1957), p. 36.
16. Allen, C. K. "Jurisprudence—What and Why?" Legal Duties p. 1.
17. Jolowicz, H. F., *Lectures on Jurisprudence* (London: University of London, The Athlone Press, 1963), p. 11. See also p. 2.
18. Stone, *op. cit.*, p. 25.
19. Chapter 10; see also, Part 3 on theories of law.
20. Professor Elias outlines the possible role of law and the lawyer to be envisaged in a developing society in an inaugural lecture delivered at the University of Lagos on 17th January, 1969. See Elias, T. O., *Law in a Developing Society* (Nigeria: Ibadan University Press, 1969), p. 26 in particular.
21. Laski, H. J. *A Grammar of Politics* (London: 1925), p. 377; see also Hall, J. "A 2-2-2 Plan for College-Law Education" (1942) 56 *Harv. L. Rev.*, 245, especially pp. 251–256, 264 ff.; Reisman, D., Jr., "Law and Social Science" (1940) 50 *Yale L. J.* 636.
22. Quoting Holmes' Friedmann, in *Law in a Changing Society* (London: Stevens and Sons Ltd., 1959), p. xiii.
23. Customary Law here includes Islamic Law for the Moslems Areas.
24. Professor Elias has suggested that in Nigeria, for example, the Legal Education Act, 1962, and the Legal Practitioners Act of the same year are both inspired by some philosophy of legal education and of the proper task of law in society—Elias, *op. cit.*, p. 26.
25. Friedmann, *op. cit.*, p. ix.
26. Buckland, W. W. *Some Reflections On Jurisprudence*, p. 2; see also Julius Stone's views on the need for a redefinition of the scope of jurisprudence. *Stone, op. cit.*, p. 41, et seq.
27. On definitions of law, see Part 3, Theories of Law.
28. Karl Marx, *Introduction to Critique of Political Economy*, p. 11.
29. Friedmann, W. *Law in a Changing Society* (London: Stevens and Sons Ltd., 1959), p. 6.
30. See Chapter I on the Sources of Law in the new states.
31. See, for example, the Nigerian Interpretation Ordinance, Cap. 89, s.45 (1); The Eastern Nigerian High Court Law, No. 27 of 1955; s.14; Northern Nigeria High Court Law, No. 8 of 1955, s.28; Law of England (Application) Law, Cap. 60, No. 9 (Western Region) of 1959, s.3. By s.4 of the same Law, Imperial Acts hitherto in force in that Region are no more in force. In Ghana the same principle is contained in the Ghanaian Courts Act, 1960. This practice is equally true of the local statutes of other English-speaking Africa. In Francophonic Africa, French law is in similar position.
32. This repungnancy test which to this day is applied to customary law, was introduced in English-speaking Africa in the earlier days of the colonial era. See, for example, Ordinance No. 13, March 28, 1844 (Gambia), s.5; The Supreme Court Ordinance of the Gold Coast, 1876 s.19; The Supreme Court Ordinance of the Colony of Lagos No. 4 of 1876, s.19; also Supreme Court Ordinance, 1914 s.19(1). Similar provisions are to be found in the laws of Sierra Leone, Northern Rhodesia. etc.
33. See Duncan M. Derrott, "Justice Equity and Good Conscience" in *Changing Law in Developing Countries*, Anderson, J. N. D. (ed.) (London: Allan and Unwin, 1963), p. 148.
34. *Waghela v. Sheikh* (1887) 14 I.A. pp. 89, 96. P. C.
35. 9 W. R. (1868) pp. 230, 232 (italics added). The qualification of "justice" by the introduction of the adjective "natural" in the prevalent statutes in Africa undoubtedly confirms the formula as having a universal meaning deducible from a consultation of various systems of law.
36. Dicey, A. V. *Law and Public Opinion in England During the Nineteenth Century*, (London: Macmillan Co., 1926, 2nd Edition), p. 33.

37. See Read, J. S., "Women's Status and Law Reform" in *Changing Law in Developing Countries, op. cit.,* p. 215.

38. Examples in Nigeria are: The Abolition of the Osu System Law (Eastern Nigeria) No. 13 of 1956; The Limitation of Dowry Law (E. N.) No. 13 of 1956. In practice these laws are not being observed by the people. In Ghana, the proposed Nudity Law met with very strong opposition. In Ethiopia, The Penal Code, drawn from outside Ethiopia and not considering Ethiopian conditions, still has to be put to a test. Among the Iteso of Uganda, the maximum limit for marriage payment fixed by law is being evaded "wholesale," the men finding it profitable to pay the legal penalty of 150/- fine in the unlikely event of being detected. See *Lawrence,* J. C. D., *The Iteso,* (1957), pp. 202–203. Cf., the Ngwato of Bechuanaland, where a chief's edict prohibiting bride price appears to have been effective. See also Schapera, I., *A Hand Book of Tswana Law and Custom,* (London: International Institute for African Languages and Culture, 1955) *2nd Edition,* pp. 145–146.

39. Holmes, Oliver Wendell, *The Common Law* (Boston: Little Brown & Co, 47th printing), p. 211.

40. Marshal, O. R. The statement was made at the Conference of African Law Teachers held at the University of Ife, Ibadan Branch, April 17–19, 1965.

41. Rheinstein, "Education for Legal Craftsmanship," (1944–45) *Iowa Law Review,* p. 408.

42. It is not the authors intention to deal with these views in their historical order. An attempt is made to show the historical significance of the views in the section dealing with the theories of law.

43. Kelsen, H. *General Theory of Law,* p. 116.

44. *Ibid.*

45. d'Entreves, A. P., *Natural Law* (London: Hutchinson University Library, 1963, 7th impression), p. 79.

46. See Report of Presidential Commission on the Establishment of a Democratic One-Party State, 1965, (Dar Es Salaam Government Printers), p. 6. The National Ethic is described as "certain *ethical principles* which lie at the basis of the Tanganyikan Nation, and the whole political, economic social organisation of the State must be directed towards their rapid implementation." *Ibid.,* p. 3. These principles are nothing more than the fundamental rights of the citizen, which in some countries are entrenched in the Constitution itself and thus derive their validity from the Basic Law. But in Tanganyika they stand above the law itself, forming the basis of the existence of the Constitution and of its validity.

47. Rousseau, J. J. *The Social Contract* (transl.) G.D.H. Cole (London: Everyman's Library, reprinted by permission of E. P. Dutton & Co Inc.), Book II, Chap. VI).

48. St. Thomas Aquinas (1226–1274) later held the same view. According to him, inasmuch as human laws are based on reason, they reflect Eternal Law, and there is a duty to obey them. He, like Aristotle, however, called for obedience to positive law even when it is seemingly wicked, in order to avoid social disturbance.

49. Diamond, *Primitive Law* (London: 1935), Diamond A. S. Primitive Law (London: Watts & Co, 1935), pp. 49–53.

50. Maine, Sir Henry S., *Ancient Law.*

51. Hegel, G. W. F., "Uber die Wissenschaftlichen Behandlungsarten des Naturrechts," (The Scientific Treatment of Natural Law)", in his *Schriften zur Politik und Rechtsphilosophie, Samtliche Werke,* Vol. VII, ed. Lasson, 1913.

52. Thompson, Samuel, "The Authority of Law," in *Ethics,* an International Journal of Social and Legal Philosophy (Chicago: University of Chicago Press, Oct. 1964), Vol. LXXV, p. 17.

53. Thompson, *ibid.,* p.18.

PART II
THE CORPUS JURIS

Chapter 1

Sources of Law

Meaning of the Term "Source"

Generally, the word "source" means the "starting-point," the "origin" or the beginning. Literally, the term *source of law* means source of authoritative statement, such as the Law Report and the Statute Book.[1] In strict legal phraseology, it means any source from which the substance of the law is derived.

Salmond classified sources of law into *"formal"* and *"material."* The former he gave as the source of validity of law, i.e., the source from which a rule derives its legal force, and this source is nothing other than "the will and power of state" which is manifested in the court of justice. Such a distinction is meaningful only with legal positivism. The "common consciousness" of the people or the "general will" and the "Divine-will" would all, in effect, pass as formal sources of law, but Salmond excluded them in his classification.[2]

Material sources are those sources from which the substance of the law, as opposed to its validity, are derived. Salmond further subdivides this into historical and legal sources. *Historical* sources are remote sources. They are not regarded as legal, but become law only by reception into the legal sources. Until received into the law, historical sources remain merely persuasive and have no authority. Examples of these are the writings and opinions of lawyers, or the rules and principles of foreign law.

Legal Sources are those sources "which are recognized as such by the law itself."[3] These comprise Legislation and Precedent in particular, with custom coming next. For our purpose we shall be concerned with the *material-legal-sources*, i.e., those sources from which the substance of law is drawn. These sources are authoritative. We may term such sources formal sources (with apologies to Salmond), in the sense that from them we derive formulated legal rules and principles which are authoritative and binding. The other sources we may term non-formal sources because they are merely persuasive and lack authority.

Formal Sources of Law in Africa

The laws of English-speaking Africa (and to some extent French-speaking Africa) are derived mainly from three sources, and these sources are *Legislation, Precedent* and *Custom.* Accordingly, by reference to its source of derivation, the *corpus juris* is divisible into three parts. The first part consists of *enacted law* having its sources in:

(a) received English statutes of general application,[4] and, (b) local legislation.

The second part consists of *case law,* which has its source in judicial precedent and is made up of:

(i)   the received English Common Law and the doctrines of Equity, and,

(ii) local judicial precedent.

The third part consists of *customary law* which has its source in diverse traditional customs. To be binding rules of conduct, such customs must fulfill the modern requirements laid down by law as the condition of their recognition.

The Nature and Authority of the Legal Sources

Enacted Law

Enacted Law, otherwise known as Legislation, is in general terms, a law made by formal and express declaration of rules of conduct by Parliament or some other authority. Both the Parliament and any other authority making the formal and express declaration of the rules of conduct must be recognized for that purpose by the political and legal machinery of the State. Without such a recognition the enactment lacks legality. As Salmond has aptly stated, "it is such an enunciation or promulgation of principles as confers upon them the force of law. It is such a declaration of principles as constitutes a legal ground for their recognition as law for the future by the tribunals of the State."[5] This means that the legal rules, once duly declared by a competent legislature, are binding. Their authority is not questionable on moral grounds, unreasonableness, bad faith, or non-compliance with the "general will" or the common consciousness of the people.[6] It is binding simply because the legal system concerned recognizes the legislature or the relevant authority as empowered to enact laws.

For example, in the English legal system, Parliament used to be supreme. This meant that any Act of the Parliament was valid and binding, provided it was passed through the normal legislative process. In a country with a written Constitution, unlike England, the position is slightly different. The Constitution forms the Basic Law and is therefore supreme. All laws enacted by Parliament to be valid and binding must conform with the provisions of the Constitution.[7]

Parliament can, however, amend or entirely change the Constitution. But to do so effectively it must follow the procedure laid down by the Constitution itself for its amendment or change. Failure to follow the procedure will render the amendment or change unconstitutional and therefore illegal and of no binding effect. This is the position in all new African States with written Constitutions.

We may therefore conclude that enacted laws in a country with a written Constitution are subordinate to the Constitution and derive their authority from it. In any other case it is the express declaration of the rules of conduct by Parliament or a competent legal authority that gives them the legal force. The legal precepts created deliberately by the competent authority are given articulate expression in each formalized legal document known as Statute or Act.

Case Law

Case Law is created through the application and adoption of new rules by the courts in the process of the administration of justice. Its authority as a source of law rests on the doctrine of binding precedent, otherwise known as *stare decisis*. In English-speaking Africa, as in England today, the judicial hierarchy is established and settled. The general judicial practice is that courts below the hierarchy are bound by the decisions or judgments of the courts above them. A judgment or decision of a court which serves as an authority for the legal principles embodied in it therefore becomes law, which must be followed in subsequent cases having similar set of facts.

In addition to a well-established judicial hierarchy, it is important for the establishment of the doctrine of *stare decisis* that there must exist reliable reports of decided cases. Such law reports literally constitute the source of authoritative legal statements. By case law, therefore, we mean that body of law which is built up through authoritative and binding precedents, and which is usually contained in law reports.

Case law is often referred to as judge-made law. This does not mean that judges are legislators or that the court is synonymous with the legislature. *Judge-made law* is a phrase used to indicate that it is the rule or the principle as laid down by the judge in the process of judicial administration that is binding. It is only the *ratio decidendi* of the case which is authoritative and binding, and an opinion expressed obiter may be persuasive but never binding.

Unlike enacted law, case law cannot be made in *vacuo*. A case with real facts, or a legal instrument with a doubtful authority or meaning, must be brought before the court to offer the judge an opportunity to make an authoritative and binding pronouncement. Such a case may involve the interpretation of a statute, thus offering the judge an opportunity to attach a specific meaning to the word used in the statute by the legislator. At this juncture, the judge's power to make law would seem to be greater than that of the legislator.

However, the extent of a judge's power to make law depends much on the method he adopts in deciding a particular issue. Where he adopts the deductive method, i. e., where he bases his decision upon fixed and certain legal rules, he has a negligible power to make law. On the other hand, he may adopt the inductive method, i. e., he may work from the particular to the general and refuse to conceive any legal rule as being applicable directly by simple deduction. With this method a judge has greater potentiality to make law. He may make reference to his own personal views, especially when they are not limited by any previous decisions arrived at through the inductive method that have mostly earned for the court the position of a law-making machinery. Because of such decisions, the American Realists, as we shall see later, tend to see law as nothing short of "the prophecies of what the courts do in fact...."[8]

In legal philosophy, however, no unanimity has ever been achieved as to the true nature and authority of case law as a source of law. In *civil law* countries, as in France and French-speaking Africa, for example, prominence is given to codification and case law is not regarded as a formal source of law.[9] Their attitude toward case law as a source of law is one that favors the Justinian maxim that "cases should be decided on basis of laws not precedents."[10] Apparently, however, there is now a trend[11] among those countries in favor of recognizing precedent as a formal and authoritative source of law. But the trend seems to be to gradual crystallization through persistent and unqualified approval of precedents by the courts[12] rather than to any radical change to give force and effect to precedents.

In common law countries, viz., England and other Commonwealth countries, and the United States, opinion is strongest in favor of the court as a law-making organ of the government. There is no doubt now that those countries regard case law as a formal source of law, but the victory of the court as a law-creating organ was not achieved until quite recently.

In the United States jurists and judges of the 19th Century and early 20th Century regarded precedent as mere evidence of the law, whose authority and force lie beyond the pronouncement made by the judge.[13] James Cooklidge once referred to precedent as nothing more than an "authoritative custom."[14] And Justice Holmes, summarizing the purpose and end of judicial enquiry in *Prenties v. Atlantic Coast Line Co.*, had the following to say: "A judicial inquiry investigates, declares, and enforces liabilities as they stand on present or past facts and *under laws supposed already to exist.* . . . Legislation, on the other hand, looks to the future and changes existing conditions by making a new rule, to be applied thereafter to all or some part of those subject to its power."[15]

In England, we have a clear picture of the importance of a settled judicial hierarchy in the development of case law. Before the Judicature Act settled the hierarchy of the courts in England in 1875, earlier English jurists maintained the positivist approach to the nature and authority of the law. "The decisions of courts of justice," said Sir Matthew Hale, "do not make a law properly so-called (for that is the function of only the King in Parliament); . . . they have a great weight and authority in expounding, declaring and publishing what the law of this kingdom is, especially when such decisions hold a consonancy and congruity with resolutions and decisions of former times, and though such decisions are less than law, yet they are a greater evidence thereof than any opinion of many private persons as such whatsoever."[16]

Thomas Hobbes (1588–1679), a renowned English legal author, presented the strongest view of his time against precedent. "No man's error," he said, "becomes his own law; nor obliges him to persist in it. Neither, for the same reason becomes it a law to other judges, though sworn to follow it. . . . Therefore, all the sentences of precedent judges that have ever been, cannot altogether make a law contrary to natural equity."[17]

Even the English common law judges refused to support the idea of precedent as a formal source of law. Lord Mansfield, in *Jones v. Randall*, remarked that "the law of England would be a strange science indeed if it were decided upon precedents only." Precedents he continued, "serve to illustrate principles and to give them a fixed certainty. But the law of England, which is exclusive of positive law, enacted by statute, depends upon principles, and these principles run through all the cases according as the particular circumstances of each have been found to fall within the one or other of them."[18] Earlier, in 1762, the same judge had maintained that "the reason and spirit of cases make law, not the letter of particular precedents."[19]

In modern times, as we have noted earlier, the place of precedent as a formal source of law is firmly established in the common law countries. The idea that legislation, as against precedent, is the only formal source of law has been discarded. The "courts are constantly making *ex post facto law.*"[20] The rules and principles laid down in court decisions are regarded both as sources of law and the law itself.

We must however note that in contrast to the legislator, the creation of new law is for the judge an *ultima ratio* only, to which he must resort when the existing positive or non-positive sources of the law give him no guidance, or when the abrogation of an obsolete precedent becomes imperative.[21] The legislature exists mainly for the making of new rules to guide man's future actions in society. Sometimes, however, the legislature is compelled by past facts to legislate retrospectively.

The authority of the court to interpret legislation involves to some extent a power to make law, especially where the court is the highest tribunal of the land. In the words of Bishop Hoadly, "whoever hath an absolute authority to interpret any written or spoken laws, it is he who is truly the law-giver to all intents and purposes, and not the person who first wrote or spoke them."[22] *Ex Cathedra*, a judge of the highest tribunal who inductively interprets a statute is more of a law-giver than the legislator.

Customary Law

Primarily, Customary Law is that body of law deriving from local customs and usages of traditional Africa. As a source of law in the English-speaking Africa, customary law now includes Islamic law, and only those local customs which are not repugnant to *"natural justice, equity and good conscience."*

When held not repugnant to natural justice, equity and good conscience, the quantum of enforceable customary law is reduced further by such other criteria as:

(a) it must not be incompatible with any law at the time in force,[23]
(b) it must not be contrary to public policy.[24]

The criteria of incompatibility with any law in force simply means that where statute has adequately provided for cases formerly covered by customary law, the latter should yield place to the former. This is a case of choice and preference which, strictly, does not question the initial legality of the abrogated customary law.

The criterion of public policy has become synonymous with the repugnancy test which was introduced by various ordinances of the colonial period. The issue raised by these criteria is the true nature and basis of authority of customary law as a source of law.

Primarily, a customary rule reflects the common consciousness of the traditional if not the modern African. Thus far its authority stems from the ethos and beliefs of the people. When, however, its application is subject to a basic principle of law acceptable by countries other than Africa, or a subjective test by the judge, its nature of authority becomes an issue.

When a rule of customary law fails the test of repugnancy, i. e., when it is rejected on the ground that it is repugnant to natural justice, equity and good conscience, or public policy, it falls outside the scope of an enforceable law.[25] On the other hand, where it is accepted because it is deemed not to be repugnant to natural justice, equity and good conscience, we have to look for more facts to determine whether or not its authority is affected by the test.

Judicial Attitude

The attitude of the Privy Council is to either accept a native custom whole and entire and enforce it, or to reject it. It is not the intention of the Board to try to modify any native custom in order to give it effect. In *Eshughayi Eleko v. Officer Administering the Government of Nigeria,* the Board took the view that "the court cannot itself transform a barbarous custom into a milder one. If it still stands in its barbarous character it must be rejected as repugnant to "natural justice, equity and good conscience."[26]

More recently, the Privy Council, by implication, seems to welcome the idea that customary rules should not be subjected to exotic or universal standards of values. Thus, in *Danmole v. Dawodu*[27] where the deceased died intestate leaving four wives and nine children, and the issue was whether his property should be distributed *per capita* in accordance with a modern Yoruba practice of "Ori-Ojori," or *per stirpes* in accordance with an older custom known as "Idi-Igi," the Privy Council in arriving at a decision drew a distinction between the principles of natural justice, equity and good conscience applicable in a polygamous society, and those applicable to a monogamous society. Rejecting the lower court's decision of Jibowu, J. which favored equality of treatment among the children as opposed to equality of treatment among the wives, the Board stated

The principles of natural justice, equity and good conscience applicable in a country where polygamy is generally accepted should not be readily equated with those applicable to a community governed by the rule of monogamy.[28]

If the opinion of the Privy Council represents the views of the courts in English speaking Africa today,[29] a rule of customary law is enforced by the courts because it is an authoritative rule with a binding force. The test has only the effect of reducing the quantum of enforceable rules, while leaving the source of their authority unimpaired.

There have been instances, however, where the local courts adopted the view that customary law must be adapted to changing conditions of modern Africa. Thus, in a Ghanaian case Linley, J. maintained that "this court cannot allow local customs to override general principles and practice in these days of changing conditions."[30]

In *Wokoko v. Molyko*[31] The issue appearing before a Nigerian Court was whether or not in Buea (Cameroons) the principle of non-alienation of land had yielded place to one of alienation. Pearson, Assistant J., stated obiter that "it may be observed that in the past native custom has been by no means static, indeed a great many native customs in West Africa are manifestly of European origin, and it is eminently desirable that native custom should be progressive, as in this case, where the older and, as I hold, superseded custom would restrain development."[32]

Earlier, in 1909, Osborne, C. J. in *Lewis v. Bankole* observed that "one of the most striking features of West African native custom ... is its flexibility; it appears to have been always subject to motives of expediency, and it shows unquestionable adaptability to altered circumstances without entirely losing its individual characteristics."[33] If the above is true of West African native custom, it is equally true of the native customs of at least all English-speaking Africa.

The fact remains, however, that law is a social fact. It is, as Professor Elias has very aptly stated, "an expression of the social consciousness of every people subject to its authority." It cannot, therefore, be judged by exotic standards.

> What is by one people regarded as possessing the attributes of law may not impress another people as such, if the rules of social behaviour and the juridical sentiment of the latter are different from those of the former.[34]

It may also happen that, with the same people, time may so change their social values and standards that what was regarded by them as sound law at an earlier stage may be held obnoxious at a later stage of their development.

To adapt and modernize rules of customary law to meet changing conditions is a worthwhile venture. It is the objective of every progressive society to alter and modify its social and legal institutions and rules to meet the needs of the time. But, as in chemistry, two matters which when mixed and inseparable form a compound the nature of which is different from those of its components, so a customary rule that is given a new facet by the injection of modern ideas and principles ceases to be what it was originally. When courts apply and give effect to such a rule, they are not enforcing customary law in the sense that we know it. The judge is creating new rules whose authority belongs to case law and not customary law.[35]

Where, of course, the hardship of a customary rule is simply minimized without the custom losing its essential character, the case is different. The rule remains a rule of customary law, deriving its force and authority from the assent of the community. Such changes are evolutionary and are in keeping with the theory of the historical school.

Lord Atkin summarized the effect of this trend in *Eshughayi Eleko v. Government of Nigeria,* when he said:

> Their Lordships entertain no doubt that the more barbarous customs of earlier days may under the influence of civilization become milder without losing their essential character as custom. It would however, appear to be necessary to show that in their milder form they are still recognised in the native community as custom, so as in that form to regulate the relations of the native community inter se. ... *It is the assent of the native community that gives a custom its validity,* and therefore, barbarous or mild, it must be shown to be recognized by the native community whose conduct it is supposed to regulate.[36]

A court of law cannot in itself create customary law.

Thus far the true position seems to be that the nature of a custom remains in doubt until ascertained by judicial enquiry. This is so because it is an unwritten law. The function of the court is to determine whether or not the community holds a custom as binding, and not whether or not the court would give it the force of law. Where a court is satisfied that the community holds a custom as binding, it ought to enforce it.

The mode of proof of customary law in the common law countries supports the view that the purpose of judicial enquiry on custom is merely to ascertain it and not to give it validity. Any book or manuscript recognized by the natives as a legal authority is relevant to the proof (ascertainment) of customary law. Also, a custom may be without further proof before it is applied by the court "if it has been acted upon by a court of superior or co-ordinate jurisdiction in the same area to an extent which justifies the court asked to apply it in assuming that the persons or the class of persons concerned in that area look upon the same as binding in relation to circumstances similar to those under consideration."[37] This is not a case of precedent. It is rather a question of judicial notice of the custom based on its certainty.

Even in civil law countries, the object of judicial enquiry on custom seems to be its ascertainment, to recognize a custom and give it effect as a rule of law, the court sees to it that the custom is accompanied by *opinion juris* or *opinion necessitatis.*

Some countries in Africa are taking steps to assimilate customary rules into the law, once they are ascertained to exist. In Ghana, for example, the Courts Act[38] has elevated the status of customary rules from a matter of fact to a matter of law and the courts are requested to apply and uphold a customary rule once it is proven. The repugnancy test is no more invoked in Ghana, but the test of public policy, remains, which could be used, in fact, to the same end as the repugnancy test.

The Shifting Trend

Notwithstanding, the true position is that customary law as a formal source of law in Africa today has undergone many changes which affect its validity. Its source of authority has parted company with the Savignian School and the theory of the Volksgeist. An examination of what the courts do, in fact, with customary rules will show that no customary rule is regarded as binding until accepted by the court as such. The emphasis as to the validity of customary law has shifted from the assent of the native community to the opinion of the judge, as a result of the repugnancy test. Traditional customary rules have become historical sources of the law, while customary law as a formal source of law is taking the form of judge-made law.

In administering customary law, judges do not stop at the mere factual finding as to what the rule is. They go beyond this. To uphold a customary rule, they seem to be influenced more by factors, such as the result which the application of the rule will bring than the fact that the customary rule truly does exist and is accepted by the community.

For example, in *Edet v. Essien*[39] a Nigerian Divisional Court, applying the test of repugnancy, rejected a customary rule which gives the custody of a child of a union between a woman and an intervener to the husband who is deprived of his wife by the intervener, who paid no dowry for her. The rule as accepted by the community is based on the ground that a marriage under customary law subsists until a refund of the dowry is made to the husband; and that any child of a woman born while the marriage subsists is deemed an offspring of the husband (the customary law concept of illegitimacy being different from the English concept). The court's attitude can only be explained on the ground that it is just fair and equitable for a natural father to have the custody of his child.

Induced by similar considerations, in a more recent case: *Mariyama v.*

Sadiku Ejo[40], a rule of the Igbirra custom which gives the custody of a child born within ten months after divorce to the former husband of its mother was rejected by the court. After finding that the custom does exist, the court took the view that the child should go to its putative father, adding that:

> We must not be understood to condemn this native law and custom in its general application. We appreciate that it is basically sound and would in almost every case be fair and just in its result.[41]

In *Re Effiong Okon Ata*,[42] *Butler Lloyd, J. rejected a customary rule which entitles the former owner of a slave to administer his property after his death. Upon similar facts in Ghana, the West African Court of Appeal gave the same ruling in Kodieh v. Affram.*[43] The view of the courts in both cases was that the rights claimed were those of slave owners, and that since slavery has been abolished (not necessarily under traditional customary law), the rights asserted cannot be upheld. There are other cases[44] similar to those given above in which the courts have rejected a proven customary rule and arrived at a decision which amounts to the creation of a legal norm or the substitution of the law that ought to be.[45] Thus the position of customary law at present can be summarized as follows:

(a) A rule of customary law may not be known to exist until discovered through judicial enquiry;

(b) an existing rule of customary law is valid law if accepted and pronounced upon by the courts;

(c) a rule of customary law is invalid and unenforceable if rejected by the courts; and

(d) a rule of customary law ceases to be law if it is incompatible with statute law.

The result of the above analysis is that the term customary law now means that part of the *corpus juris* which embodies those rules of traditional custom, which are discoverable by judicial enquiry and are enforceable because they conform to the current values in society as determined by the judge. If the validity of customary law rests on the assent of the native community, the mere existence of a customary rule will be enough to give it the force of law and the court will be compelled to enforce it. But the attitude of the court which picks and chooses between an enforceable customary rule and a non-enforceable one seems to have shifted the basis of its validity from the consensus of the community to the opinion of a handful of judges.

Analysis of the Legal Sources

For a better understanding of the analysis of the function of laws in English-speaking Africa it will be necessary to reclassify the source under headings which reflect their social and geographical origin or source of derivation. Thus, we can reclassify the *corpus juris* as follows:

1. *Received Law,* which includes the English Common Law, the doctrines of Equity, and the Statutes of general application;
2. *Laws produced by British established Local Institutions* namely, local statutes and local precedents;
3. *Customary Law* which embodies mainly the rules of traditional custom, and Islamic Law.

As Sir Oliver Wendell Holmes once said, *"The actual life of the Law has not been logic; it has been experience."* The felt necessities of the time, the prevalent moral and political theories, intuitions of public policy, avowed or unconscious, even the prejudices which judges share with their fellow men, have had a good deal more to do than the syllogism in determining the rules by which men should be governed.[46] The corollary of this statement is that for law to fulfill a useful and adequate function in society, it must be based on the felt social, economic, moral and political needs of that particular society at the relevant time. It is on this basis that we intend to examine the function of the legal sources in English-speaking Africa.

The Received Law

The Common Law that was received in Africa was founded on the local customs and usages of very early English communities. By the Middle Ages the local systems had disappeared and a body of rules common to the whole of England was developed. "Common Law" then became the basic law of the land, which the judges of the common law courts[47] developed. Ultimately the Common Law derived from the "Common Customs of the Realm" and the principles that were built around it by the English judges of old.

It cannot, however, be said that common law grew spontaneously from customary rules of England, nor can we hold that it is an artificial creation of English judges. What is more important to note is that it had its roots deeply engrained in the national ideas, ways of life and institutions of the British people.[48] Throughout the history of its development, the guiding principle for the judges was the felt necessities of their time in England, as was dictated by the political, moral and economic conditions.

While common law remained the basic law of England, its rigors became pervasive, because of its stringent application. To temper the pervading rigors, Equity was developed by the Lord Chancellor in the Court of Chancery. It operated within specific areas of the law, both to supplement and alleviate the harshness of the existing common law rules within those areas.

The Chancellor was the keeper of the King's great seal; as a result, original writs issuing from the Chancery were issued by him. He was also known as the keeper of the King's conscience, and a prominent member of the *Curia Regis,* which was the English Council of the 14th Century. Because of his position the Chancellor was right at the hub of legal administration. He was, as a member of the Curia Regis, deputed to hear petitions addressed to it, that body being closest to the Supreme authority of the King.

The petitions arose from failure of the petitioner to obtain justice in the common law court. The failure usually could be due to any of the following reasons:

(i) The common law was in some way defective or rigid. For instance, an aggrieved person in tort or contract might not succeed in bringing action for redress unless there were an existing form of action into which his action could fit in.

(ii) The only remedy obtainable at common law was the remedy of damages, and damages were not always a satisfactory form of relief, particularly where restitution was possible.

(iii) Very powerful and influential parties in the early days could overawe or intimidate the court to give judgment in their favor.

The petitions were at first judged on matters of conscience. The conscience of the Chancellor controlled the decision he would give. Using his discretion thus, he gradually evolved a set of rules to remedy the defects in the common law, and, forms of action to correct the rigidities in the common law. It is the rules and the principles so evolved by the Chancellor in the court of Chancery that became known as Equity.

Generally the doctrines of equity had no direct application upon factual situations. Being originally a matter of conscience, its general approach was to use a common law rule on a particular subject as a base upon which equitable rules and principles were engrafted and subsequently developed. It took some two hundred years after the common law courts were established before the court of Chancery came into existence. Both the common law and the principles of equity continued to be administered in those two separate courts until the year 1875, when the Judicature Act brought their administration within a single court. In any case of conflict between the two systems, it was stipulated that equity should prevail.[49] When, therefore, both systems were received in English-speaking Africa, their administration was fused together, but their rules remained separate and distinct.

The doctrine of equity, like the common law which was received, is part of the British legal experience. The experience was national and therefore particular. Though equity, being originally a matter of conscience, has some universal appeal, its development in Britain was affected by the character of its people, its laws, and the value system. It reflects the British Chancellor's frame of mind in dealing with legal questions of his time. It cannot therefore be correctly maintained that the doctrine of equity, which was received in English-speaking Africa, is so universal as to fit into the African environment and experience.

Statutes, unlike the common law and the doctrines of equity, evolved neither from the judges nor from the Chancellor's conceptions of justice. They are laws made by formal and express declaration of rules by Parliament to regulate human conduct. Statutes are therefore sometimes arbitrary, reflecting values which the legislator has seen or would like to see in society, and which more often than not are results of national experience.

English statutes applicable to English-speaking Africa are of two kinds. The first group are rules enacted by the Crown pursuant to powers delegated to it by the Foreign Jurisdiction Acts dating from 1890 to 1913. The second are statutes of general application enacted before a particular date, the operative date corresponding generally with the date when the colony first had its local legislature.[50] The former Imperial Statutes are of specific application and are a source of law only in those countries specified by the particular statute.[51] As part of the received law, they do not form a considerable portion of the law as the statutes of general application. Also, due to their specific nature, the application of imperial statutes of this kind are not subject to local conditions. Except, therefore, to the extent that the British Parliament before enacting the laws took cognizance of the prevailing conditions in a colony through its legal experts (most of whom had never visited the colony nor possessed adequate knowledge of its social life and institutions), the imperial statutes are generally arbitrary enactments which often wrought injustice.

On the other hand, statutes of general application are in force "so far only as the limits of the local jurisdiction and local circumstances shall permit."[52] In theory, it would seem that this phrase offers an adequate opportunity for the adaptation of statutes to meet the local needs and requirements within the particular matter covered by each statute. In practice, however, the precise meaning and effect of the phrase remain unsatisfactory, and existing judicial decisions have not done much to improve the situation. There are no known decided cases to determine the precise meaning and effect of the "limits of the local jurisdiction," and the judicial decisions on the *"limits of the local circumstances"* show the phrase as having the effect only of excluding a particular statute of general application from the corpus juris. Where the phrase is held not sufficient to exclude a statute, the qualification does not operate to reduce it into a flexible instrument of social order based on the social and economic values of the "colony."

In *Lawal v. Younan*,[53] for example, local practical incongruity arising in the application of the Fatal Accidents Act was held not to be enough to exclude its application. The Act enables the widow of a man killed by the tortious act of another to sue that other for the tort, but bars her right of action if she remarries. The court, in applying the Act, was of the view that the practice of levirate or widow inheritance, which is a feature of customary law marriage, does not bar a widow's right for action under the Act.

There was nothing in the decision to suggest that the Act was unsuitable to the traditional form of marriage, even though it was by its very nature designed for compensation to the woman for losing her husband and not having a substitute to provide for her. Where, however, the Act would produce manifestly unreasonable results or results which would be contrary to the intention of the statute, it would be rejected.[54]

Where the subject matter dealt with by the Act does not exist in the colony, or where the Act requires special administrative and judicial machinery which is non-existent in the colony, the Act is assumed not to apply.[55] Also, the courts would exclude a statute where local phrases do not exist to permit of meaningful formal verbal alterations. Thus, in *Adeoye v. Adeoye*[56] it was held that section 18(1)(b) of the Matrimonial Causes Act 1950 is not in force in Northern Nigeria. It was observed that in the Nigerian local circumstances there was nothing equivalent to the phrase "in any other part of the United Kingdom, or in the Channel Islands or in the Isle of Man," in connection with the residence of the petitioning wife's husband, under the Act. Verbal alterations must be formal only to be acceptable and are not intended to affect the substance of the enactment,[57] which quite obviously reflect more of the social milieu of England at the time of its passing than that of the receiving territory.

The courts are sometimes aware of the fact that a statute may be framed for reasons affecting life in England and may exclude it on that ground. In *Jex v. Mckinney*,[58] the Mortmain Act of 1735, prohibiting in England the acquisition of land by certain institutions including the nonconformist churches, was excluded in British Honduras on the basis that it was framed for reasons affecting the land and society of England and not for reasons applying "to a new Colony."[59] This is certainly true of most if not all statutes of general application. The courts have also taken into consideration some special features of the local traditional law which do not conform with English rules. In some such circumstances it avoids a strict application of the English rule which could cause considerable hardship to both or either of the parties.[60] Nevertheless, this attitude has not been uniformly followed. Thus, in *Green v. Owo*[61] and *Mills v. Renner*[62] (Gold Coast) the Real Property Limitation Act, which was rejected by Webber J. in 1910 in *Chief Young Debe v. African Association*,[63] was regularly applied.

Several views have been expressed as to the meaning of the general applicability of a statute in the context. Some of the proposed criteria are based on general applicability throughout the United Kingdom (i.e., Scotland, Ireland and England)[64] or in the Colonies.[65]

Also, the courts have set forth some relevant factors which are pertinent to the determination of the generality of a statute, such as the persons to whom the statute apply, the subject matter of the statute, and its geographical generality throughout England.[66] None of the views and decisions suggest that general applicability has anything to do with any kind of universality of the English principles purporting to regulate human and social conduct within the subject matter of the particular statute. The motivating force and the rules of conduct of these statutes remain essentially British. The statutes remain part and parcel of the British social and institutional experiences which are quite alien to the receiving colonies.

In 20th Century Britain, some of these statutes have become anachronistic as they no longer meet the needs of the time. To keep abreast with the social requirements and changes, Parliament takes the initiative by repealing outdated Acts. Such repeal Acts, if made outside the reception date, are of no effect in the erstwhile colonies.[67] The Act of Independence of each colony does not alter the position of the old laws. Only, the enactments of the local legislatures in English-speaking Africa show more reluctance than dynamism over altering received British laws and the British legal tradition.

Law Produced by British Established Local Institutions

Local statutes and local Case Law which make up this group have increased and are still increasing both in number and in importance. With local statutes, in particular, the increase after Independence seems to be at the expense of the received law. However, a closer analysis of both types of law would show no true radical change of legal conception, nor a real attempt at legal autochthony in the new independent countries.

In the Western Nigerian States, (former Western Region, including the Mid-West), for example, all the English statutes of general applications were, on the eve of the Nigerian Independence, repealed. The local legislature reenacted some of the pre-1900 statutes, modernizing them by incorporating recent English statutes in conformity with legal reform in England. Common law and equity were retained as part of the received law.[68] The idea was aimed at certainty rather than legal autochthony. Since a statute of general application may not be known to apply in the country until a case turns up in which it is invoked, a catalog of all applicable and acceptable English statutes was deemed necessary for the convenience of legal practice and legal administration. Thus, the exercise in Western Nigeria, the first of its kind in the country, was not only incomplete, but also fell short of bringing the law in line with a conception that is indigenous to the people. Its aim was not even to modernize the substance of applicable English laws and statutes to suit the Nigerian circumstance.

Similar developments can be seen in East Africa where, as in Tanganyika, the inherited Indian Law[69] has been repealed by a local statute and reenacted in the law of Contract Ordinance. In Ghana, the Constitution of the Republic includes, among the various sources of Ghanaian law, the "common law"[70] which, by virtue of local enactments,[71] is no more confined to English common law.

> The common law, as comprised in the laws of Ghana, consists, in addition to the rules of law generally known as the common law, of the rules generally known as the doctrines of equity and *of rules of customary law included in the common law under any enactment providing for the assimilation of such rules* of customary law as are suitable for general application.[72]

The local enactment gives prominence to assimilated rules of customary law that "in the case of inconsistency, an assimilated rule shall prevail over any other rule and a rule of equity shall prevail over any rule other than an assimilated rule."[73]

Since, in Ghana, no rules of customary law have been assimilated, and it is not easy to find any such rules of customary law which are generally observed and are suitable for elevation into a national law, no indigenous common law has been developed, and none (if at all) will be developed in the immediate future. Thus, in practice, the common law as defined by the local enactment remains English law. The exercise, therefore, seems to be of less practical effect in revolutionizing the law. The Ghanaian courts, of course, are by virtue of the Courts Act not bound by the decisions of any foreign court. This normally affords the courts a great opportunity to adopt a more realistic and practical approach to the exposition of the law, but in practice they are so overwhelmed by British legal tradition that the Bench and the Bar are less effective in evolving any legal notion that is more adequate to the social milieu than the received laws.

Further, a close analysis of some of the local legislation will show, generally, that attempts were not necessarily made to oust received foreign law. Where English law was sought to be replaced by local enactment, the latter still owes its origin to sources outside the country concerned. Outstanding examples abound in the field of criminal law. In Southern Nigeria, the Criminal Code[74] replaced the English common law of crime. The Code is based closely upon the Queensland Criminal Code of 1899 which made its debut in Africa in Northern Nigeria in 1904.[75] The Penal Code now applicable in Northern Nigeria was introduced in 1959 and is of the Sudan Model, which in turn was derived from the Indian Penal Code of 1860.[76] The change was more for a unitary criminal code to replace both the old criminal code and the Islamic law of crimes in that Region than for a unique code to reflect the indigenous notions of the law of crimes.

In East Africa the original Indian Penal Code of 1860 was by the early 1930's replaced by the Nigerian Queensland model code which now applies in Tanganyika, Uganda, Kenya, Zanzibar, Zambia (formerly Northern Rhodesia), Malawi (formerly Nyasaland, and the Gambia. It had been suggested that these local enactments aimed at bringing the law of crimes in those territories nearer to the English Common Law of crimes and to give effect to current principles of English Criminal Law.[77]

In Ghana, where the local criminal code can be said to be unique in itself, it shows no originality in the principles it contains. In fact, the code is more of an extensive revision of the St. Lucia Code of 1889, which was derived from a draft Jamaican Code.[78]

Even though in some cases the idea was to replace English Common Law of crimes by a local code, in practice the codes are mainly interpreted, and the extent of their provisions determined, in accordance with the principles of English Law.[79] Where a local statute is not specific as to the principle of law applicable for the determination of its provisions, it may operate to exclude the received law.[80] However, to supplant English statute a local statute must be comprehensive and complete in itself. Where, for instance, a local penal code fails to include certain concepts of the English common law of crime, examples show that the concepts will nevertheless be enforceable in that country.[81]

The courts seem to be the least effective machinery in English-speaking Africa to create and promote legal autochthony. They apply the English common law, the doctrines of equity, and the applicable statures of general application. In interpreting local statutes they show a bias for the English legal principles and rules. In their application of customary law they have further shown trends of trying to modernize its rules to fall in line with certain accepted notions and standards of English law.

The main creative area should be with the interpretation of statutes. Progress in this direction, however, has been greatly hampered by the conservatism of the Bench and the Bar, enhanced by the doctrine of *stare decisis*. The courts in the main cling tenaciously to English common law rules to interpret local statutes, where the statutes fail to define certain words or phrases contained therein. In *R. v. Edge.*,[82] for instance, the English Common law rule (which was expounded in *R. v. Bourne*)[83] was relied upon to interpret the word "unlawful" used in s. 230 of the criminal code.

Even in the field of traditional law, certain doctrines of the English law which are quite unknown to traditional Africa have been manipulated by the courts to achieve similar results. In *Agbo Kofi v. Addo Kofi*[84] it was held by the West African Court of Appeal, in unmistakeable terms, that the doctrine of laches does not apply to land holding under the customary law of land tenure. Nevertheless, through subsequent decisions[85] the courts have applied the principle of estoppel to deprive acquiescing owner of the right of redemption of her land. The aim of the courts, as was stated by De Comarmond, S. P. J. in *Onisiwo v. Fagbenro,* appears to be

> to obviate hardship in cases where, owing to the fact that prescription and limitation of actions are unknown to native law and custom, occupiers of long standing would have been deprived of land of which they had had undisputed possession for a very long time, and in respect of which they had acted as owners with the knowledge and acquiescence of those claiming belatedly to be the rightful owners.[86]

This overlooks the point of inalienability[87] of land under customary law, and where possession, no matter for how long, is never taken to be nine points of the law.

It would appear that, instead of fostering legal autochthony, the courts are imbued with the notion of civilizing the new states through laws whose concepts are quite alien. Inherent in the conservatism of the judges and their attitude toward indigenous conception of law is the belief that the African states are made up of tribes, some of which "are so low in the scale of social organization that their usages and conceptions of rights and duties are not to be reconciled with the institutions or the legal ideas of civilized society."[88] It has however been acknowledged that among the African states "there are indigenous peoples whose legal conceptions, though differently developed, are hardly less precise than (those of the English). When once they have been *studied and understood* they are no less enforceable than rights arising under English law."[89] The fact however remains that a conservative English judge or an African judge who is deeply steeped in the British legal tradition can hardly find it easy to understand the indigenous legal conceptions involved in the case before him. The idea of legal autochthony in Africa may not only be unusual to him, but he may find it repulsive as well.

Customary Law

It is not to be disputed that customary law, like any early law, functioned to compel certain acts and to prevent others. Its ultimate aim was to maintain the established order and enhance social equilibrium. The function of much contemporary law in Africa is aimed at making possible the achievement of rapid developments in all spheres of nation-building. New goals must be achieved, and law becomes one of the best machinery for introducing the required new values for the much-needed rapid development.

Because it has its roots in traditional Africa, customary law is often regarded as law *per excellence,* as reflecting the common consciousness of the people. This is a historical approach to the conception of law. It has the binding force of law and its efficacy as two major preoccupations. The main question, however, is how does customary law fit into the scheme of things in a modern African State that is aspiring toward more industrialization and the development of modern technology?

Undoubtedly, customary law retains its useful function within the subsistence sector of the community. Its flexibility and adaptability to altered circumstances have been recognized by the courts in a series of cases, from *Lewis v. Bankole*[90] to *Mariyama v. Sadiku Ejo.*[91] A rule of customary law may not be allowed by the courts "to override general principles and practice in these days of changing conditions," nevertheless its subjection to motives of expediency is limited by the fact that it is not allowed to lose its character entirely as to the usages and custom of traditional Africa.

We may therefore conclude that customary law is inadequate to solve the needs of any modern African State aspiring toward modern industry and the development of modern technology. The development of a national law in Africa calls for assimilation of customary law rules. The old and the new ought to be blended together in a way that would represent the general will of the people, as well as help forward the social purposes of the African modern State.

Notes to Chapter 1

1. Textbooks do not come within this meaning; instead they are regarded as unauthoritative sources.
2. This distinction is regarded as insignificant, and Glanville Williams, in the 11th edition of Salmond, Sir John, *Jurisprudence* (London: Sweet and Maxwell, 195) p. 530, gave reasons why. See further, Jolowicz, H. F., *Lectures on Jurisprudence, op. cit.,* p. 192.
3. Salmond, Sir John. *On Jurisprudence,* 11th edition by Williams, Glanville (London: Sweet and Maxwell, 1957).
4. In French-speaking Africa, the French Codes which derive from the Code Napoleon form the Basic Law.
5. Salmond, *op. cit.,* p. 139.
6. The Basic Law, i. e., the Constitution, may however provide otherwise.
7. A written Constitution is generally, but not always, an Act of Parliament.
8. Holmes, Oliver Wendell, *The Path of the Law* (Boston: 10 Harvard Law Review, 1897) p. 461; *Collected Legal Papers,* p. 173; see further, Llewellyn, K. *The Bramble Bush,* p. 3.
9. See Szladits, Charles, *A Guide to Foreign Legal Systems; French, German, Swiss* (New York) (1959).
10. Codex vii. 45, 13.
11. See Esser, Josef, *Crundsatz and Norm* (Tubingen: 1956), p. 23; also, David, Rene and de Vries, H. P., *The French Legal System* (New York: Oceana Publications, 1958), pp. 79–121.
12. Enneccerus, Kepp and Wolf, *Lehrbuch des Burgerlichen Rechts,* 1, 168; Veny, Francois, *Methode D'interpretation et Sources en Droit Prive Positif,* (Paris: 1954), 2nd edition II, pp. 51–52.
13. See for example, Kent, *Commentaries on American Law,* 14th ed.
14. Carter, *Law: Its Origin, Growth and Function* (New York: 1907), p. 65.
15. 1908, 211 U. S., 210 at p. 226. Emphasis added.
16. Hale, Sir Matthew, *History of the Common Law* (London: 1939), 4th ed., p. 67.
17. Thomas Hobbes, *Leviathan* (London: Everyman's Library, 1914) Ch. XXVI. See also (Oxford: Oxford University Press, 1957) ed., p. 181.
18. (1 / /4), Cowp. 37. See 98, *English Report* 954 at p. 955.
19. *Fisher v. Prince* (1762), 3 Burr 1363; 97, *English Report* 876.
20. Gray, J. C., *Nature and Sources of the Law* (New York: 1948), p. 100; also pp. 84, 94–95, 104.
21. Bodenheimer, Edgar, *Jurisprudence* (Cambridge, Mass: Harvard University Press, 1962), pp. 272–273.
22. Hoadly, Benjamin, Bishop of Bangor, Sermon preached before the King, 1717, p. 12.
23. See for example, Nigeria; section 27(1) High Court Law of Lagos Act. There are similar provisions in the Regional High Court Laws and elsewhere in former British territories.
24. Nigeria; Section 14(3) Evidence Act Cap. 62.
25. Quere if its rejection denies it the force of law, even in the traditional sense.
26. (1931) A. C. 662 at p. 673.

27. (1962) 1 W. L. R. 1053.
28. *Ibid.,* p. 1060. See also (1958) 3 F. S. C. 46 for the Federal Supreme Courts earlier decision on the case, which was upheld by the Privy Council.
29. The Privy Council has ceased in many of those states to be the last court of appeal and its decision now is persuasive in those states. But it is arguable that the principle of the *Eshugbayi Elekn's Case* has already become part of the law through the doctrine of *stare decisis.*
30. Biei v. Akonea (1956) 1 W. A. L. R. 174.
31. (1938) 14 N. L. R. 42.
32. *Ibid.,* p. 44.
33. (1909) 1 N. L. R., pp. 100–101.
34. Elias, T. O., *Nigerian Legal System* (London: 1962), p. 6.
35. Contrary views have been expressed by some writers on this topic. See for example, Ojo Abiolu, "Judicial Approach to Customary Law," in *Journal of Islamic and Comparative Law,* 1969 Vol. 3, p. 44, and especially p. 51; also, Olawoya, "Customary Law and the Repugnancy Provision," in *The Lawyer* (Journal of Law Society, University of Lagos) May 1970, Vol. 4, No. 1, p. 6.
36. (1931) A. C. 622 at p. 673. Emphasis added.
37. Evidence Act (Nigeria) s. 14(2).
38. Courts Act 1960. See also, the Senegalese Ordinance of November 14, 1960 Arts. 11 & 14. Some States of French-speaking Africa go further, drawing up a list of customs to be assimilated into the law. See, for instance, the Senegalese arrete of Feb. 28, 1961.
39. (1932) 11 N. L. R. 47.
40. (1961) N. R. N. L. R. 81.
41. *Ibid.,* p. 83. See also, *Re. Whyte* (1946) 18 N. L. R. 70.
42. (1930) 10 N. L. R. 65.
43. (1930) 1 W. A. C. A. 12. Ghana was then known as the Gold Coast.
44. For example, *Amachree v. Kallio* (1914) 2 N. L. R. 108, where a customary rule giving exclusive right to fish in a navigable river to a section of the Nigerian community was rejected on the ground that it was unfair and against public policy for any section of the community to have such a right over a navigable river which, in the court's view, belonged to all. See further, *Guri v. Hadejia Native Authority* (1950) 4 F. S. C. 44, illustrating the attitude of the Court toward rules of the Islamic Law.
45. *Cf.,* the more recent cases of *Dawodu v. Danmole* (1958) 3 F. S. C. 46; (1962) 1 W. L. R. 1053 (P.C.); *Nezieanya v. Okagbue* (1963) 1 All N. L. R. 352; *Salako v. Salako* (1965) L. L. R. 136; *Ogiamien v. Ogiamien* (1967) N. M. L. R. 245, particularly, p. 247; and *Nwaribe v. President, Registrar East Oru (Omuma) District Court, Orlu* (1964) 8 E. N. L. R., p. 24.
46. Holmes, Oliver Wendall, *The Common Law* (Boston: Little Brown & Co, 1923) p. 1. See also, pp. 213, 312. (Emphasis added.)
47. These were the Court of Kings Bench, the Court of Common Pleas, and the Court of Exchequer.
48. For a detailed account of the history and development of the Common Law, see, Allen, C. K., *Law in the Making,* (Oxford: Clarendon Press, 5th edition) Potter, Harold, *A Historical Introduction to English Law and its Institutions* 3rd ed., pp. 253–549 (London: Butterworths, 2nd edition) James, P. S., *An Introduction to English Law.*
49. Judicature Act 1873. s.25(1); now Supreme Court of Judicature (Consolidations) Act 1925, s. 44.
50. The operative date in Nigeria is 1st January 1900. In other countries the dates are as follows: Ghana, July 24, 1874; Sierra Leone, January 1, 1880; Uganda, 11th August

1902; Kenya, 12 August 1897; Tanzania (Tanganyika) 22nd July, 1920. For more details and other dates, see Allot, A. N., *Judicial And Legal Systems in Africa* (London: Butterworths, 1962).

51. Such powers of the British Crown to legislate for the colonies ceased after each colony has achieved independence.

52. This phrase is present in most of the local acts enabling the application of Imperial laws coming within this group. See, for example, Nigeria, Interpretation Act, Cap. 89 s.45(2); Eastern Region High Court Law No. 27 of 1955, s.20(1); Northern Region High Court Law No. 8 of 1955, s.28A(1). Also, East African Protectorate Order in Council, 1902.

53. (1961) 1 All N. L. R. 245.

54. *Ibid.,* p. 257.

55. See, *Halliday v. Alapatira* (1881) 1 N. L. R. 1, where Smith, J. rejected the application of the Bankruptcy Act in the Colony of Lagos apparently for the lack of the existence of the necessary administrative and judicial machinery.

56. (1962) N. R. N. L. R. 63.

57. See *Apatira v. Akanke* (1944) 17 N. L. R. 149 where the Court rejected the suggestion by Counsel that the question of attestation and validity of a will under the Wills Act 1837 ought to be determined in the light of local circumstances and the local (Mohammedan) Law.

58. (1889) 14 App. Cas. 77.

59. *Ibid.,* p. 82.

60. See *Balogun v. Balogun* (1935) 2 W. A. C. A. 291; further, *Nyali Ltd. v. Attorney-General* (1955) 1 All E. R. 646, (1966) I BI (CA), where it was held that an implied grant under an agreement was sufficient in Kenya for the English rule which requires a grant by the Crown at a franchise of Pontage to be by matter of record, i. e., by Charter or letters patent.

61. (1936) 13 N. L. R. 43.

62. (1940) 6 W. A. C. A. 144.

63. (1910) 1 N. L. R. 130.

64. See *Young Dede v. African Association* (1910) 1 N. L. R. 30; *In Resholu* (1932) 11 N. L. R. 37 of *Young v. Abina* (1940) 6 W. A. C. A. 180.

65. See *Att. General v. John Holt & Co.* (1910) 2 N. L. R. 1. The view which was submitted was, however, rejected by Osborne C.J.

66. See, per Osborne, C. J., in *Att. General v. John Holt Co., ibid.,* p. 21; *Ribeiro v. Chahin* (1954) 14 W. A. C. A. 476 (a Gold Coast case); *Inspector General of Police v. Kamara* (1934) 2 W. A. C. A. 185; *Labinjo v. Abake* (1924) 5 N. L. R. 33; *Adam v. Duke* (1927) 8 N. L. R. 88.

67. See *Stephen v. Pedrocchi* (1959) N. L. R. 76 where Smith Ag. S. P. J. rejected counsel's submission that a repeal of a statute of general application by the English Parliament after the reception date in Nigeria makes the law inoperative in that country. Further, in *Young v. Abina* (1940) 6 W. A. C. A. 180, it was held that the Land Transfer Act of 1897, which was repealed in England in 1925, still remains part of Nigerian Law; and in *Ribeiro v. Chahin* (1954) 14 W. A. C. A. 476 ss. 210–212 of the Common Law Procedure Act, 1852, which was repealed before 1900 but after the reception date in the Gold Coast (July 24, 1874), remains part of the law of Ghana.

68. See Law of England (Application) Law Cap. 60 sections 3 and 4.

69. The Indian Contract Act.

70. The Constitution of the Republic of Ghana, 1960 s.40. Several Acts of the United Kingdom and statutes of general application which hitherto were in force in Ghana were retained by the Constitution.

71. See, for example, the Interpretation Act (CA.4) 1960.
72. *Ibid.,* s.17(1), Emphasis added.)
73. S. 17(2).
74. No. 15 of 1916.
75. No. 23 of 1904.
76. This Code also applies in the Northern Region of the Somali Republic.
77. Read, J. S., "Criminal Law in Africa of Today and Tomorrow," J. A. L. Vol. 7, No. 1, 1963, p. 7.
78. Read, *op. cit.,* p. 5. In Ethiopia, the Penal Code is entirely foreign to that country and was in fact drafted by someone who had never visited the country nor knew of the prevailing conditions there.
79. See, Tanganyika Penal Code, Cap. 16 ss.4 & 18; Malawi (Nyasaland) Penal Code Cap. 23 s.17 & 3; See further, Penal Codes of Uganda, Kenya, and Zanzibar.
80. See *Wallace-Johnson v. R.* (1940) A. C. 231 (Gold Coast Appeal) to the Privy Council; *Ogbuagu v. The Police* (1953) 20 N. L. R. 139.
81. See *Magingi v. R.* (1955) 22 E. A. C. A. 387 (a Tanganyikan case), *R. v. Nwanjoku of Umuhu* (1937) W. A. C. A. 208; *R. v. Cooker* (1927) 8 N. L. R. 7; *Shorunke v. R.* (1946) A. C. 316.
82. (1938) 4 W. A. C. A. 133.
83. (1939) 1 K. B. 687.
84. (1933) 1 W. A. C. A. 284.
85. See, for example, *Awo v. Cookey Gam* (1913) 2 N. L. R. 100; *Onisiwo v. Fagbenro* (1954) 21 N. L. R. 3.
86. (1954) 21 N. L. R., p. 6.
87. See also, *Golightly v. Ashrifi* (1955) 14 W. A. C. A. 676, where the court relied on flexibility of Native Law to uphold alienation; 1961 J. A. L. 52 (P. C.); and *Alade v. Aborisade* (1960) 5 F. S. C. 167. These and other similar cases show the courts increased inclination toward alienation of family land. This is another process of modernizing customary law.
88. See, per Lord Summer delivering the report of the Judicial Committee of the Privy Council, in re *Southern Rhodesia* (1919) A. C. 211 (P. C.), p. 233.
89. *Ibid.,* p. 234. (Emphasis added.)
90. (1909) 1 N. L. R. See, per Osborne, C. J., pp. 100–101.
91. (1961) N. R. N. L. R. 81. See further, the Nigerian and Ghanaian cases of *Amachree v. Kallio* (1914) 2 N. L. R. 108; *Kodieh v. Affram* (1930) 1 W. A. C. A. 12; Re Effiong Okon Ata (1930) 10 N. L. R. 65; *Biei v. Akomea* (1956) 1 W. A. L. R. 174; and *Guri v. Hadejia Native Authority* (1959) F. Sc. 44.

Chapter 2

The Technique
of the Judicial Process
in Dealing with
the Legal Sources

No unanimity has been achieved in legal philosophy as to the true function of a judge in the administration of the law. Under the English and the American systems the argument so far has been centered on two questions:

Is the judge's main role to maintain stability in the law? Or does his role embrace a law-making process? If, as is the view of Chief Justice Holmes, the law is "the prophecies of what the judges will do in fact and nothing more pretentious," then the judge is the only true law-giver. Legislation and customary law consequently become historical sources of law which would derive their legality from the pronouncement of the court.

As a choice between alternatives, law in the hands of the judge assumes the character ascribed to it by the court. However, the judge in selecting his alternative is normally bound by certain rules and principles which may limit his powers as the ultimate law-giver. Judges have a dual function in administering the law. These functions are:

(a) the maintenance of stability in the law, and,
(b) effecting changes in the law to meet current social needs.

It is in these functions that the relevance of the judicial process to legal philosophy may be found.

The fitting aphorism is that "law must be stable and yet it cannot stand still."[1] Stability and change in the law are necessary. The judge maintains stability in law by adherence to the principles and rules of the judicial process. His contribution to the use of law as a machinery of social change lies in:

(1) his power to interpret statutes for social engineering,
(2) his power to overrule old and outmoded precedents, and,
(3) his power to sift rules of customary law.

Thus, in any developing country the law-making powers of the judges may aid legislation to effect changes in the law to meet the current social, political, and economic needs of the time. They may use such powers also to give new blood to the law outside legislation by their dealings with decided cases and rules of customary law.

We can therefore consider the technique applied by the judge in his functions to effect stability and change in the law under three heads:

(1) Statute Law
(2) Precedent
(3) Customary Law

Statute Law

In dealing with a statute, the judge may be bound to place a certain interpretation on the statute. Examples of such authentic interpretation may be seen in statutes which define some words or phrases used in the statute itself, or which define the meaning to be attached to some expressions in other statutes.[2] Also, as a result of the doctrine of binding precedent, a judge may be bound in accordance with the doctrine to place particular meaning on the words of a statute. In both instances there is an actual rule of law which binds the judge in interpreting the statute. Here the scope of his power is very limited as he has no other choice but to adopt the authentic, or usual analytical approach to statutory interpretation.

The approach is authentic because the statute has already established the true meaning of the expression used. Where the meaning of the expression used has been established in a previous case and later adopted by a judge in a subsequent case, the approach is often referred to as usual. Both approaches are purely analytical, as the judge has to apply the law that is, and not the law that ought to be.

On the other hand, the judge may not be so fettered. He may be called upon simply to interpret the statute. He then has two courses open to him:

(a) He may lay emphasis solely on finding the true meaning of the words used because the framers of the statute must have intended what the words mean.
(b) He may put emphasis solely, not on finding the true meaning of the expressions used, but on the intention of the makers of the ᐧ statute, so as to give effect to it. With the first course, the judge's

grammatical construction, unless that is at variance with the in...
the legislature, to be collected from the statute itself, or ...
manifest absurdity or repugnance, in which case the la...
varied or modified so as to avoid such inconvenience, ...

From decided cases[11] it seems quite obvious th...
normally would adopt the analytical approach...
cases where a grammatical interpretation w...
pugnance. In a recent case of *Prince of F*...
the court of first instance was called...
English Act of 1705 which conferre...
ants of Princess Sophia. It foun...
opinion that its strict applica...
in effect confer British na...
the operation of the Ac...
Appeal was not impresse...
the decision on appeal.[13] It t...
of the statute is clear, its absura...
no latitude to adopt the functiona...
in English-speaking Africa who follo...

Rules of Interpretation of the Analytical A...

The basic rule of the analytical approach...
the *Literal Rule*. It is the general rule followed...
words in a statute are taken to bear the usual...
dictionary. Once the meaning of a word is clear the...
meaning, regardless of the consequences. The attitud...
appeal in the *Prince of Hanover* case already referred to...
well the conservatism of the English Court with regard to th...

In that case the appellant, born in 1914, and descending fro...
Sophia, claimed British citizenship based on a British statute o...
The statute provided as follows:

> Princess Sophia Electress and Duchess Dowager of Hanover, and the issue
> of her body, and all persons lineally descending from her, born or hereafter
> to be born, be and shall be to all intents and purposes whatsoever, deemed,
> taken and esteemed natural born subjects of (the United Kingdom).

The court of first instance, applying the technique of the Golden Rule,
saw in the Act an absurdity in extending United Kingdom citizenship to
descendants of the princess *ad infinitum*. The Court of Appeal, however,
stuck to the grammatical or literal interpretation...

---

approach is again analytical, but the second is functional.[3]
The judge in a functional approach, may be inclined either to determine the social purpose and policy of the statute in order to give effect to
it, or to use his free intuition. Where he refers to the social purpose and
policy of the statute, the judge gives himself a limited latitude than when
he adopts the free intuitional approach. The former gives him latitude to
make law which is confined only to the social purpose as seen from the
wordings of the statute.

The main distinction between the analytical approach and the functional is that, while the former primarily aims at stability in the law, the
latter aims at effecting changes in the law to suit the needs and circumstances of society.

Rules of Interpretation of the Functional Approach

We can see from the above that the technique of the functional approach may be logical, free intuitional, or a look at the social policy. The
emphasis is on effecting the intention and purpose of the statute. The
words of the statute are interpreted in such a way as to give effect to the
intention of its framers.

The English courts fall back on two main rules to give effect to the
social purpose and policy of the statute; namely:

(1) *The Mischief Rule*, and
(2) *The Golden Rule*

The Mischief Rule is to the effect that judges are to construct the statute
in such a way as to suppress the mischief of the common law, which the
statute sought to remedy, and to promote the remedy. The Golden Rule,
on the other hand, is a more cautious application of the functional approach. It demands that the ordinary meaning of the words used in a
statute be adhered to, unless this would lead to absurdity, in which case
the literal sense may be modified.

The main contents of the Mischief Rule were summarized by the English court in *Heydon's Case*. In considering the rule it is the duty of the
court to discuss and consider four things:

...as the Common Law before the making of the Act?
...the mischief and defect for which the Common Law did
...h Parliament resolved and appointed to cure the
...nwealth?
...remedy.

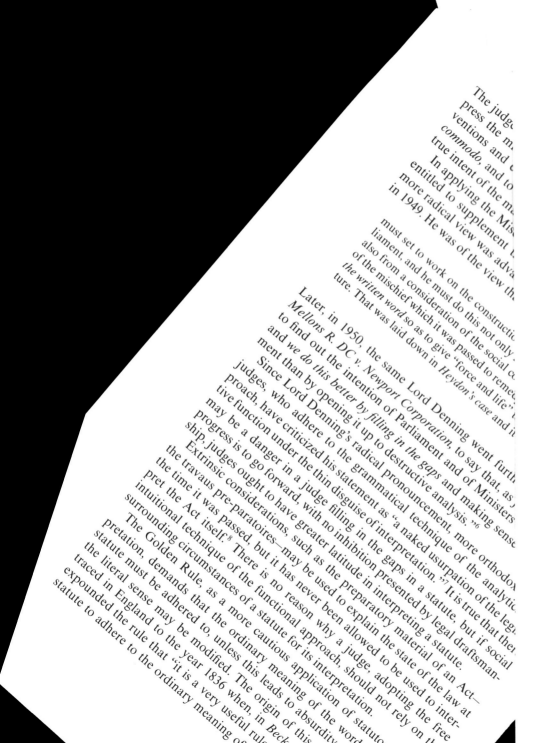

The judge... press the m... ventions and... commodo, and to... true intent of the m...

In applying the Mis... entitled to supplement... more radical view was adva... in 1949. He was of the view th...

must set to work on the constructio... liament, and he must do this not only... also from a consideration of the social co... of the mischief which it was passed to reme... the written word so as to give "force and life";... ture. That was laid down in *Heydon's case* and i...

Later, in 1950, the same Lord Denning went furth... *Mellons R. DC v. Newport Corporation*, to say that, as... to find out the intention of Parliament and of Ministers... *and we do this better by filling in the gaps and making sens*... ment than by opening it up to destructive analysis."[6]

Since Lord Denning's radical pronouncement, more orthodox... judges, who adhere to the grammatical technique of the analytic... proach, have criticized his statement as "a naked usurpation of the legi... tive function under the thin disguise of interpretation."[7] It is true that the... may be a danger in a judge filling in the gaps in a statute, but if social... progress is to go forward, with no inhibition presented by legal draftsman-... ship, judges ought to have greater latitude in interpreting a statute.

Extrinsic considerations, such as the preparatory material of an Act—... the *travaux pre-paratoires*—may be used to explain the state of the law at... the time it was passed, but it has never been allowed to be used to inter-... pret the Act itself.[8] There is no reason why a judge, adopting the free... intuitional technique of interpretation... surrounding circumstances of the functional approach, should not rely on the...

The Golden Rule, as a more cautious application of statuto... pretation, demands that the ordinary meaning of the word... statute must be adhered to, unless this leads to absurdity... the literal sense may be modified. The origin of this... traced in England to the year 1836 when, in Beck... expounded the rule that "it is a very useful rul... statute to adhere to the ordinary meaning o...

clear and unambiguous, their effect could not be restricted even by consideration of inconvenience or incongruity consequential on the enactment, such inconvenience or incongruity not following immediately on the passing of the statute, but rather arising through the statute being left unrepealed for so long.

As Celsus once said, "to know the law does not mean to be familiar with their words, but with their sense and significance. Laws should be liberally interpreted in order that their intent be preserved."[16] A rigid analytical approach is a plug on social change through the law. Statutes ought to be interpreted in such a way as to give effect to the intention of the framers, but more so in a way that will be in keeping with the spirit of the time.

The only instances where the English Courts could depart from applying the literal rule are:

(a) Where the expression used in the statute in question is so faulty that no sense can be made of it at all, or

(b) if the literal sense is so unreasonable *in the context* that it cannot possibly be regarded as corresponding to the will of the legislature.

The position was summarized earlier by Tindal, C. J. in *Sussex Peerage Case*[17] as follows:

> If the words of the statute are in themselves precise and unambiguous, then no more can be necessary than to expound those words in their natural and ordinary sense. The words themselves alone do, in such case, best declare the intention of the law giver.[18]

In consequence of both their place and method of legal training, most judges in English-speaking Africa, like their English counterparts and legal trainers, regard legislation as a closed logical source of law in which correct decisions are deducible only from the words used in the statute. The chief tool of Jurisprudence is, to their mind, analysis in the positivist or analytical sense. Thus, the major pursuit of lawyers, and the main function of the judge in English-speaking Africa today is to take the law as it stands and not as it ought to be.

Over the years the English courts have developed sub-rules in aid of the literal approach to statutory interpretation, among which are:

(i) The usual meaning is taken at the time when the statute was passed

This operates to prevent the adaptation of a statute, especially out-

Statutes of general application come within this category.

In the United Kingdom, Parliament may take steps to repeal an Act that has become anachronistic in order to remove a later inconvenience or incongruity. In the erstwhile colonies, such Acts, as we have seen, may continue to be law regardless of the repeal, if made outside the relevant date. Thus, in *Young v Abina*,[19] the West African Court of Appeal held that the Land Transfers Act of 1897, which was repealed in England by the Property Act of 1925, still remained part of Nigerian Law. In *Ribeiro v Chahin*,[20] another decision of the West African Court of Appeal, sections 210–212 of the Common Law Procedure Act 1852, which were repealed in England before 1900, but after the reception date (July 24, 1874) in the then Gold Coast, remains part of the law of Ghana.

Strict adherence to the application of the literal rule in interpreting Acts, such as we have seen, would result in the perpetuation of the incongruity and inconvenience which time has brought to the Act. The incongruity and inconvenience would be compounded by the fact that the outdated statute is made to apply in a society whose social and economic backgrounds differ greatly from those of England for which it was intended originally. The judge is left with no room to maneuver to modernize the law. As long as the words of the statute remain clear and unambiguous, even though out of tune with the time, he has a "sacred" duty to interpret the Act, giving the words the meanings they bore at the time the Act was passed.

(ii) The statute itself may provide special meaning for words used in it, or, it may give directives as to the technique or the principle of law to be applied.

The court has no alternative but to apply the special meaning as provided by the statute. An example of this is the Interpretation Act of 1889. Here again, in English-speaking Africa, such an authentic legal approach to statutory interpretation limits any scope the court may have to bring a long-standing statute in line with the realities of modernization.

Local statutes sometimes specify that the principles of statutory interpretation in England should apply, thereby making it impossible for any judge to depart from the analytical approach which is the general rule of statutory interpretation in England. For example, section 4 of the Penal Code of Tanganyika provides as follows:

This Code shall be interpreted in accordance with the principles of legal interpretation obtaining in England, and expressions used in it shall be presumed, so far as is consistent with their context and except as may be otherwise provided, to be used with the meaning attaching to them in accordance therewith.

Similar provisions could be found in the Penal Codes of the Gambia[21] and in most East and Central African Codes.[22]

Far from giving the courts more scope to deal with local statutes to reflect the social milieu, most local statutes go further and tie the judges to the apron strings of the English law. Certain offenses are to be defined merely by reference to the law "for the time being in force" in England;[23] and some legal concepts are to be determined in accordance with the *principles* of English law. Thus the Tanganyika and Nyasaland Penal Codes provide that the "criminal responsibility for the use of force in the defence of person or property shall be determined according to the principles of English law."[24]

The effect of the above technique is that current English decisions are cited and relied on in courts. In *Mawji and Ors. v R*[25] the Privy Council took the view that since in English Criminal Law the words "conspires" and "conspiracy" are not applicable to husband and wife alone, the words "other persons" in section 110(a) of the Tanganyikan Penal Code dealing with conspiracy cannot in the context include a spouse whose marriage was potentially polygamous, if English Criminal Law is applied, to their "interpretation" and "meaning."[26] Consequently, it held that the English rule applied to spouses of any marriage valid under the laws of Tanganyika.

One would think that for received English statutes the general clause usually present in the enabling statute, viz, "such Imperial laws shall be in force so far only as the limits of the local jurisdiction and local circumstances shall permit,"[27] would be sufficient to allow the courts to adopt the free intuitional approach. We have however seen above that the precise meaning and effect of the phrase, *the limits of the local jurisdiction* is unknown, and that the meaning of *"limits of local circumstances"* remains a mute point. Brett, F. J. is of the view, however, that "the court would be free to hold that local circumstances did not permit a statute to be in force if it produces results which were manifestly unreasonable or contrary to the intention of the statute."[28] This view is only helpful where it is the applicability of a statute and not its method of interpretation that is in question. Notwithstanding, where local difficulties arise in the practical application of a general act, the court has adopted the view that it is not enough to make it inapplicable to the colony. Thus, in Nigeria the practice of levirate (widow inheritance) has been held not to bar a widow's right of action under the Fatal Accidents Act.[29]

Another aspect of the literal rule is that technical words are given their usual technical meaning, unless specified otherwise by the statute itself.[30] The usual meaning either of technical words or other words is taken subject to the context. This means that the statute must be taken as a whole in order to determine the usual meaning of the word used. As a guide to this "context" rule the English courts developed other sub-rules. For example, if a phrase or word has two possible interpretations in a given context, the express mention of one of the possible meanings in a similar context excludes the other possibility. This rule is often remembered by the Latin tag *expressio unius est exclusio alterius.* Thus, in *Lead Smelting Co. v. Richardson*[31] the express mention of the word *coalmines,* after *lands,* was held to exclude other mines, even though "land" in its usual meaning would include all mines.

The next sub-rule, referred to as the *ejusdem generis rule,* is to the effect that where, after mentioning a list of specific items a statute follows it up with a general concluding clause, this general clause is deemed not to include in its meaning things that are not of the same kind as those specified in the list. Following this rule, in *Sandiman v Breach,*[32] it was held that a coach proprietor does not come within the meaning of "other persons whatsoever" used by the Sunday Observance Act of 1677, which provided as follows:

> no tradesmen, artificer, workman, labourer, or *other person whatsoever,* shall do or exercise any labour, business, or work of their ordinary callings upon the Lords' Day.[33]

There are other rules and sub-rules of the literal approach to statutory interpretation developed by the English Courts, which are not discussed here.[34] The few rules selected are enough to illustrate the rigidity of the analytical approach and the conservatism of the judges in following the rules. The judges are mainly concerned with trying to solve questions where statute law is vague or ambiguous. The question that judges in English-speaking Africa must always solve first is: by what test the ambiguous is to be resolved. The adoption of abstruse or immutable principles of the English law neglects the social effect of the court's decision. Law has a double role to play in society. The one function is to strengthen and stabilize social relationship, and the other is to promote social change to meet the demands of a progressive and forward-looking society. These functions should coincide with the intention of any true and patriotic legislator and should be the concern of judges whose duty it is to determine that intention.

Case Law

Stare Decisis

Case law, as we have noted earlier, rests on the doctrine of binding precedent otherwise known as *stare decisis*. This doctrine imposes an obligation on lower courts to follow relevant decisions of a superior court *as a matter of law*. Also a similar obligation, though to a modified degree, as we shall see later, is imposed on the superior court to follow its previous relevant decisions. Thus, speaking on the doctrine with regard to the House of Lords, the Highest Court of the land in England, Lord Campbell in *Bright v. Hutton* said, "this House cannot decide something as law today and decide differently the same thing as law tomorrow...after there has been a solemn judgment of this House, laying down any position as law, I apprehend that that is binding upon the rights and liabilities of the Queen's subjects until it is altered by an Act of the Commons, the Lords, and the Sovereign on the throne."[35]

In 1861 the same Lord Campbell, emphasizing on the absoluteness of the doctrine, had further stated that the law laid down by a previous decision of the House of Lords, "being clearly binding on all inferior tribunals, and on all the rest of the Queen's subjects, *if it were not considered as equally binding upon your Lordships, this House would be arrogating to itself the right of altering the law, and legislating by its own separate authority.*[36] In *Young v. Bristol Aeroplane Co.*[37] the rule was firmly laid that the English Court of Appeal is absolutely bound, not only by its own decision, but by those of older English Courts of coordinate authority, such as the Court of the Exchequer Chamber. "We have come to the clear conclusion" said Lord Green "that this court is bound to follow previous decisions of its own as well as those of courts of coordinate jurisdiction."[38]

To understand the scope of the doctrine of binding precedent in English-speaking Africa, one has to study first its operation in England, and then by analogy draw the necessary conclusions. The prerequisites of the doctrine are two:

(a) an established hierarchy of courts, and
(b) a system of law reports.

These are present both in the legal systems of England and in English-speaking African States. In the latter they are relics of the colonial heritage. It is true that in some independent States of Africa, such as Ghana and Nigeria, attempts have been made to sever connections with the Judicial Committee of the Privy Council,[39] but the national legal system remains the English pattern.

The Hierarchy of the Courts

The following diagram illustrates the hierarchy of the English Courts since the Judicature Act of 1875.

SUPREME COURT OF JUDICATURE

COURT OF CRIMINAL APPEAL (Appeals to House of Lords)	COURT OF APPEAL (Appeals to House of Lords)	HIGH COURT OF JUSTICE
COMMISSION OF ASSIZES	CHANCERY DIVISION (Appeals to Court of Appeal)	KINGS BENCH DIVISION (Appeals to Court of Appeal)
		COMMON PLEAS DIVISION EXCHEQUER DIVISION
		PROBATE DIVORCE AND ADMIRALTY (Appeals to Court of Appeal, except in prize cases)

Older Courts Now merged since 1880 into the King's Bench Division

The House of Lords is the highest judicial authority in the United Kingdom, and as a matter of law its decisions are binding on all courts inferior to it. It is also bound to follow its own previous decisions, as we have seen in the cases mentioned above.[40]

However, there are cases where it is doubtful whether the House is bound as a matter of law by its own previous decisions. Apparently the House of Lords is not bound by its previous decision in peerage cases.[41] It is also presumed that where a decision was clearly made by the House in ignorance of an existing Statute, such a decision would be regarded as a mistake of fact and thus would not be binding on the House.[42] Generally, the decision of the House with regard to appeals from Scotland does not bind English courts, and the House itself is not bound by it when it hears appeals from English courts. However, such a decision may be binding on English courts if the Scottish law on the point is declared by the House to be the same as the law of England.[43]

Of recent, however, the House of Lords seems to be having second thoughts about following its past decisions, which all along were aimed at producing finality and maintaining certainty in the law. In a *practice statement* of the House made in 1966, the Lords took a rather dramatic view that

Their Lordships regard the use of precedent as an indispensable foundation upon which to decide what is the law and its application to individual cases. It provides at least some degree of certainty upon which individuals can rely in the conduct of their affairs, as well as a basis for orderly development of legal rules.

Their Lordships nevertheless recognise that too rigid adherence to precedent may lead to injustice in a particular case and also unduly restrict the proper development of the law. They propose, therefore, to modify their present practice and, while treating former decisions of this House as normally binding, to depart from a previous decision when it appears right to do so.

In this connection they will bear in mind the danger of disturbing retrospectively the basis on which contracts settlements of property and fiscal arrangements have been entered into and also the special need for certainty as to the criminal law. *This announcement is not intended to affect the use of precedent elsewhere than in this House.*[44]

To what extent this policy statement of the House would bring about confusion as to which of the Houses previous decisions the lower courts would follow is yet to be seen. So also is its effect on the certainty of the law, if in actual practice it brings about a true deviation from the normal practice of the House with regard to the doctrine of Stare decisis.

The English Court of Appeal is absolutely bound to follow, not only its own previous decisions, but also the decisions of those older and now obsolete courts of coordinate authority, such as the Exchequer Chamber.[45] There are only three exceptions when the court is not bound by its previous decisions:

(a) The court is entitled, and must decide which of two conflicting decisions of its own it will follow.

(b) The court may refuse to follow in a subsequent case a previous decision of its own which, though not expressly overruled, cannot in its opinion, stand with a decision of the House of Lords.

(c) Where the court is satisfied that a previous decision of its own was given *per incuriam,* it is not bound to follow it. For example, the court may not follow its own decision where a statute, or a rule having statutory effect, or other binding authority which would have affected the decision if noted, was not brought to the attention of the court in the earlier case.

The Court of Appeal binds all inferior civil courts, and possibly the inferior criminal courts. It does not bind the Court of Criminal Appeal, and the latter does not bind it.

The Court of Criminal Appeal binds all inferior criminal courts. It is not clear whether it binds civil Divisional Courts of the High Court.

Generally, the Court is bound to follow its previous decision, and is bound by those of the older courts for Crown cases Reserved.

Where the Court, however, deals with questions involving the liberty of the subject, *before a full court,* it is under a duty to reconsider its earlier decision, where in its opinion there was a possible misapplication or misunderstanding of the law. The court in such a case, said Goddard, C. J. in *R v Taylor,*[46] has to deal with questions involving the *liberty of the subject,* and if it finds on reconsideration that, in the opinion of a *full court assembled* for the purpose, the law has been either misapplied or misunderstood in a decision which it has previously given and that, on the strength of that decision, an accused person has been sentenced and imprisoned, it is the bounden duty of the Court to reconsider the earlier decision with a view to seeing whether that person had been properly convicted. The exceptions which apply in civil cases ought not to be the only ones applied in such a case as the present.[47]

The English High Court binds all the lower courts, i. e., the Magistrate Courts and the County Courts, with the following exceptions:

(a) Generally, decisions made at *nisi prius*[48] do not possess great legal authority and as such are not binding. So far, only the case of *Baker v Bolton*[49] which decided that the death of a human being *per se* does not constitute an injury for which action could lie in a civil court, and which was a decision at *nisi prius,* has gained legal weight.

(b) One High Court judge is not bound by another High Court judge. Further, since they are of equal jurisdiction, one cannot overrule the other. The normal practice is that a High Court judge is at liberty to refuse to follow a previous decision of another High Court judge with which he disagrees. In that case their conflicting decisions will stand side by side until resolved by a higher court.[50] *Divisional Courts of the High Court* practise the following:

(1) A decision of a Divisional Court of the Queens Bench Division binds a judge of the Queen's Bench Division.

(2) A decision of a Divisional Court of the Queen's Bench is not binding on a judge of the Chancery Division.[51]

(3) A single High Court judge does not bind a Divisional Court.[52]

(4) The Divisional Court regards itself as bound by its previous decisions, but it may choose which of its two conflicting previous decisions to follow.[53]

(5) A Divisional Court in civil matters is bound by the Court of Appeal.[54] Probably, it is not bound by the decisions of the Court of Criminal Appeal.

(6) A Divisional Court in criminal matters is bound by the Court of

Criminal Appeal and by the decisions of the obsolete Court for Crown Cases Reserved.[55]

The Privy Council in theory is an advisory committee. In practice, however, it functions as the highest court of appeal in England, but only for certain overseas British or former British territories. Some independent English-speaking African States have retained the services of the Privy Council after political independence, while others have discarded it.[56]

The Judicial Committee of the Privy Council, not strictly forming a part of the English courts hierarchy, does not hold its previous decisions as binding on English courts. The English judges, however, do respect them, and they could have some persuasive effect on their decisions. The Privy Council is generally never bound by its own previous decisions. It appears, however, that on constitutional matters of great importance it will be bound by its previous decisions.[57]

The general rule in English-speaking African States is, that as the last court of appeal, the Privy Council's decisions bind all courts below it in any territory when it sits as a final court of appeal for that particular territory. Other courts in English-speaking Africa will also follow as a general practice the decisions of the Board on appeals not coming from their territory, but where the decision is *in pari materia* with the case before them. Even after dispensing with its services as the final court of appeal by a territory, the previous decisions of the Board made for the territory and before its abolition as the last court of appeal continue to be part of the laws of the territory that has dispensed with its services. Such previous decisions, though in theory they should have only persuasive effect, are accorded full recognition by the local courts.

Pattern of The Hierarchy of the Courts in English-speaking Africa

The hierarchy of the courts in English-speaking Africa takes on the pattern of the English Courts. We have already discussed the position of the Board of the Judicial Committee of the Privy Council as the final court of appeal for the former British African territories. Immediately below the Privy Council are what may be called "Zonal" Courts of Appeal, like the former West African Court of Appeal, or the Court of Appeal for Eastern Africa. The former was serving as a court of appeal for the English-speaking West African territories, while the latter played the same role for a group of East African territories.

Under the Zonal Courts of Appeal came the national court hierarchy of each territory; the Supreme Court, the High Court, the subordinate Courts and the Native Courts generally come in that order.

As a matter of law, and following the British practice, the Supreme

Court normally is bound by its previous decision, and the High Court is also bound to follow the decision of the Supreme Court. The same applies to all courts inferior to the Supreme Court. As a result of the attainment of political independence, the Privy Council is no longer regarded as a court of final appeal by some territories. This makes the local Supreme Court the final court of appeal in any territory which has taken the above step.[58]

In Ghana, for example, Article 42(4) of the 1960 Republican Constitution provides that:

> The Supreme Court shall in principle be bound to follow its previous decisions on questions of law, and the High Court shall be bound to follow the previous decisions of the Supreme Court on such questions, *but neither Court shall be otherwise bound to follow the previous decisions of any court on question of law.*[59]

The searching question is: What is the position of the previous decision of the courts which, before the Constitution, bind the Supreme Court? It would appear that, since at independence all the existing laws are retained by the Act of Independence, the previous decision of the superior, but now abolished courts, will continue to be part of the national law and therefore will remain binding on the Supreme Court.[60]

In territories where the Constitution failed to spell out the relationship, there are two possible ways of looking at the issue. Firstly, as in the above, all the binding previous decisions which remain law on Independence are therefore binding on the Supreme Court. Secondly, whether the Supreme Court can overlook a previous decision of the Privy Council or the Zonal Appellate Court like the former West African Court of Appeal, will depend on the answer to the question whether the Supreme Court is a successor to the Privy Council and/or the abolished Zonal Appellate Court. If a successor, then by analogy, the decision of those old courts will be regarded as the decision of the Supreme Court and the conclusion will depend on whether or not those two courts were bound by their previous decisions.

In criminal matters again, following the British principle based on the liberty of the individual, it is apparent that the Supreme Court is not bound by its previous decision. Thus, in the Nigerian case of *Maizabo v Sokoto Native Authority*,[61] the Federal Supreme Court refused to follow either of its two previous decisions. *Maizabo v Sokoto Native Authority* was a criminal case involving the death penalty. At the trial there was evidence of provocation which, if accepted, could under the criminal code have reduced the offense to manslaughter. Appellants were tried under Maliki law, which does not recognize provocation as a defense. The Appellants appeal to the High Court was dismissed, with the court stating that: "Questions of manslaughter might have arisen if this case had been tried under the Criminal Code. But in the light of the Federal Supreme Court decisions in

(1) *Jalo Tsamiya v. Bauchi Native Authority.*[62]
(2) *Fagoji v. Kano Native Authority*[63]

this court is precluded from considering the question of manslaughter."

The Federal Supreme Court, however, held that notwithstanding its decision in *Jalo Tsamiya's case* and the subsequent decision based on it in the case of Fagoji, "where a person had been properly convicted of intentional homicide in a Native Court applying Maliki Law and sentenced to death, but that the offence might have been manslaughter under the Criminal Code, the High Court in its appellate jurisdiction ought not to order a retrial so as to make it possible for a verdict of manslaughter to be found." *Having regard "to the great importance of this matter and in particular since it affects the life of the subject,* we felt it right to hear fresh argument with a view to considering if necessary the decisions of this court in the two cases under reference."[64] The case was accordingly remitted to the High Court to consider the question of retrial. It is true that the Federal Supreme Court, while it existed, was not the final Court of Appeal in Nigeria, whereas the Supreme Court is; nevertheless, at the appropriate time both itself and the Supreme Court stand at the apex of the hierarchy of the Courts operating within the territory. By analogy, at least, the same principle which is applicable to the former court would also apply to the latter.

The position of the High Court sitting on appeal is to be looked at from the position of a Court of Appeal in England. By analogy, the rules in *Young v. Bristol*[65] will apply. The court would have a choice between two conflicting decisions of its own; it would be bound to refuse a previous decision which, though not expressly overruled, cannot in its opinion stand with a decision of the House of Lords (in this case the Supreme Court). It would not be bound to follow decisions made *per incuriam.* In criminal matters the analogy would be drawn from the court of Criminal Appeal.

It may be necessary to state that in Federal Territories like Nigeria the effect of federalism may alter the position a little. For example, in Nigeria the State High Court may not be bound by the decision of the other. The decisions of one State High Court are, however, of persuasive authority in other States.

In the exercise of his original jurisdiction, a judge of the High Court is entitled to refuse to be bound by another court of first instance.[66] It is most likely that a first instance judge will be bound by a previous decision of the High Court made on appeal, but not by a single judge.[67]

The West African Court of Appeal is viewed as being succeeded in respect of each country by the Supreme Court. If this view is correct[68] it follows that, while the WACA binds all other inferior courts in English-speaking West Africa, it does not bind the Supreme Courts. If so, its decisions will only constitute persuasive precedent to the Supreme Courts.

The West African Court of Appeal has been known to reconsider its decision on civil matters.[69] If the view that the Supreme Court is its successor is accepted, then it may follow that the latter Court will be prepared to reconsider its decisions on civil matters. However, an analogy drawn from the practice of the English Court of Appeal may not favor such a practice.

As regards Criminal matters, the court, in *Matayo v Commissioner of Police*[70] adopted the principle enunciated by the Engish Court of Criminal Appeal in the case of *R. v. Taylor*.[71] It took the view that where an issue involving the liberty of the subject was brought before it in full session, it would not regard itself as being invariably bound by its previous decisions.

In East Africa, the Court of Appeal for Eastern Africa is the counterpart of the West African Court of Appeal. As an Appellate Court it served the former British territories in East Africa, which included Kenya, Tanganyika, Uganda and Zanzibar. The court, which was constituted under the Eastern African Court of Appeal Orders in Council (1921-1947) served those territories as a Zonal Court of Appeal. Appeals lie from it to the Judicial Committee of the Privy Council.

On the question of being bound by its own past decisions, the Court of Appeal for Eastern Africa has adopted, in the main, the principles followed by corresponding English Courts. It gave a summary of its position in criminal cases in the case of *Kabui v R*[72] as follows:

> The principle of *stare decisis* should be followed, unless the court is of opinion that to follow the earlier decision which is considered to be erroneous would involve supporting an improper conviction. The Court of Criminal Appeal in *R v Taylor*[73] based its decision on the principle of liberty of the subject and we think that this court should not ordinarily depart from a previous decision merely because it appears that the view taken of the law in that decision may involve acquittal where there should be convictions.[74]

In civil matters, the Court has also adopted relevant English rules as were laid down by the Court of Appeal in England in the famous case of *Young v Bristol Aeroplane Co.*[75] It is bound to follow previous decisions of its own, subject to the limits laid down in *Young's case*. Also, decisions of any of the old appellate courts now treated as having similar authority to decisions of the Court of Appeal are regarded as binding on the Court.[76]

The powers of a judge and his ability to overrule, or at least distinguish old and outmoded precedents, are the yardstick for measuring his contribution to social changes through the law. A judicial technique which imposes an obligation on the courts to follow relevant decisions of superior courts as a matter of law, tends to curb the judge's potentiality as a law-making agent. No binding precedent can be so easily disregarded in favor of views concerning contemporary social conditions and values. Thus, the doctrine of binding precedent in English-speaking Africa appears to be a more formidable tool for upholding the positivist view of law in African courts. It may promote certainty and stability in the law, but it certainly does not enhance radical social change through the action of judges in court.

Ratio Decidendi

No discussion on the doctrine of binding precedent will be comprehensive without a consideration of that which is binding in a case. It is not everything that a judge of a superior court says during the course of his judgment that is binding. Before reaching his conclusion in any case, a judge says a lot of things. Some of what he says may be an enunciation of a rule, or principles of law which he expressly or by implication treats as necessary in reaching his conclusion. It is this rule or principle alone on which a judge decides a case that is binding as precedent, and is known as the *Ratio Decidendi* of the case. Other pronouncements of the judge, constituting a proposition of the law which are not necessary for his decision, are *obiter dicta*.

The distinction between a *ratio decidendi* and an *obiter dictum* has always remained a subtle distinction. When a judge expressly states his reason or reasons for giving his decision, no problem is created. That which he regards as the ratio, forms the ratio undisputably. At times, however, he may rest his decision on more than one reason, or he may give no reasons at all. If he gives several reasons, so long as he bases his decision on those reasons, all of them constitute the ratio of the case. If he gives no reason at all, the problem is how to find the ratio.

In finding the *ratio decidendi* of a case, generally, Professor Wambaugh suggests that it may be discovered by inserting a word reversing the proposition of law put forward by the court and inquiring whether the decision would have been the same notwithstanding the reversal. He states:

First frame carefully the supposed proposition of law...then insert in the proposition a word reversing its meaning...then inquire whether, if the court had conceived this new proposition to be good and had it in mind, the decision would have been the same. If the answer be affirmative, then, however excellent the original proposition may be, the case is not a precedent for that proposition, if the answer be negative, the case is authority for the original proposition and possibly for other propositions also. In short, when a case turns only on one point, the proposition or doctrine of the case, the reason of the decision, the *ratio decidendi,* must be a general rule without which the case must have been decided otherwise.[77]

Professor Goodhart, differing from Wambaugh, lays emphasis on the material facts of the case: the *ratio decidendi* is nothing more than the decision based on the material facts of the case. He maintains that the reason which the judge gives for his decision is never the binding part of the precedent. The reason, he argues, may be false, while the decision nevertheless retains its authoritative force.[78] He is also of the view that the ratio decidendi is not necessarily the proposition of law stated in the judgment, since some judgments may contain no expressly enunciated rule or rules, or, as in appellate judgments, different rules, and yet arrive at the same conclusion. He further argues that the rule stated may go far beyond the facts of the case in question[79] or be too narrow[80] to constitute the ratio.

Also, criticizing Professor Wambaugh on this score, Lord Simond refers to cases where a judge has passed judgment based on two alternative grounds, either of which can sustain the decision in spite of the reversal theory.[81]

It is not intended here to go in detail into the academic dialogue as to what constitutes the *ratio decidendi* of a case and what is *obiter dictum.* What we regard as important is that for a previous case to be authoritative in a subsequent case there must be a substantial coincidence of material facts in both cases, or the facts of the later case must be such as could be contained within the material facts of the previous case. Since the issue of what constitutes the ratio of a previous case does not call for a determination until a similar case comes before the court, we submit that it is the judge in the subsequent case who determines the ratio of the previous decision. His task is only made easier where there was an express and clear statement by the previous court on the ratio; otherwise he has room enough to maneuver in finding out the ratio decidendi.

With the modern usage of words in at least three senses,[82] it would not always be correct to assume that judges agreeing as to the collection of individual facts will always form the same impression of the facts as a body, or agree on a common reason for the decision of a previous decision of a court based on the words in which the reasons given are couched. Cases have been known to be distinguished in a most subtle way[83] where the facts are very identical, in order not to be bound by a disagreeable precedent, or at least to obviate the hardship of the former decision without disrupting the doctrine of *stare decisis.* But these are orthodox judicial techniques which are very much in favor of maintaining stability in the law and which are too hesitant to radical legal changes through court decisions.

It is a known fact that too much adherence to precedent may lead to injustice and hardship in particular cases. In 20th Century Africa it undoubtedly restricts progress and the development of the law to suit the realities of the modern and developing new independent countries. "It is revolting to have no better reason for a rule of law than that so it was laid down in the time of Henry IV. It is still more revolting if the grounds upon which it was laid down have vanished long since and the rule simply persists from blind imitation of the past."[84] If this statement is true of the Anglo-Saxon law, it is more true of the laws of the new States in English-speaking Africa today. The colonial heritage, of which the English legal system and legal methods form part, should be reoriented toward solving the unique African social, political, and economic problems of the modern times.

Customary Law

The section of the *corpus juris* known as customary law stems from the indigenous customs of various communities of the African peoples. Customary rules are the habitual practices of the generality of a local community. Every community in Africa, long before the advent of Western civilization, evolved a kind of practice which became unavoidably binding on every member of the community. These, unlike ordinary social habits and observances, carried along with them local sanctions for their breach.

Like the common customs of the realm of old England, our customary rules are *lex non scripta,* or unwritten law. As a result of the colonial heritage from the English system, however, most of these rules (as we have seen earlier in this work) are now being assimilated into judicial precedent or denied legality altogether. The technique of the English-speaking African courts in dealing with local customs are comparable with the technique used by the English courts during the early Middle Ages in England to build up a body of English Common Law out of general Customs. Nevertheless, considering the judicial attitude and the techniques, the perennial question as to when does a rule of customary law become law still remains.

Hitherto the notion has been that customary rules derive their authority from the consent of the community. Consequently, the judge is generally believed to be a mere fact finder whose duty is to discover a rule of customary law and apply it. Generally, customary law is regarded as a matter of fact that is provable by expert witness, with the possible exceptions where:

(i) a rule of customary law is contained in any book or manuscript recognized by the natives as a legal authority;

(ii) a rule of customary law has been acted upon by a court of superior or coordinate jurisdiction in the same area to an extent which would justify the court to regard it as a binding rule within the area; and

(iii) where a customary rule has been assimilated into the law.

In practice however the judicial attitude and technique do not seem to favor the analytical approach, as the above portrays. The tendency seems to be that of trying to modernize customary law rules.

The English Tests

The acceptance of a local custom by the English Courts is surrounded with a number of conditions which must be satisfied before they are accepted as forming part of the common law. These conditions have been laid down over the centuries by the courts. Some English writers, like Blackstone, Salt, and Sir Carleton Allen[85] have listed and examined these tests. The tests mentioned are various and many, but for our present purposes here we only mention the following:

(a) The custom must be of immemorial antiquity, i. e., it must have existed before 1189.[86]

(b) It must be certain;[87]

(c) It must have been enjoyed as of right, *nec vi nec clam nec precario* (without force, not clandestinely and without permission);[88]

(d) The custom must be reasonable;[89]

(e) It must not conflict with a fundamental principle of the common law,[90] though when accepted by the court, it may operate in derogation of the common law without attacking its fundamental principles;

(f) A local custom must not conflict with any statutory rule.

The General Tests in English-speaking Africa

Before an analysis of the attitude of the judiciary of enumerated tests adopted by the English judiciary, we would like to restate immediately some of the conditions applicable to customary rules in English-speaking Africa:

(a) A rule of customary law is a matter of fact that is provable by expert evidence in court before its adoption;

(b) A rule of customary law to be applied by the courts must not be repugnant to equity and good conscience;

(c) It must not be incompatible with any law at the time in force, and

(d) It must not be contrary to public policy.

Without going into the details of the unique interpretation that the English judiciary gives to the various tests it applies to a local custom before its assimilation into the common law, broadly one sees some striking similarities between these tests and those adopted by the English-speaking Africa courts. For instance, the English tests that a custom must be of immemorial antiquity, that it must be certain, and that it must have been enjoyed as of right *nec vi, nec clam, nec precario,* when taken together, have the true existence and certainty of the customary rule as the main objective.

For example, during the permissible period for the existence of a recognizable custom, the custom must have been enjoyed continuously. The continuity does not necessarily mean that a cessation in the active enjoyment of the custom will defeat its claim as a binding customary rule. The test is only there to assure that it has not been abandoned as a custom. Furthermore, since the binding force of a customary rule stems from its antiquity and the generality of its practice by the people and their consensus to hold it as binding, a customary rule is supposed to be notorious. A clandestine observance of any rule of custom is therefore a sure indication that it lacks the generality needed for its existence.

In English-speaking Africa the certainty of the existence of a customary rule is determined by its proof through expert evidence. The generally accepted notion is that the judge is a fact finder in dealing with customary rules. His main function is to discover a rule of customary law and apply it. This view is based on the notion that customary rule derives its authority and validity from the indigenous practice and consent of the community.

The test that a custom must be reasonable in order to be assimilated into the English common law has similar effect to the "repugnancy" and the "public policy" tests applied by the court in English-speaking Africa to a rule of customary law. In theory the tests of reasonableness as in the English case, or repugnancy in the case of English-speaking Africa ought to be decided in accordance with standard of the period when a customary rule started. In the case of an African community, both the standard of the time and the social values of the people at the time the custom came into existence ought to be the criteria. In practice, however, it would appear that the judges judge the issue by the contemporary standard of the time when a case involving the custom comes to be heard before the court,[91] and in English-speaking Africa, were by standards and social values that are alien to the people.[92]

The test that a customary rule must not be contrary to public policy, which seems to be a unique test for customary rules in English-speaking Africa, confirms further the statement that customary rules are judged more by contemporary standards in Africa than by the standards and social values of the time of their origin and existence. It is true that there has been no distinction drawn by the courts between the public policy test and the test of repugnancy, but the mere use of the statement that a customary rule must not be contrary to public policy suggests a contemporary test. For, if it is the assent of the native community that gives custom its validity, inasmuch as a customary rule remains the practice of the local community, one sees nothing contrary in it *vis a vis* the policy of the community whose practice it is.

The questions of repugnancy and public policy, like the question of reasonableness under the English law, are questions of law and not of fact to be determined by the court. Thus the courts have, through them, gained a greater measure of control over the assimilation of customary rules into the *corpus juris*. In applying these tests the courts reserve to themselves the right of discrediting or abrogating a customary rule. It seems that in English-speaking Africa, the discretion of the courts are more far-reaching than in England. In the particular question of reasonableness, the English courts very seldom reject a custom on the ground of unreasonableness in its origin. On the other hand, in English-speaking Africa the tendency, while applying the repugnancy test, is to initially regard the *origin* as primitive and the custom barbarous unless, under the influence of civilization, it has become milder while still retaining its character as custom.

It remains to consider the tests that custom must not conflict with the fundamental principles of the common law or be incompatible with any statutory rule. Where a customary rule is clearly incompatible with statute law, the custom is deemed to be abrogated. Where, however, as in English law the court is to determine whether or not a customary rule is incompatible with any law in force other than statute law, it has a discretion to exercise. The exercise of this discretion could have the same effect as when the court applies the repugnancy or public policy tests.

Summary

An evaluation of the judicial technique in dealing with the legal sources shows some response by the courts to contemporary demands of economic, social, and political changes in Africa in their application of the rules of customary law. With the interpretation of statutes, the courts by and large still adhere to the analytical approach. The conservatism of the Bench in this connection may have the adverse effect of defeating the purpose of legislation and impeding rapid social and economic changes.

The doctrine of binding precedent as adopted from the English legal practice, though promoting legal stability, has become anachronistic to the African situation. It can no longer meet adequately the needs and requirements of a modern African State. There is a great need for a functional or teleological approach to the judicial techniques in dealing with all the sources of law in Africa.

Notes to Chapter 2

1. Pound, R. *Interpretation of Legal History*, p. 1.
2. See, for example, the Interpretation Act, 1889.
3. Friedmann sees three indistinguishable approaches; namely, The Pseudo logical or textbook approach, the Social policy approach, and the Free Intuition Approach. See Friedmann, W., *Law and Social Change in Contemporary Britain* (1951), p. 239 et seq. The last two approaches are in fact functional, while the first is analytical.
4. 3 Co Rep 7a at p.7b. For more recent English cases reiterating this canon of interpretation, see *Eastman Photographic Materials Co. Ltd. v. The Comptroller General of Patents*, (1898) AC 571, per Lord Halsbury, L. C., p. 573; *London and County Property Investment, Ltd., v. A. G.* (1953) 1 All E. R. 436, per Up John, J., p. 441; *Barnes v. Jarvis*, (1953) 1 All E. R. 1061, per Lord Goddard, C. J., p. 1063.
5. *Seaford v. Asher* (1949) 2 All E. R. 155, p. 164; (1949) 2 KB 481, pp. 498-499. (Emphasis added.)
6. (1950) 2 All E. R. 1226, p. 1236. (Emphasis added.)
7. Per Lord Simonds on appeal, *Magor and St. Mellons RDC v. New Port Corporation* (1953) 2 All E. R. 839, p. 841; (1952) AC 189, p. 191. See also to the same effect, per Lord Goddard, C. J. in *R v. Wimbledon Justices Ex parte Derwent*, (1953) 1 QB 380, p. 384.
8. In *Hilder v Dexter* (1902) AC 474, Lord Halsbury refused to deliver a judgment on the ground that he had participated in drafting the Act under consideration. *Cf.*, Hengham, C. J. in 1305 (Year Book of 33 Edw. 1, M. Term Rolls Ed., 82) where he said to a counsel, "Do not gloss the statute for we know better than you, we made it." See further, *Admiralty Commrs v. North of Scotland & Orkney & Shethland Steam Navigation Co. Ltd.* (1947) 2 All E. R. 350, p. 353, 1948, AC 140, p. 149—a case embracing the law reform (Contributory Negligence) Act, 1945. Viscount Simon referred to the Report of the Law Revision Committee on Contributory Negligence to ascertain causation in relation to the last opportunity rule; *British Coal Corp. v. R.* (1935) AC 500; the Privy Council referred to the resolutions of the Commonwealth Conference in order to interpret the statute of Westminster, *Edwards v. A. G. for Canada* (1930) AC 124, p. 143; the Privy Council consulted a report in *Hansard* of a Parliamentary debate.

9. 2 M & W 191; 150 English Reports 724.
10. *Ibid.*, 2 M & W, p. 195; 150 English Reports, p. 726.
11. See, for instance, the following English cases: *Gray v Pearson* 1857, 6 H. L cas. 61, p. 106; *Vacher & Sons Ltd v London Society of Compositors,* (1913) A. C. 107, p. 117; *Re Sigsworth Bedford v. Bedford,* (1935) Ch. 89 at p. 92; *Francis Jackson Development Ltd v. Hall* (1951) 2 All E. R. 74, pp. 79–79; (1951) 2 KB 488, pp. 494-495; *Summer v Priestly (Robert L) Ltd.* (1955) 3 All E. R. 445, p. 447; *Thompson v Thompson* (1956) 1 All E. R. 603, p. 607.
12. (1955) 1 All E. R. 746, (1955) Ch. 440.
13. (1955) 3 All E. R. 647; (1956) Ch. 188.
14. 4 & 5 Anne, c. 4 (or c 16).
15. (1955) 3 All E. R. 647; (1956) Ch. 188. And see (1955) All E. R. 746; (1955) Ch. 440.
16. Celsus, Dig. 1.3.17;1.3.18.
17. 11 Cl & Fin 85; 8 English Reports, 1034.
18. *Ibid.,* p. 143; 8 English Reports, p. 1057.
19. (1940) 6 WACA 180.
20. (1954) 14 WACA 476; see also *Stephen v Pedrocchi* (1959) NRNLR 76, where Smith, AG. S. P. J. rejected counsel's argument that a repeal of a statute of general application by the English Parliament after the reception date in Nigeria makes the law inoperative in Nigeria.
21. S. 3(1).
22. See, the Penal Codes of Uganda s.3; Kenya s.3; Zanzibar s.3; Northern Rhodesia, s.4; and Nyasaland s.3.
23. See, for example, the Kenya Penal Code Cap. 24, s.40; Criminal Code of the Gambia Cap. 21, s.35; the Uganda Penal Code Cap. 22 s.53; and the Northern Rhodesia Penal Code Cap. 6 s.61, where the offenses of treason and piracy are specifically stated as being defined by reference to English Law.
24. See the Codes, Cap. 16 s.18 and Cap. 23 s.17, respectively.
25. (1957) AC 126; 23 EACA 609.
26. (1957) AC 126, pp. 134, 135. Cf., the Nyasaland case of *Mphumeya v R* (1956) R & N 240, where Southworth, Ag. C. J. held that the English rule that a wife is incapable of stealing from her husband while cohabitation continues operates in Nyasaland, but its operation to customary law marriages seems doubtful.
27. See, Interpretation Act, Cap. 89 s.45(2); Eastern Region (Nigeria) High Court Law No. 27 of 1955; s.20(1); Northern Region (Nigeria) High Court Law No. 8 of 1955, s.28A(1); Tanganyika Order in Council 1920, Art 17(2).
28. (1961) 1 All N. L. R. at p. 257.
29. *Lawal v Youngs* (1961) 1 All N. L. R. 245.
30. See *London and North Eastern Rail Co. v Berriman* (1946) 1 All E. R. 255; (1946) AC 278.
31. (1762) 3 Burr 1341, 97 English Reports 864. For further applications of the rule see *North Central Wagon & Finance Co. Ltd. v. Graham* (1950) 1 All E. R. 780; (1950) 2 KB 7; *Dean v. Wiesengrund,* (1955) 2 QB 120; *Marczuk v Marczuk,* (1956) 1 All E. R. 657, (1956), 127.
32. (1827) 7B & C 96; 108 English Reports 661.
33. See also, *Palmer v Snow* (1900) 1 QB 725, where the Act was also held not to apply to a barber on the ground that his calling was not similar to those specified in the preceding list; and *Powell v Kempton Park Racecourse Co. Ltd.* (1899) AC 143.
34. On these, see Maxwell, P. B., *On The Interpretation of Statutes* (London: Sweet & Maxwell, 1962), especially p. 3, et seq.

35. (1852) 3 H. L. C. 341, p. 392; 10 E.R. 133, p. 153.

36. *Beamish v. Beamish* (1861) 9 H. L. C. 274, p. 338. (Emphasis added.) See also, 11 E. R. 735, p. 761, and *cf.* the attitude of the House in a Policy Statement read by Lord Gardiner, L. C. on 26 July 1966, to the Lords.

37. (1944) K. B. 718; (1946) A. C. 163.

38. *Young v. Bristol Aeroplane Co.* (1944) K. B. 718 at p. 729. Also (1946) A. C. 163. For exceptions to this rule, see pp. 85–86.

39. For colonial English-speaking Africa, this was the final court of appeal and it has remained so for some even after Independence.

40. *Bright v. Hutton* (1852) 3 H. L. C. 341; 10 E. R. 133; *Beamish v Beamish* (1861) 9 H. L. C. 274; 11 E. R. 735. See further, *London Street Tramways Co. v. L.C.C.* (1898) A. C. 375, *Nash Inspector of Taxes v. Tamplin & Sons' Brewery Brighton Ltd.,* (1951) 2 All E. R. 869, p. 880; (1952) A. C. 231, p. 250. Dworkin, R. G. has suggested that there is now a relaxation of the attitude of the House of Lords toward following its own decisions. See Dworkin, "'Stare Decisis' in the House of Lords" (1962) 25 M. L. R. 163.

41. See, *St. John Peerage Claim* (1915) A. C. 282, p. 308; *Viscountess Rhonddas Claim* (1922) 2 A. C. 339, p. 376.

42. See, *per Lord Halsbury in London Street Tramways v L. C. C.* (1898) A. C. 375, pp. 380–381.

43. See the case of *M'Alister (Donoghue v Stevenson,* (1932) A. C. 562.

44. Statement read by Lord Gardiner, L. C. for and on behalf of himself and the Lords of Appeal in Ordinary on 26 July 1966 before the delivering of Judgments. (Emphasis added.)

45. See again, *Young v. Bristol Aeroplane Co.* (1944) K. B. 718, per Lord Green, M. R., p. 729.

46. (1950) 2 K. B. 368; (1950) 2 All E. R. 170.

47. *Ibid.,* p. 371, and 172, respectively.

48. A trial at *nisi prius* is a trial by a jury before a single judge, either at sittings held in London or Middlesex for that purpose, or at assizes. Originally, all common law actions were tried at bar, that is, before the full court, consisting of several judges. The writ for summoning the jury used to be addressed to the Sheriff commanding him to bring the jurors from the country where the cause of action arose to the court at West Minster. When, later, Statute 13 Edw. 1 directed that the justices of assize may try the cases in the county where they arose, the form of the writ of summons was changed accordingly. The Sheriff was commanded to bring the jurors to Westminster on a certain day "unless before that day" (nisi prius) the justices of the assize came into the county.

49. (1808) 1 Camp. 493; 170 English Reports 1033.

50. See, *per Lord Goddard, C. J. in Huddersfied Police Authority v Watson* (1947) 2 All E. R. 193; also (1947) K. B. 842. However, compare *Metropolitan Police District Receiver v Croydon Corp.* (1956) 2 All E. R. 785; *Monmouthshire C. C. v Smith* (1956) 2 All E. R. 800.

51. *Elderton v. U.K. Totalisators Ltd* (1945) (No. 2) All E. R. 624, (1946) Ch. 57.

52. *Bretherton v U.K. Totalisators Ltd.* (1945) 2 All E. R. 202; (1945) K. B. 555.

53. See, *Huddersfield Police Authority v Watson,* (1947) 2 All E. R. 193; (1947) K. B. 842; *Younghusband v Luftig* (149) 2 All F. R. 72, especially p. 75; (1949) 2 K. B. 354, especially p. 361; *Broughton v Whittaker,* (1944) 2 All E. R. 544, p. 547; (1944) K. B. 269, pp. 274–275.

54. *Read v Joannon* (1890) 25 QBD 300, pp. 302–303; *Scott v D. P. P.* (1914) 2 K. B. 868, p. 879.

55. See, *per Lord Alverstone, C. J. in Hawke v Mackenize* (1902) 2 K. B. 225, p. 231.

56. For example, it was not until October 1963, three years after her political independence, that Nigeria was able and willing to dispense with the services of the Privy Council as her final Court of Appeal within the hierarchy of her courts.

57. See, per Viscount Simon in *A. G. for Ontario v. Canada Temperance Federation* (1946) A. C. 193, p. 206. Compare *Nkambule v R.* (1950) A. C. 379, an appeal from Swaziland, where the Privy Council refused to follow its previous decision.

58. This is true of Ghana and Nigeria.

59. (Emphasis added.)

60. For Ghana, see Asante, S. K. B., "'Stare Decisis' in the Supreme Court of Ghana" (University of Ghana L. J. 1964) Vol. 1 No. 1. The position in Nigeria is discussed by Brett, Sir Lionel, "'Stare Decisis' in Nigeria, Some Random Thoughts" (*Nigeria Bar Journal,* 1965) Vol. VI, pp. 74–77); Ijalaiye, "Precedent in the Nigerian Courts" (1965) (*Nigerian Law Journal,* 1965) Vol. 1. No. 2, p. 284.

61. (1957) 2 F. S. C. 13.

62. (1957) N. R. N. L. R. 73.

63. (1957) N. R. N. L. R. 57.

64. *Ibid.,* at p. 14. (Emphasis added.)

65. (1944) K. B. 718 (1946) A. C. 163.

66. *Olawoyin v A. G. of Northern Region* (1960) N. R. N. L. R. 53. See also *Okolie Chime and Anor. v Ofili Elikwu and Anor.* (1965) N. M. L. R. 71.

67. *Agbalaya v Bello* (1960) L. L. R. 109 following *Anah v Owudunni Trading Co.* (1956) L. L. R. 20.

68. It is to be noted that the WACA, when it existed, was not the last Court of Appeal (the Privy Council was); whereas in some countries, like Nigeria, the Supreme Court came into existence after the Privy Council has ceased to be the last court of appeal for that country. It is arguable, therefore, that for Supreme Courts like that of Nigeria, if there be a successor of any court, it must be the Privy Council. For other Supreme Courts, which came into existence before the Privy Council ceased to exist as a Court of Final Appeal, the view that each succeeded the WACA sounds correct.

69. See, *Re Adadevoh* (1951) 13 WACA 304; but see an earlier decision of the WACA, in *Osumanu v Seidu* (1949) 437, where it accepted and acted upon the Court of Appeal's decision in *Young v Bristol Aeroplane Co. Ltd.* (1944) K. B. 718, (1946) A. C. 163.

70. (1950) 13 WACA 114.

71. (1950) 2 K. B. 368 (1950) 2 All E. R. 170.

72. (1954) 21 H. A. C. A. 260.

73. (1950) 2 K. B. 368.

74. *Ibid.,* p. 261.

75. (1944) K. B. 718. See, per Lord Greene, M. R., p. 729.

76. See, per O'Connor, P. in *The Kiriri Cotton Co. Ltd v Dewani* (1958) E. A. 239, pp. 245–246. See further, *Commissioner for Lands v. Bashir* (1958) E. A. 45; *R v Norman Godinho* (1950) 17 E. A. C. A. 132.

77. Wambaugh, *Study of Cases* (2nd ed.), pp. 17–18.

78. See his *Essays in Jurisprudence and the Common Law,* p. 1. He gives as an example the case of *Priestly v Fowler* (1837), 3 M & W1; 150 English Reports 1030, which was a decision turning on the rule of "Common Employment."

79. As in *Lickbarrow v Mason* (1787) 2 Term Rep 63; (on appeal 1790) 1 Hy. Bl. 357, Ex Ch; (1793), 4 Bro Parl Cas. 39 2 English Reports 39; 100 E. R. 35. *R v. Fenter* (1830), 1 Lew 179.

80. *Barwick v English Joint Stock Bank* (1866) L. R. 2 Ex. 259. There Willes, J. stated that "the master is answerable for every such wrong of the servant or agent committed in the course of [his] service and for the master's benefit even in the absence of express command or privity of the master."

81. See *Jacobs v London County Council* (1950) 1 All E. R. 737, p. 741; (1950) A. C. 361, pp. 369–370.

82. One is the sense in which the speaker uses the word. The second is the usual meaning of the word, which need not necessarily be the same as the first; while the third is the sense in which the person addressed understood the word.

83. Compare for example, *Phillips v Brooks* (1919) 2 K. B. 243, with *Ingram v Little* (1961) 1 Q. B. 31.

84. Holmes, Oliver Wendall, *Collected Legal Papers* 1920, p. 187.

85. See for example, Allen, K. C., *Law In The Making* (Oxford: Clarendon Press, 1946 4th edition) p. 124, et seq.

86. *Simpson v Wells* (1872); L. R. 7 Q. B. 214.

87. *Wilson v Willes* (1806), 7 East 121; 103 Eng. Rep. 46.

88. *Mills v Colchester Corporation* (1867), L. R. 2 C. P. 476; 144 English Reports 254.

89. *Bryant v Foot* (1868), L. R. 3 Q.B. 497; cf. *Lawrence v Hitch* (1868), L. R. 3 Q.B. 521.

90. *Johnson v Clarke* (1908) 1 Ch. 303.

91. See again, the English cases of *Bryant v Foot* (1868), L. R. 3 Q. B. 497, and *Lawrence v Hitch* (1868), L. R. 3 Q. B. 521.

92. See again, section on Customary Law in the preceding Chapter dealing with the nature and authority of the legal sources. In the celebrated case of *Dawodu v Banmole*, however, the Privy Council refused to follow this line of assessment when it stated that "the principle of natural justice, equity and good conscience applicable in a country where polygamy is generally accepted should not be readily equated with those applicable to a country governed by the rule of monogamy," (1962) 1 W. L. R. 1053, p. 1060.

PART III
THEORIES OF LAW

Introductory

The knowledge of the past and prevalent notions, theories, and conceptions of Law should be regarded necessary, *only* as tools of analysis, examination, and the search for a legal theory that is most appropriate for social, political, and economic developments in Africa. Generally, theories of law are affected by basic assumptions underlying overall theories of justice and legality. Specifically, a theory of law should concern itself with a search for a concept of law which is most adequate for man in society and which meets adequately man's aspirations for better conduct and treatment for better life.

Among the main preoccupations in Africa today, are social and political stability and economic advancement. To these is added the general education of the masses as a basis for the creation and the inception of new values that will help promote social progress. In all these, the role of law toward the achievement of the new goals is second to none.

The problem confronting the African legal philosopher in this era of "the winds of change" is whether he can afford to indulge in the perennial argument about the universal and permanent underlying basis of law, or to take the law as it stands, and not as it ought to be. Should he concern himself mainly with the values that should underlie the law and its function in society without bothering about the soul of its legality? Whatever may be the answer to these questions, development (individual, socioeconomic and political), progress, and stability should form the matrix of our assessment.

There are two elements in law; the compelling element—*vis coactiva*—and the directing element—*vis directiva.* In the view of the Schoolmen it is the latter, the element of justice in the law that ultimately matters. But the African is caught in the web of both the compelling and the directing elements because of his contemporary needs and values, and the two elements are not always in harmony. The compelling element often (though not always) reflects the desires of those who prevail in the struggles between the conflicting interest classes in the new African States. This is what our kind of jurisprudence should avoid. As a structure of human relationships in society, law must not lose sight of the directing element. Among its main objectives should be the balancing of the conflicting interests (both individual and State interests) in a developing nation.

Law in our own case should not be regarded, to use the words of Lloyd, as "an abstract set of rules simply imposed on society, but...an integral part of that society, having deep roots in the social and economic habits and attitudes" and we may add, aspirations "of its past and present members."[1] If we accept the above as our guidelines, our attitude toward the study of legal notions so far advanced by legal philosophers throughout the ages should be that of critical analysis. Our legal philosophy should be based on the result of empirical study of those notions in the light of our past and present experiences, our individual needs in society, and our national or state requirements.

Chapter 3

Metaphysics and the Law

Natural Law

Man, according to the Bible, was created in the image of God. This statement, though an assumption, has become the major premise in human thought and action. All human actions are to be judged in accordance with man's image of the Divine and the values and principles that are ascribed to it. Unlike the Deity, however, man found himself living in society, where interests are competing as well as conflicting. Consequently, the very early legal philosophers, viewing law as a formidable machinery for regulating human actions in society, sought for a philosophy of law that could deal with the Divine character of man as well as his secular social needs.

The early legal philosophers of the Greek and the Roman world resorted to ideas of natural law to meet both man's celestial and secular requirements. Their major concerns were therefore,

  (i) the universal and permanent underlying basis of law;
 (ii) the relationship of law to justice; and
(iii) the problem of social stability.

The Greek Philosophers

As the architects of the *natural law* theory, the Greek philosophers sought for a theory of law which would suit the needs of their time and their city states. One of the greatest problems of the Greek world was social and political instability. To the Greeks, therefore, a true philosophy of law was that which would suit the much-needed stability.

The Sophists, led by Trasymachus, Protagoras, and Callicles, adopted a purely secular approach to legal philosophy. Law to them was a matter of social and political expediency not involving any absolute standards. The belief was that the compelling element in the law was the interests of the ruling class who emerged as the stronger in society. The weaker class, the subjects, had no other choice but to obey the law, in their own interests too. Thus, as a matter of expediency, the basis of law was in each case the self interest of both the governor and the governed.

On the second element of law, the directing element, Trasymachus postulated a theory of justice which heavily favored the ruler. Justice, in his view, "is to the advantage of the stronger in society." In each city, whether it is tyranny, or democracy that prevails, the rulers lay down laws in their own interests. The subject, the ruled, who obeys the law, is said to be a just man acting justly, while he who does not obey the law is punished as a law-breaker and an unjust man.[2]

Glaucon, in the second book of Plato's *Republic,* propounded a theory of justice which could rightly be said to be the origin of the idea of the *social contract theory.* Justice, he maintained, is unnatural to man, for by nature each man tries to take advantage of others. Even the so-called just man, if you gave him the magic ring of Gyges, whereby he could become invisible at will and escape detection in wrongdoing, would act precisely in the same way as the unjust man. But when men discovered that "there is more evil in suffering injustice than there is good in inflicting it," after experiencing both the doing and the suffering, they entered into a mutual pact. They formed the opinion "that it is more profitable that they should mutually agree neither to inflict injustice nor to suffer it."[3]

Such was man's compromise between the best thing, that of doing injustice without paying the penalty, and the worst thing, which is to suffer injustice while being unable to take revenge. This compromise was the beginning of law. "Hence, men began to establish laws and covenants with one another and they called what the law prescribed lawful and just. This then is the origin and nature of justice. It is a means between the best—doing injustice with impunity—and the worst—suffering injustice without the possibility of requittal. Thus justice, being a mean between these extremes, is looked upon with favor, not because it is good, but because the inability to inflict injustice makes it valuable."[4]

The Sophists' theory failed to gain ground with the Greek populace because of its lack of an appealing postulate for the second element in law, *the directing element.* It failed to appeal to the psychology of the Greeks. It divested law of the psychological mechanism for obedience, which in the Greek world was an absolute standard identifiable with the Deity. The legal postulate of the Sophists called for force to command obedience. Force, particularly when misapplied, could lead to resistance, which in turn might bring more chaos. But the Greeks needed more of stability at the time than anything else.

Socrates (470–399 B.C.) and Plato (429–348 B.C.), on the other hand, advanced a legal theory which was more appealing to the Greeks. Their theory postulated a more appealing and acceptable reason for obedience to law. They maintained that law was guided by *uniform principles.* These uniform and directing principles are unchangeable moral principles which form a criterion for human conduct.

Human actions were not, as the Sophists maintained, governed solely by man's inclinations and desires. To Socrates, man possessed insight into the nature of conduct. He equates the insight with man's knowledge of goodness. Compelled by a desire for the much-needed social stability, Socrates and Plato minimized the revolutionary effect of their theory with consideration of both the directing and the compelling elements in the law. On the other hand, man's insight, his knowledge of goodness, demands that the acceptance of positive law be preceded by a critical examination of its contents, for it is man's knowledge of goodness that is the criterion by which all human conduct is to be assessed.

This was a more appropriate theory for the Greeks of their time. It took cognizance both of the immediate needs of the Greek world and the question of the efficacy of the law. The Greeks needed positive law to achieve and maintain social stability. An inefficacious law could hardly be useful for these objectives, for to maintain obedience to it brute force has to be used, and force begets resistance, which in itself brings more instability and greater suffering.

Aristotle, elaborating on the doctrines propounded by Socrates and Plato, distinguished between two kinds of law: natural law which is universal and particular, and conventional law. The former embodies natural justice, that is invariable in its content, and the latter manifests conventional justice, which is a variable; which varies according to situations and place, and is binding only because it is decreed by a particular authority. "By the two kinds of law," said Aristotle, "I mean particular law and universal law. Particular law is that which each community lays down and applies to its own members; this is partly written and partly unwritten. Universal law is the law of nature. For there is....a natural justice and injustice that is binding on all men, even on those who have no association or convenant with each other."[5]

Of political justice, Aristotle was of the view that it is partly natural and partly legal. The natural is

that which everywhere has the same force and does not exist by peoples' thinking this or that; legal, that which is originally indifferent, but when it has been laid down, is not indifferent, e. g., that a prisoner's ransom shall be a mina, or that a goat and not two sheep shall be sacrificed, and again all the laws that are passed for particular cases, e. g., that sacrifice shall be made in honour of Brasidas, and the provisions of decrees. Now some think that all justice is of this sort, because that which is by nature is un-changeable and has everywhere the same force (as fire burns both here and in Persia), while they see change in the things recognized as just. This however, is not true in this unqualified way, but is true in a sense; or rather, with the gods it is perhaps not true at all, while with us there is something that is just even by nature, yet all of it is changeable; but still some is by nature, some not by nature. It is evident which sort of thing, among things capable of being otherwise, is by nature; and which is not but is legal and conventional, assuming that both are equally changeable. And in all other things the same distinction will apply; by nature the right hand is stronger, yet it is possible that all men should come to be ambi-dextrous. The things which are just by virtue of convention and expe-diency are like measures; for wine and corn measures are not everywhere equal, but larger in wholesale and smaller in retail markets. Similarly, the things which are just not by nature but by human enactment are not ev-erywhere the same since constitutions also are not the same, though there is but one which is everywhere by nature the best.[6]

Like Socrates, Aristotle had great consideration for stability, the great social need of their time. Natural law, therefore, demands obedience, in his view, to positive law, regardless of what may be the latter's short-comings. Where positive law is imperfect or bad the individual or citizen should aim at its reform, not its breach.[7]

We may equate Aristotle's *natural justice* to Justice, and his *conventional justice* to Legality in the modern sense. The former should be the directing element in the law. To achieve and maintain social stability the latter should take into consideration the question of efficacy of the law. Laws based solely on the compelling element, as seen by the law-giver alone without cognizance of the people's feelings, can hardly be just, and therefore very seldom, if at all, promote social stability.

The Stoic School of Zeno (350–260 B.C.) developed further the legal philosophy of Aristotle and his group. To the Stoic, positive law is neces-sary because of man's degeneracy. Originally, they maintained, man lived in a state of nature—a state of perfection, but afterwards this was destroyed by man's greed and selfishness.

The theme of Stoic philosophy was: *live according to nature*. Life in accordance with nature is virtuous. Virtue was a life according to reason. The virtuous submits himself to the world order, a submission not as to something external to man himself, but as to a law of man's own nature.[8] The great aim of the law-maker is, in the Stoic view, to approximate positive law—the law which man's destruction and perversion of his orig-inal state of perfection has brought into being—to ideal natural law.

The Roman Writers

The Roman writers were not original thinkers, unlike their Greek counterparts. Therefore they were satisfied with merely relating each accepted philosophy of the Greeks to the factual situation in Rome. No attempt was made theoretically to evolve a philosophy of law that would adequately explain the Roman situation.

The result was that their legal method led to contradictory and inadequate results. Some of their accepted ways of life and institutions could not fit in with the adopted alien legal philosophy, the empiricism of which belonged to the Greek world.

The *Roman lawyers,* adopting the view that law is a set of rules discoverable by man's reason as expressing the nature of things, divided their *corpus juris* into two main divisions, vis., the *Ius civile* and the *Ius Gentium.* The former was law available only to the Roman citizens; the latter was law available to all persons in Rome, regardless of their nationality. The magistrate, the *praetor peregrinus,* whose assignment it was to evolve the rules of the *Ius gentium* (law of nations), was to rely mainly on reason and common sense.

Ius Gentium was equated to *Ius Naturale,* for both were held to be founded on reason and were of universal application. But, as we have stated earlier, an adopted foreign philosophy more often than not has inherent contradictions which may make it inadequate to explain certain local conditions. The Romans accepted the institution of slavery, which contradicted the natural law principle that all men are born free. Failing to explain this contradiction, the Roman lawyers upheld the right of masters to own slaves as something which agrees with the rules of nature, in spite of the general principle of the freedom of birth. They merely adopted the palliatory view that the slave owner has a duty to treat his slave fairly.

The Christian Fathers, particularly Irenaeus (2nd Century), St. Augustine (354–430), and George the Great (6th Century) A.D., took over the teachings of the post-Aristotelian philosophy sometimes referred to as the neo-Platonist philosophy. They traced and extended the authority of natural law to a divine origin. Natural law became an unchangeable moral code.

St. Augustine (one-time professor of the neo-Platonist philosophy) maintained that mankind was in a state of moral death from which only Christian Grace could save it. The Church must, as the exponent of divine law, interfere with the State and override its acts.

Like the Stoics, the Christian Fathers conceived the original state of man as a sort of golden age, tranquil, happy, and innocent. Then came the fall of man. To cure the evil results of man's fall and wickedness, God created the institutions of law and the State. Thus, slavery and private ownership of property (forms of domination unknown in man's golden era) which are unnatural, are instituted by God to correct man's new sinful tendencies resulting from his fall.

The above sounds more plausible than the views of the Roman lawyers to explain the institution of slavery. The Christian Fathers' idea of law and the government being the products of man's sinful behavior and God's instrument, in effect makes both the law and the State divine sanctions imposed on man to correct him. However, they maintained, like their Greek teachers, that positive law which clearly contradicts the law of God could be disregarded.[9]

Notwithstanding their adoption of Greek legal philosophy, the Romans, being practical men, were able to adjust themselves so as to benefit from it. By trial and error and political conflict they were able to find their way through the states predicted by the Greek philosophers. They experienced various types of government, from monarchy, oligarchy, and democracy to tyranny, each in its turn bringing with it a different form of law. It was left to the senate, the courts, the tribunes, the prefects and other legal organs to evolve practices which refined and revised the *corpus juris* to suit prevailing circumstances.

Perhaps it was the Romans' adaptability and practicality, and undoubted experience that caused Cicero to state that:

> The variety of laws in different states proves that these codes must be based on utility, which differs in different places, not on justice. Changes in the laws of a single State prove the same thing. There is no natural justice or law, but men as well as all other living creatures are governed naturally by utility. There is therefore no such thing as justice, or if it exists, it is the height of folly, inasmuch as it leads us to injure ourselves to the advantage of others. The best proof of this is found in history, particularly in that of Rome. She has won her empire by injustice both to gods and men; a policy of justice would make her again what she was originally, a miserable poverty-stricken village. What is commonly called justice in States is nothing but an agreement for mutual self-restraint, which is a result of weakness, and is based on nothing whatever but utility. Rulers of all sorts rule for their own advantage solely, not in the interest of the governed.[10]

The above statement could well represent the views of an African legal writer who has experienced both colonialism and neo-colonialism in Africa and the laws generated by both. The Roman concept of law, however, did not depart from the ideal law. The Romans continued the search for true law. "True law is right reason in agreement with nature," said Laelius:

> ...it is of universal application, unchanging and everlasting it summons to duty by its commands, and averts from wrong doing by its prohibitions. And it does not lay its commands or prohibitions upon good men in vain, though neither have any effect on the wicked. It is a sin to try to alter this law, nor is it allowable to attempt to repeal any part of it, and it is impossible to abolish it entirely. We cannot be freed from its obligations by senate or people, and we need not look outside ourselves for an expounder or interpreter of it. And there will not be different laws at Rome and at Athens, or different laws now and in the future, but one eternal and unchangeable law will be valid for all nations and all times, and there will be one master and ruler, that is, God, over us all, for He is the author of this law, its promulgator, and its enforcing judge. *Whoever is disobedient is fleeing from himself and denying his human nature, and by reason of this very fact he will suffer the worst penalties, even if he escapes what is commonly considered punishment.*[11]

The Medieval Period

The Medieval period saw the fall of the Roman Empire in Western Europe.[12] It covers the period between the fall of the Empire and the Renaissance of the end of the 15th Century. The years from the end of the 5th Century to about the middle of the 10th Century is the period known as the "Dark Ages." There was a decline in civilization, law, and knowledge. The Papacy took advantage of the diminishing power of the Emperors and the reduction in size of the Roman territories to become a political power to be reckoned with. Papal States which emerged during this period claimed superior authority to that of the secular rulers. Natural law was adopted in the *Decretum Gratianum* and identified with the law of God. It became a reflection of Divine reason, which governs the universe.

The whole concept was, as usual, based on the social needs of the time. There were the need to establish firmly the authority of the Church, and to preserve social stability. These two great needs of the time, in the main, influenced the theory of Natural Law. The Middle Ages regarded positive law as something to be built on natural law. Natural law was made the superior law and its principles formed the criterion for judging the validity of positive law. Such views bound the monarch by natural law, though he stood above the positive law.

St. Thomas Aquinas (1226–1274), attempted to put in reconcile the philosophies of the ancient Greek writers with the teaching of the Church. In this attempt he categorized law into eternal law, *Lex aeterna*—natural law, *Lex naturalis*—divine law, *Lex divina*, and human or man-made law, *Lex humana*, in that order. He equated eternal law with the law of God. Natural law became eternal law revealed to man by reason, and divine law became eternal law revealed to man through the Scriptures. Positive law, or man-made law, to be valid must be reasonable and thus conform with eternal law.

He maintained that social stability demands obedience to positive law. Being a law based on reason and reflecting eternal law, the citizen was obliged to obey it. Following the views of Aristotle and Socrates, St. Thomas Aquinas called for obedience to positive law even seemingly wicked, in order to maintain stability and avoid social disturbance.

Positive law continued to be measured in terms of natural law ideas until the *Reformation* and the *Renaissance* when changed social conditions brought about a rethinking. With the decay of the Holy Roman Empire and the emergence of modern municipal States, legal philosophers started to advance legal theories based on sovereignty.[13] The emancipation of the individual, coupled with the great desire for harmony in society as the main need of the time, influenced men's thinking. The concept of Sovereignty was evolved in legal philosophy and the consolidation of the powers of the national sovereign became an additional factor influencing legal thought.

Modern Notions of Natural Law

The Greek philosophers followed by the Roman lawyers advanced a doctrine of natural law which was expressive of their time and social conditions. They concentrated more on a search for the origin of law and its historical development. Modern legal philosophers have advanced doctrines of law that are purely secular. Unlike their Greek and Roman predecessors, they have witnessed additional human problems in society, one of which (and the most outstanding) is man's economic wants.

Man's economic pursuit has become an additional need which in many ways has had the unsavory effect of unbalancing social stability. In the 20th Century economics has emerged as the base, and law a mere superstructure imposed on it for social ordering. Different political ideologies have sprung up from man's economic wants, and positive laws have been geared to meet the main objective of each particular ideology.

However, some constant features of the doctrine of natural law have persisted which modern philosophers have not been able to disengage from legal notions. Rather, there seems to be a revival of the doctrine as modern man discovers that there are certain moral principles which seem indispensable if man is to be saved from the inhumanity of his fellow man. As H. J. Laski said to Holmes:

The truth is that we are witnessing a revival of "natural" law and natural is the purely inductive statement of certain minimum conditions we cannot do without if life is to be decent.[14]

The modern concern of jurisprudence has assumed a wider dimension featuring other considerations. The essence of law is one of these features. It has culminated in the problem of the definition of law. The line of enquiry has been to find out to what extent law rightly constitutes an act of will, or that of intellect. In other fields the examination is to find out whether the existence of a superior and an inferior is a necessary pattern of legal development. However, many results show that the essence of law is not to be derived solely from parliamentary acts, judicial decisions, or military decrees and edicts. Man in the 20th Century has become aware that there is something much deeper in law than all the above sources.

In our modern times legal notions seem to favor the revival of the idea of a higher law. The modern legal writer can say today, in the words of Atticus and Marcus, that in studying jurisprudence

we are not trying to learn how to protect ourselves legally, or how to answer client's questions. Such problems may be important, and in fact they are.... But in our present investigation we intend to cover the whole range of universal justice and law....[15]

The revival of the natural law concept is evidenced by modern legal phraseologies which take us back to conscience and morality. The question of Fundamental Human Rights, the principles of natural justice, which are to be observed in cases where an administrative tribunal or a minister is exercising a judicial or quasi-judicial function, are concepts of natural law. So also are the use of phrases such as "the due process of law" in the United States Constitution, "repugnant to natural justice, equity and good conscience" found in most enabling Acts in English-speaking Africa;[16] and the test of the "reasonable man" as applied by English judges.

The modern concepts of "public policy," "democratic society," "the national ethic,"[17] "justice according to law and ethics," are all vestiges if not innovations of the Natural Law doctrine. These show that the association of law with morals is still an important feature of legal concept.

Modern legal philosophers do not any longer see law as merely a command, be it of Austin's Political Superior, or Machiavelli's Prince. The Sovereign is no more regarded as having unquestionable absolute power over the subject. The end of law is being constantly sought in the society itself in a way that eulogizes (even though perhaps unconsciously) Bentham's principle of utility. Sociological background has come to be recognized as an indispensable part of modern legal experience. Law may be a command, but a command with a difference, a command that must be the embodiment of recognized and accepted values in society. The difference in positive laws lies in the society and the way it accepts and recognizes those values.

Law as generally conceived by modern writers has become a variable, varying in accordance with the social values of the particular society. Whether as in the views of Ihering, law is regarded as an instrument for balancing competing interests in society, or has social solidarity, according to Duguit, as its sole objective, the trend is shifting toward what is equitable and just in society, and thus a search for justice.

Undoubtedly, it has come to be recognized in our modern times that "legality is an aspect of moral experience which extends far beyond the legal field proper." The modern legal philosopher cannot afford to ignore such conceptions which, in the words of A. P. d'Entreves, "can still enrich our minds, and—the old discussions about the essence of law should not be wilfully ignored."[18]

Public opinion is fast becoming the yardstick for legal validity. This is in agreement with natural law idea that there must be a standard for measuring positive law. Public opinion rests on the moral values of the society. This is perhaps where the modern idea of natural law differs from the concept of earlier times. The earlier writers went beyond the society itself to determine the moral principles or the absolute standard which ought to govern positive law. Their modern counterparts, like Ehrlich and Pound, find the center of gravity of law and its development in society itself. These and other writers of the Sociological School are not, of course, exponents of natural law, but inherent in their theories is the fact that law exists or ought to exist for the furtherance of what is good and equitable in society.

The main objective of law as well as the end of all political associations in modern times is to preserve man's natural and imprescriptible rights. As Professor Lloyd said, "behind all these attempts to find a place for a higher law may be discerned a feeling of discontent with justice based on positive law alone, and a strenuous desire to demonstrate that there are objective moral values which can be given a positive content and expressed in normative form, and that law which denies or rejects these values is self-defeating and nugatory."[19]

So long as man searches for lasting peace, and peace depends on both individual and collective satisfaction of man's political, economic, social, and religious needs, modern man can hardly disentangle himself from the web of moral values and moral principles. Justice gives satisfaction and promotes peace. The quest for justice is a search for absolute and satisfying values in society. The questions that still elude us are: What is justice? And what are the fundamental or inalienable rights of man? If we can find the definite and satisfying answers within the law itself, then we are done with natural law. But as long as there is that need for us to look outside positive law to find our answers, we are still caught up with the doctrine of natural law.

Notes to Chapter 3

1. Lloyd, Dennis, *Introduction to Jurisprudence* (London: Stevens and Sons, 1959), p. 333.
2. Plato's *Republic* (London: Everyman's) Bk. I. See in particular, pp. 15, 21.
3. *Ibid.* Bk. II, pp. 36–38.
4. *Ibid.,* p. 37.
5. Aristotle's *Rhetorica* Bk. I. Ch. 13, p. 1373b.
6. Aristotle's *Ethica Nicomachea.* Translated by H. Rackham (The Loeb Classical Library. Reprinted by permission of Howard University Press in The Great Legal Philosophers (Philadelphia: University of Pennsylvania Press, 1959) Bk. V, Ch. 7, pp. 1134–1135a. pp. 1134–1135a.
7. Aristotle tried to explain away slavery with the belief that it is a natural institution. Slaves must accept their lot. But he urged on slave owners humanitarian treatment of their slaves.   ,
8. See, Zeller, *Philosophic der Griechen* iii(1) (1865).
9. This sounds contradictory, judging from their view on the origin of the law and the state, unless, if by law in the original sense, they excluded positive law.
10. Cicero, *De Re Publica* Book III, XI, p. 201. Translated by C. W. Keyes.
11. *Ibid.,* XXII, p. 211. (Emphasis added.) The Romans were ardent believers in retributive justice. The act of breaking the law was a sacrilege. In most cases the offender was punished for fear that non-punishment of him would bring the anger of the gods on society, not necessarily because his act was a danger to society, which must be prevented.
12. 476 A. D. is usually taken as a convenient date.
13. See Chapter 4 on The Development of Sovereignty, and the Social Contract Theory.
14. See *Holmes–Laski Letters,* 1, 116–117.
15. A conversation between Atticus and Marcus, in *De Legibus* 1, V. 17.
16. See for example, Nigeria, The Supreme Court Ordinance, 1876, which established the Supreme Court of the Colony of Lagos. It provided, under laws applicable by the Court, that the Court shall apply local laws and customs "*not repugnant to justice, equity and good conscience* (S.19)"; Native Courts Proclamation Ordinance No. 9 of 1900 abjures statutory native courts and other minor courts to apply local laws and custom "*not opposed to natural morality and humanity* (s.6)"; High Court Law 1955 (Western Nigeria) (S.17) provides for the enforcement of existing native laws and custom when "*not repugnant to natural justice, equity and good conscience.*" See further, similar enabling acts in English-speaking East and Central Africa.

17. See, for instance, the *Report of the Presidential Commission on the Establishment of a Democratic One-Party State in Tanzania.* There it was stated that "there are certain ethical principles which lie at the basis of the Tanganyika Nation, and the whole political, economic and social organisation of the State must be directed towards their rapid implementation." This means that the ethical principles must provide the basis for the Constitution, and the framework of the government's political, economic, and social policies and activities. Dar-es-Salaam: Government Printers 1965, pp. 3, 6)

18. d'Entrèves, A. P., *Natural Law: an Introduction to Legal Philosophy*—(Hutchinson University Library: London, 1963), pp. 78–79.

19. Dennis, Lloyd, *Introduction to Jurisprudence* (London: Stevens and Sons, 1959), p. 60.

Chapter 4

Sovereignty and the Law

The origin of sovereignty in legal thought can be traced down to the 15th and 16th centuries when eminent writers like Machiavelli, Bodin, Hooker, Grotius, and Thomas Hobbes started to conceive of law in terms of a sovereign act. From there it was developed steadily throughout the 17th and 18th centuries and on into the 19th Century by John Locke and Jean Jacques Rousseau, and later by Jeremy Bentham, the analytical side of whose postulates John Austin finally brought to a climax by conceiving of law as solely an act of the sovereign.

Behind the facade of the legal thinking of this period was Aristotle's epitome of the nature of man. As far back as the third century before Christ, Aristotle saw man in his nature as a political animal, and postulated that

> he who by nature and not by mere accident is without a State, is either above humanity, or below it, he is the *tribeless, lawless, heartless one,* whom Homer denounces—the outcast who is a lover of war; he may be compared to an unprotected piece in the game of draughts.[1]

However, we see from a study of the legal notions of this period, that man's political activities were more of a matter of expediency rather than the dictates of his assumed nature as a political animal.

A look at man in his true image revealed him, even as at present, to be a selfish animal whose main consideration in life was quite in accord with Cicero's First Principle: the principle of self-preservation. As expounded and expatiated on by Hugo Grotius:

> ...an animal, from its birth, is urged to care for and preserve itself, *to choose the means of preserving its good condition, to shun destruction, and everything which leads to its destruction.* Thus there is no one who does not prefer to *have the parts of his body sound and whole, rather than maimed and distorted.* The first business of each is to preserve himself in the state of nature: the next, to retain what is according to nature, and to reject what is contrary to it.[2]

Thus it could be maintained that man's action, be it the formation of a political society, the election of a political sovereign, or the promulgation of laws, is impelled by this first principle of nature: to preserve himself, his very existence.

Ironic as it may seem, war, with all its devastations and destructive elements, conforms with the first principle. The declaration and execution of war, whether a civil war, a war between nations, an interstate or tribal war, or even a fight between individuals, is fully in accordance with man's nature and his desire to preserve himself. As Hugo Grotius once stated, "...there is nothing which is repugnant to war: indeed all things rather favour it; for the end of war, the preservation of life and limb, and the retention or acquisition of things useful to life, agrees entirely with that principle."[3]

However, unlike other gregarious animals, man, being endowed with the faculty to reason, soon discovered that an individual or a unilateral use of his power in furtherance of the first principles to preserve his life and interests often became a means that defeated his very ends. He realized out of experience that the evil of suffering injustice was greater than the advantage of acting unjustly.[4] With further awareness that, since in his original state of anarchy no one is so strong that he may claim any benefits and live without fear of others at all times, so is there no one so weak that he could not, if only by stealth or conspiracy, constitute a danger to others,[5] man decided to come to terms with his fellow man. Thus he conceived a notion of government in an organized society as something more important than those things to which alone his first impulse for self-preservation tended.

The origin of the concept of the State and the Law, and the emergence of the sovereign, have been attributed, and rightly too, to man's right reason and his experience from the practice of the first principle, which turned out an ill wind that does no one any good.

Following this basic premise, let us therefore consider the major factors for the identification of the law with the Sovereign, thus leading to the development of the concept of legal positivism.

The Development of Sovereignty

Jeremy Bentham and John Austin, were not, as it sometimes appears, the first writers to relate the law to sovereign act. From the 15th Century up to the early 18th Century the dominant theme in political and legal thinking was the concept of the Sovereign. The modern idea could be said to start with the Italian writer Machiavelli (1469–1527). His political thinking culminated in the State being an end in itself. The principles of State government which should guide the rulers of any State must be conditioned purely by the end. This end is the success of the State.

Having abstracted the State as an end in itself, Machiavelli postulated that the ruler of the State is bound at times to use means which may appear immoral to most men in order to achieve that end. However, he found it praiseworthy for the ruler to keep faith with the people—the masses—in order to maintain political power, even though he might resort to deceit and hypocrisy as indispensable tools. "The Prince must appear all sincerity, all uprightness, all humanity..." but he must condition and discipline his mind so well that once it is a question of the preservation of the State he can act regardless of these.[6]

The ideas of Religion and the notions of morals or ethics are, in Machiavelli's view, mere instruments of policy in the hands of the ruler. They are subordinate to the ruler's objects. No organization and no law stands above that of the State. Thus he ruled out the idea of divine or natural law as the supreme law.

During Machiavelli's time Italy had the problem of State expansion. It has been suggested by Jolowicz that it is possible Machiavelli's chief object was to further the unification of Italy by the expansion of one of the States in the peninsula at the expense of the other.[7] From this it would be apparent why his postulates on politics and law were purely secular. Since the end must be attained at all costs and by any means, the connection of morals and ethics to law and legality is a mere matter of trying to keep faith with the people. It is a device in statecraft which must disappear when the interest of the State demands it.

Machiavelli's abstraction of the State as an end in itself, and his notion that the principles of State government by which the ruler should be guided must be conditioned by State's ends, would appear quite attractive to new and developing countries, particularly in Africa. Rapid technological, industrial, and economic developments would call for very strong State powers. Scientific socialism, which appears to be the third force in Africa today battling with imperialism and neo-colonialism, may gain from the Machiavellian principle. But the problem is how best can we define *State ends* for the principle to ensure stability and progress if adopted.

The dilemma, however, appears when we come to distinguish the State ends from the idea that the State and the law exist merely to regulate competing interests in society. To see law as an instrument of social engineering is to think of the totality of individual interests in society. The ends of an abstract State may not necessarily be the same as the totality of the individual interests within it.

The person regarded in political theory as the first to formulate a definite theory of sovereignty is Bodin (1530–1596). According to Pollock, Bodin postulated to the effect that no independent community governed by law exists without some authority, "whether residing in one person or in several whereby laws themselves are established, and from which they proceed." Being the source of law, the authority must itself be above the law:[8]

> Find the person or persons *whom the Constitution of the State permanently invests with authority, under whatever name,* and you have found the sovereign. Sovereignty is a power over citizens and subjects, itself not bound by the laws.[9]

According to Bodin, "it is the distinguishing mark of the sovereign that he cannot in any way be subject to the commands of another, for it is he who makes laws for the subject, abrogates law already made, and amends absolute law. No one who is subject either to the law or to some other person can do this. That is why it is laid down in the civil law that the Prince is above the law, for the word *law* in Latin implies the *command of him* who is *invested* with sovereign power."[10] The Prince is neither bound by his own laws, nor by the laws of his predecessors, and even if he wishes he cannot bind himself, for his laws are the free exercise of his own will.

Undoubtedly Bodin's Sovereign is bound by the Constitution, since his power derives from the Constitution. Also the sovereign, though the source of positive law and therefore a power that is above it, "is not above duty and moral responsibility." Thus Bodin recognized the existence of a supreme authority that is outside the law itself. It is implied in Bodin's writings that the Constitution is the basic law. Further, being man-made law, the Constitution, though above the sovereign, cannot contravene divine or natural law to which "all the Princes of the earth are subject." To contravene divine law was both treasonable and rebellious, as being against God.[11]

Further, by implication also, the Constitution to be binding must be in accord with the "Laws of God and Nature." A sovereign Prince is not subject to the laws of any alien power, neither those of the Greeks nor those of the Romans, "much less to his own laws *except in so far as they embody the law of nature which, according to Pindar, is the law to which all Kings and Princes are subject. Neither Pope nor Emperor is exempt from this law....*" From this postulate a Constitution which is based on moral and ethical principles would appear to be binding in perpetuity, and neither King nor a revolutionary leader has the right to set it aside.

Bodin drew a distinction between right and law. The former, he maintained, implies what is equitable, and the latter what is commanded. Law, therefore, is nothing other than "the command of the sovereign in the exercise of his sovereign power." It would appear from Bodin's theory that what is equitable derives from nature and is therefore superior to any legal rights. Hence he concludes that no sovereign Prince has the power to take the goods of his subjects at will.

Man's fundamental rights, therefore, are absolute rights. There should be no expropriation without reasonable cause, and the safety of the State would, in the light of Bodin's postulates, be a reasonable cause. In Bodin's view:

> Absolute power only implies freedom in relation to positive laws, and not in relation to the law of God. . . . Since then the Prince has no power to exceed the laws of nature which God himself, whose image he is, has decreed, he cannot take his subjects' property without just and reasonable cause, that is to say by purchase, exchange, legitimate confiscation, or to secure peace with the enemy when it cannot be otherwise achieved. Natural reason instructs us that the public good must be preferred to the particular, and that subjects should give up not only their mutual antagonisms and animosities but also their possession for the safety of the Commonwealth.[12]

Bodin tempered his legal positivism with the absolutism of natural law, presumably because of the fear of tyranny, as was seen in his period. He wrote at a time when the French Monarchy was aspiring to make itself absolute. It was also during this period that the omnipotence of the Parliament in England was being proclaimed for the first time by Thomas Smith (1513–77).

In his book *De Republica Anglorum,* written about 1565 and published in 1583, Thomas Smith was proclaiming the omnipotence of the English Parliament:

> . . . all that ever the people of Rome might do either in *Centuriatis Comitiis or tributis,* the same may be done by the Parliament of Englande, which representeth and hath the power of the whole realme both the head and the bodie.[13]

Notwithstanding the superior position given the Sovereign in society by Bodin, and his use of the words "person or persons" in the definition of the Sovereign, his thesis could be used to support the view that the Constitution of any State which is the basic law, is the true sovereign. Firstly, Bodin's sovereign is sovereign because the Constitution invests him with authority. Secondly, his commands are laws only by virtue of the power invested in him. When these postulates are taken in conjunction with his first attribute of the sovereign Prince as "the power to make laws binding on all his subjects in general and on each in particular...without the consent of any superior, equal, or inferior being necessary..." our conclusion becomes obvious. Particularly as he maintains that if the Prince can only make law with the consent of a superior, he is a subject; if of an equal, he shares his sovereignty; if of an inferior, *whether it be a council of magnates or the people*, it is not he who is sovereign."[14]

In English-speaking African States with written Constitution and parliamentary system of government, members of Parliament have not their authority to make laws invested in them permanently, and permanency appears to be a strong attribute of Bodin's sovereign prince. Also, the members are in Parliament as a result of the peoples' exercise of their own free will through the ballot box and can only make laws in accordance with the provisions of the Constitution which expresses the people's wishes. Or, in other words, members of Parliament cannot make laws in Parliament without the consent of the people. Thus we conclude that, following Bodin's postulates, it is the Constitution, the authoritative instrument of the people, which is intended to be permanent that is sovereign, or else the people themselves collectively constitute the sovereign.

The Social Contract

The conception of Law as a sovereign act was developed further by Hooker (1554–1600) and other writers of the 16th and 17th centuries. Their main preoccupation was to find the origin of the State and the Sovereign, and thence the law. Hooker and his contemporaries evolved the modern idea of the theory of the *Social Contract*. They saw the origin of the sovereign as the result of a union between men in society, and the product of man's desire to protect *collectively* his personal life and property in society.

As one of the first exponents of this new line of political and legal thinking, Hooker bases the institution of government on an agreement entered into by men, "touching the manner of their union in living together." Before the union, man lived by himself. In his state of individualism, man lacked most of the essentials of a life that is fitting for the dignity of man. This period was followed by an era of social contract which, though not free from the evils of the past period, nevertheless was better than it.

Hooker maintains that the contract by which men set up the ruler was, once entered into, binding in perpetuity. Though more of a natural law enthusiast, Hooker, it has been suggested, was influenced by his support of Queen Elizabeth the First's ecclesiastical supremacy.[15] The social contract idea, which was rather a sideline to his writings, was seized upon, expanded, and expatiated on by subsequent writers during the Reformation and the Renaissance when the political theory of individualism received its distinctive mark.

The writers of this time, like their predecessors, were influenced by the problems of the period. With the decay of the Holy Roman Empire, modern municipal States emerged. Commerce and scientific knowledge[16] began to make an impression on peoples' minds. The individual sought to be emancipated. Being born free, he would need to have his freedom guaranteed in order to pursue, with assurance and safety, his commercial activities in society. A national sovereign was sought who could guarantee the individual's freedom and non-interference. To maintain independence both within and outside his society, individuals collectively sought to consolidate and strengthen the powers of a national sovereign. All the above needs and the problems they posed were to be pursued, bearing in mind the ever-recurring problems of social harmony and social stability.

The theory of the social contract, therefore, was evolved at this time to provide an adequate explanation of the circumstances of the period. Grotius (1583–1645), a Protestant and a Dutch writer, postulated the independence of natural law from metaphysics. Natural law was explained as rooted in man and his reasoning faculty. He saw the State as something which has emerged from man's desire to seek society for his own good. Man entered into a contract by which each individual gave up his personal sovereignty to the ruler as a result of social compulsion; thus the State was created.

The effect of the social contract was that the individual became obliged to obey the ruler. On the other hand, the ruler's obligation was to natural law, which Grotius described as "a dictate of right reason, which points out that an act, according as it is or is not in conformity with rational nature, has in it a quality of moral baseness or moral necessity."[17] Pursuing further the question of the individual's safety outside his own State, Grotius put forward a postulate which earned him the name of the "father of International Law." The State and its rulers, he held, are bound further to enter into a larger society, a society of nations.

Not all the writers of the social contract theory were exposed to the same social environment, but each, with his own local background and general experience, developed a particular theory. The fact that their individual theories culminated in the search for the origin of society, the sovereign, and the law stems from their general knowledge of humanity and the main problems of a universal nature which confronted men in their period. This is a positive proof that law is a social phenomenon made for man, not man for it.

Thomas Hobbes (1588–1679), who saw and lived through the horrors of the civil war in his country, England,[18] started off his theory with the depiction of the life of man in a state of nature as something horrifying. The life of man in a state of nature was to him "solitary, poor, nasty, brutish and short."[19] Men had no pleasure, but on the contrary, a great deal of grief in society because there was no one power over all men which was able to overawe them to bring order and tranquillity.

In this state of anarchy, competition, diffidence and glory dictated men's actions. They lived in a perpetual state of war, invading each other for gain, safety, or for reputation. No man could live without fear of others. All men in the state of nature are equal, he maintained, and this equality is not upset by any differences in intelligence and strength; for "when all is reckoned together, the difference between man, and man, is not so considerable, as that one man can thereupon claim to himself any benefit, to which another may not pretend, as well as he. For as to the strength of the body, the weakest has strength enough to kill the strongest, either by secret machination, or by confederacy with others, that are in the same danger with himself."[20]

To alleviate this perpetual state of war and the danger caused by the living of men in a state of nature where each insisted on his *natural right,* "the summe of the rights of nature"—man discovered the first and fundamental law of nature, which is the desire to end the state of war "to seek peace and follow it."[21]

Man, in his anxiety to end the state of war, entered into a compact with his fellow men to create a Commonwealth. The essence of the pact, according to Hobbes, was to transfer power to the sovereign—a man or an assemblage of men—authorizing him to end the state of war and to preserve and protect the Commonwealth. Hobbes held the appointment of the sovereign to be an act quite distinct from the *pactum unionis* to which the sovereign himself was not a party.

The effect of Hobbes' theory was to assign absolute power to the sovereign. As there was no privity of contract between him and the other members of the society, *he* is not bound by the social pact, and the individual has no excuse to absolve himself from obligations imposed on him by the pact on the grounds that the sovereign himself has caused a breach of it.

> ...they that are subjects to a Monarch, cannot without his leave cast off Monarchy, and return to the confusion of a disunited; nor transfer their

person from him that beareth it, to another man or other assembly of men: for they are bound, every man to every man, to own, and be reputed author of all, that he that already is their sovereign, shall do, and judge fit to be done: so that any one man dissenting, all the rest should break their covenant made to that man, (the sovereign) which is injustice: and they have also every man given the sovereignty to him that beareth their person; and therefore if they depose him, they take from him that which is his own and so again it is injustice ... because the right of bearing the person of them all, is given to him they make sovereign, by covenant only of one to another, and not of him to any of them; there can happen no breach of covenant on the part of the sovereign; and consequently none of his subjects, by any pretence of forfeiture, can be freed from his subjection.[22]

Thomas Hobbes saw only one limitation to the absolute power of the sovereign: the right of the individual to defend his own life. Since the individual entered into the pact basically for the protection of his own life, he should (even as a criminal) resist any attempt by a sovereign command to take his life from him. Equally so, he has a right to disobey a sovereign command asking him to take the life of his fellow man.

""If the sovereign command a man, though justly condemned, to kill, wound, or maim himself; or not to resist those that assault him; or to abstain from the use of food, air, medicine, or any other thing, without which he cannot live; yet hath that man the liberty to disobey.

"If a man be interrogated by the sovereign, or his authority, concerning a crime done by himself, he is not bound, without assurance of pardon to confess it; because no man ... can be obliged to covenant to accuse himself.

"Again, the consent of a subject to sovereign power, is contained in these words, *I authorize, or take upon me, all his actions;* in which there is no restriction at all, of his own former natural liberty; for by allowing him to *kill me,* I am not bound to kill myself when he commands me. It is one thing to say *kill me, or my fellow, if you please;* another thing to say, *I will kill myself, or my fellow.*""

It followeth therefore, that:

"No man is bound by the words themselves, either to kill himself or any other man; and consequently, that the obligation a man may sometimes have, upon the command of the sovereign to execute any dangerous, or dishonourable office, dependeth not on the words of our submission...."[23]

Hobbes, however, accepted that one may fight or die for the Commonwealth, if he must, in order to save it. "When therefore, our refusal to obey, frustrates the end of which the sovereignty was ordained; then there is no liberty to refuse; otherwise there is." Nevertheless, men are not obliged to warfare, unless they do so voluntarily. For example, when one enrolls himself voluntarily a soldier, or receives money to fight, such acts are deemed as denying him the right to excuse himself from fear or cowardice, which to Hobbes are not acts of treachery or unjust behavior, but dishonorable acts. Natural timorousness is to be expected, not only of women, but of "men of feminine courage."[24]

To Hobbes, the Commonwealth is indissoluble. It follows, therefore, that the power of the sovereign should remain indivisible. To divide the power of the sovereign is to divide the power of a Commonwealth, which in effect means to dissolve it; "for powers divided mutually destroy each other." Thus, a grant or delegation of his power by the sovereign is subject to cancellation or resumption by him, unless in the meantime the sovereign itself has been removed.[25]

Hobbes' views on man in a state of nature were not shared by his contemporary John Locke (1632–1704). Unlike him, Locke saw man in a state of nature as living in a golden era, with all things free and common to all. Man could acquire a monopoly only of those things that he removes out of the state of nature, i. e., the fruits of the earth which he has mixed with his labor.[26]

Because in a state of nature man had a title to perfect freedom, everyone was a sovereign unto himself and possessed the executive power of the law of nature. "Man being born,...with a title to perfect freedom and an uncontrolled enjoyment of all the rights and privileges of the law of Nature, equally with any other man, or number of men in the world, hath by nature a power not only to preserve his property—that is, his life, liberty, and estate, against the injuries and attempts of other men, but to judge of and punish the breaches of that law in others, as he is persuaded the offence deserves, even with death itself, in crimes where the heinousness of the fact, in his opinion requires it."[27]

In such a state, Locke saw the insecurity of property as the one big defect. Upon this he based his theory of the social contract, the great and chief end of which is the preservation of property; "...because no political society can be, nor subsist, without having in itself the power to preserve the property, and in order there unto punish the offences of all those of that society, there, and there only, is political society where every one of the members hath quitted this natural power, resigned it up into the hands of the community in all cases that exclude him not from appealing for protection to the law established by it. And thus all private judgement of every particular member being excluded, the community comes to be umpire, and by understanding indifferent rules and men authorized by the community for their execution, decides all the differences that may happen between any members of that society concerning any matter of right and punishes those offences which any member hath committed against the society with such penalties as the law has established; whereby it is easy to discern who are, and are not, in political society together. Those who are united into one body, and have a common established law and judicature to appeal to, with authority to decide controversies between them and punish offenders, are in civil society one with another; but those who have no such common appeal, ... on earth, are still in the state of Nature, each being where there is no other, judge for himself and executioner; which is, ... the perfect state of Nature."[28]

Locke maintained that the surrender of man's power was to the community at large, and not to any sovereign. The sovereign has no absolute power, for if it were so he will be a judge of his own course and this, he said, will be no form of civil government at all.

He made the Legislature, appointed by the majority of those that are privy to the *pactum unionis,* the supreme power. But the Legislature, in spite of its supremacy, is to function for the common good, i. e., the main object of the community's existence. Its supreme power is merely a *fiduciary* power to act for specific ends only, while the ultimate power remains in the people who can remove or "alter the Legislative" when it acts contrary to the trust reposed on it.[29]

Locke placed four limitations on the power of the legislative. Being a creation of the people, the legislative cannot have any arbitrary power over the lives and property of the people. It is created to preserve, and never to destroy, enslave, or impoverish the citizen. Secondly, the legislative has no power to rule by "extemporary arbitrary decrees, but is bound to dispense justice and decide the rights of the subject by promulgated standing laws, and known authorized judges...." To hold otherwise would be to return to the difficulties presented by the uncertainty in the law when man lived in a state of nature. Thirdly, since the protection of property was the reason for the *pactum unionis,* ownership of property remains inviolable as the basis of the union. It would therefore be absurd for the legislative to take away from any man any part of his property without his consent. Finally, the legislative is a delegate of the people, and as such it cannot transfer the power to make laws to any other hands. "The people alone can appoint the form of the Commonwealth, which is by constituting the legislative, and appointing in whose hands that shall be. And when the people have said, "we will submit, and be governed by laws made by such men, and in such form," nobody else can say other men shall make laws for them; nor can they be bound by any laws but such as are enacted by those whom they have chosen and authorized to make laws for them."[30]

It has been said that Locke's rejection of the absolutism of sovereign power, and his idea that the legislative held a mere fiduciary power from the people, made him a champion of the 1688 revolution in England. Whether this is disputable or not, it seems quite obvious to us from his writings that he was opposed to tyranny. "Where law ends, tyranny begins,"[31] he said, and he advocates the use of force to oppose an unjust and unlawful force. Thus one could discern from his postulates that he was in favor of a revolution to overthrow a government (with a fixed tenure of office) when it acts contrary to the common good. Those who lay the foundation of a revolution, by first invading the rights of the people by force, are responsible for the overturning of the Constitution and the overthrow of the government. They are also answerable for the bloodshed, a rapine and desolation that result from a revolution.[32]

However, Locke was opposed to any secession which would result in the dissolution of the State. "The power that every individual gave the society when he entered into it can never revert to the individuals again, as long as the society lasts, but will always remain in the community; because without this there can be no community—no Commonwealth, which is contrary to the original agreement."[33] To Locke, the society remains indissoluble except by foreign conquest.

While Locke in his writings was not clear on the issue of a second pact with the sovereign, Jean Jacques Rousseau (1712–1778) ascribes to only one pact, the *pactum unionis.* He maintains that the surrender of his right by the individual was not to a single sovereign, but to the community. Thus, the individual is not obliged to any other individual but to the "general will"—*volonte generale.* The law and government that followed after the pact are mere reflections of the general will.

Rousseau, following the usual method of his contemporaries, began his postulates with the examination of man in a state of nature. He did not, like Hobbes, paint a lurid picture of man in his original state. Man in a state of nature, according to him, was free. It was man's subsequent degeneracy that altered his freedom to the extent that "everywhere he is in chains."[34]

Rousseau was precise in formulating the terms of the social compact which provided a form of association to "defend and protect with the common force the person and goods of each associate." He reduced it to the following terms:

> Each one of us puts into the common stock his person and all his power, under the supreme direction of the general will; and *we receive as a body* each member as an indivisible part of the whole.[35]

Because Rousseau did not subscribe to the idea of two compacts, (to him there is only one pact, the *pactum unionis* with the individual on the one hand, and the community which receives the individual member on the other hand), he saw no basis for the individual subjecting himself to a sovereign ruler or an assemblage of men. He held that government organs, as the creations of the people, are ordinary servants of the community.[36]

The pact, Rousseau maintained, creates a body with the function to exercise the combined sovereignty of the individuals which formed it. Thus, the individual loses nothing by entering into the pact. At the moment the individual binds himself to the civil society, he as a member receives back his share in the common sovereignty. He becomes one of the constituent parts of the "general will," thus remaining free as before. This may sound contradictory, but Rousseau uses freedom here to mean civil liberty, as opposed to natural liberty. The former is limited by the general will, while the latter is bound only by the strength of the individual.[37]

Rousseau with his idea of the general will (volonte generale), personifies the community. To him the "general will" is not the "will of all" nor is it the totality of the wills of the individuals making up the community. It is the will of the community itself, an expression of common interest requirements.

The general will in Rousseau's view is determined by the votes of the majority. It also embodies the will of the minority. The vote of the opposing minority is a mere conjecture of the general will. The minority voters are just bad guessers as to what the general will is.

> When therefore the opinion that is contrary to my own prevails, this proves neither more or less that I was mistaken, and that what I thought to be the general will was not so.[38]

All the protagonists of the social contract agreed on a general theme, and that is the permanent nature of the contract. That they held the contract to be binding in perpetuity, even when the members' rights were infringed by the custodians of the power, showed their fear and utter abhorence of disharmony which may lead to anarchy in society. Whether their initial premise of the origin of state and government is correct or not is not the basis of our enquiry. What concerns us is the happenings of their time, the human behavior as seen in their period, how those affected their legal thought, their projection of the law as an instrument for social order and what lessons we as developing states can learn from their postulates. Their concept of the sovereign and its limitations we regard as something purely symbolic; perhaps an aspect of the Oedipus complex. The early natural law theorists sought to satisfy themselves in this by resorting to the metaphysical, while their modern counterparts resort to social ethics and morality with the pious hope that social harmony, justice and peace will emerge from their consideration by the man of power—the modern law-giver. Throughout the ages man has remained by and large what he was originally, i. e., an animal whose first and foremost consideration is his individual self-preservation. If he enters into a pact, a covenant or a treaty while the stronger party he does so more because of the uncertainty of the future. He is completely aware of the fact that all secular powers are transient. Better still, he would like to maintain the status quo which is to his great advantage. If the weaker party to a pact, what guarantee has he that legality will not turn to be a mere mirage? Legality ends where the over-confidence of the ruler as to his absolute power and strength does begin.

There is no doubt that the original motivating factor for the institution of government and law was for man's mutual self-preservation and protection which could be achieved better in an orderly society where human values are generally recognized. Undoubtedly, too, there is no arguing with the fact that in some societies law has become synonymous with power, an instrument not for social engineering or for balancing competing interests, but for class domination. However, man has not given up the search for the ideal law, the law that will have force and power to curb man's natural and egoistic interests which have been to the detriment of his fellow man. The trouble, of course, is that being an abstraction of rules and principles given and administered by man, it is not the law that is powerful, it is man.

Sovereignty and the Imperative Theory

We have seen above how man's experience, arising from social problems, has influenced the political and legal thinking of the early philosophers; how the social needs of their time and the problem of a much-needed organized, harmonious, and orderly society presented the basis for their legal conception. We have also seen how the concept of law has shifted from an absolute standard and immutable universal principles to a secular consideration to meet the requirements of society. Right reason, and the practical considerations of the nature of society combined, proved to man that force is an ingredient which cannot profitably be extricated from law, while justice requires that those who had the use of organized force assigned to them, use it for the common good.

The nature of society in the periods we have considered did not admit of the prohibition of force, except when its use was repugnant to society, that is, when it is used to attack the right of others, and thus in effect jeopardize social harmony and equilibrium.

Writers like Jeremy Bentham and John Austin, following on the heels of their predecessors of the social contract theory, tried to improve on the idea of law as an act of the sovereign. Their method, which was an analysis of the mechanics of the law, resulted in a legal concept which we now refer to as legal positivism, or analytical positivism.

Jeremy Bentham (1748–1832), who is often referred to as the founder of the English analytical school, advanced a two-sided theory. Firstly, as a legal analyst he was interested in the mechanics of the legal system. Secondly, his inquiry into the ends of law in society resulted in his advancing a legal criterion of the principle of utility, that is, that every law should be tested to see how far it tends to the "greatest happiness of the greatest number."

Analyzing law as it is, Bentham defines it as "an assemblage of signs declarative of a volition conceived or adopted by the *sovereign* in a State, concerning the conduct to be observed in a certain case by a certain person or class of persons, who in the case in question are or are supposed to be subject to his power."[39] Thus, law becomes a command of the State superior. The State must be a political entity for law to exist. It emerges "when a number of persons (whom we may style subjects) are supposed to be in the habit of paying obedience to a person, or an assemblage of persons, of a known and certain description (whom we may call governor or governors) such persons altogether (subjects and governors) are said to be in a state of political society...."[40] The political superior conveys his will by the signs called words. When the expression is parol, it constitutes a direct command; when it is a tacit expression of the will of the superior, it may be styled a fictitious or quasi-command. Thus, "the statute law is composed of commands, and the common law of quasi-commands."[41]

Bentham, however, unlike John Austin (as we shall see later) did not envisage the powers of the governor as unlimited. "The supreme governor's authority, though not infinite, must unavoidably, I think, unless we are limited by express convention, be allowed to be indefinite."[42] In Bentham's view the powers of the governor would always be limited by a possible resistance of the subjects. Undoubtedly, his utilitarian principle would form the criterion of the validity of the law, and therefore a ground for the resistance by the subjects.

Nature, Bentham maintains, "has placed mankind under the governance of two sovereign masters, pain and pleasure. It is for them alone to point out what we ought to do, as well as to determine what we shall do. On the one hand the standard of right and wrong, on the other the chain of causes and effects, are fastened to their throne. They govern us in all we do, in all we say, in all we think; every effort we can make to throw off our subjection, will serve but to demonstrate and confirm it."[43] Bentham did not believe in any metaphysical limitation to the supreme governor's authority. All judgments as to the expediency or inexpediency of any act hinged on the principle of utility, "accurately apprehended and steadily applied." This alone affords the clue to guide a man through his evaluation of the law and impel him to obey or disobey it.[44]

Bentham defines the principles of utility as "that principle which approves or disapproves of every action whatsoever, according to the tendency which it appears to have to augment or diminish the happiness of the party whose interest is in question; or, what is the same thing in other words, to promote or to oppose that happiness."[45] He makes utility the mainstay of legality. The happiness of the individuals making up a community, their pleasures and their security is, to Bentham, "the end and the sole standard, in conformity to which each individual ought, as far as depends upon the legislator, to be made to fashion his behaviour."[46]

Bentham's idea of utility would be identified later with the modern teleological approach to jurisprudence, an approach which went beyond the functional to interest itself in the end to be pursued by law in society, i. e., the values that should underlie the law. On the other hand, his analysis of the law as it is lead to the pure analysts like John Austin (including Holland) to see law solely in its formal or mechanical sense.

John Austin (1790–1859), puts forward analysis as the chief tool of jurisprudence. Law, to him, must be taken as it stands, and not as it ought to be, and the idea of morals or ethics should be expunged from the law. He defines law in its general sense as "*a rule laid down for the guidance of an intelligent being by an intelligent being having power over him....*"[47]

His idea about the general nature of law leads him to classify law into two broad divisions; namely,

(a) *Laws properly so-called,* and
(b) *Laws improperly so-called.*
     The first consists of:

  (i) *The divine laws, or the laws of God which are set by God to man.*
  (ii) *Laws which are set by man to man*
      (a) *as a political superior, or in pursuit of rights conferred on him by the political superior;*
      (b) *not as a political superior, nor in pursuit of any rights conferred on him by the political superior.*

The second consists of
  (a) *Laws by analogy such as social conducts, early customary law and international law;*

(b) Laws by metaphor, e. g., scientific uniformities, such as the law of gravity.

Of Laws properly so-called, those that are set by man to man, neither as a political superior, nor in pursuit of legal rights, together with laws by analogy which are improper laws, are what Austin terms positive morality. They are positive because they are set by man as commands, but because they are not backed up by any legal sanction they are rules that are merely binding in morality.

On the other hand, with the exception of divine laws, laws properly so-called, that is, laws set by man to man either as a political superior or in pursuit of legal rights, are *positive law* "... that is to say, law which is simply and strictly so called." To Austin, it is only this kind of law that forms the proper subject matter of general and particular jurisprudence.[48]

As a visual aid, John Austin's general notion of law may be tabulated as follows:

LAW

Improperly so-called

Properly so-called

Laws by Metaphor

Set by God to man
(Divine Law)

Set by Man to Man

Laws by
Analogy

Neither as a political
superior nor in pursuit
of legal rights.

Positive
Morality

As political superior
or in pursuit of legal
rights(*Positive Law*)

The core of Austin's theory is that law is a command of a political superior. The command may be an expression or intimation of a wish that an act shall or shall not be done. The form does not matter. What matters is the visitation by the political superior with an evil in the event of a non-compliance with his wish upon the political inferior. The evil threatened is what Austin calls Sanction, and it is this that imposes a duty or an obligation on the subject to obey the law.

Austin's theory of the law and sovereignty makes positive law an act only of the political superior, whom he defines as an identifiable human being or a body of persons. The political superior can only exist in an independent political society, and it follows also that an independent political society can only exist where there is an identifiable political superior or sovereign.

He gives the following attributes to the political society:

(a) The inhabitants must not fall short of a number which cannot be fixed with precision, but, which may be called considerable, or not extremely minute.

(b) The bulk of the given society are in a *habit* of obedience or submission to a *determinate* and *common* superior; let that common superior be a certain individual person, or a certain body or aggregate of individual persons.

(c) That certain individual, or that certain body of individuals, is *not* in a habit of obedience to a determinate human superior.

"If a determined human superior not in the habit of obedience to a like superior, receives habitual obedience from the bulk of a given society, that determinate superior is sovereign in that society, and the society (including the superior) is a society political and independent."[49]

As for sovereignty, its attributes are in Austin's view, continuity, indivisibility, and the possession of an unlimited power. "Supreme power limited by positive law, is a flat contradition in terms," said Austin.[50]

How does Austin's legal philosophy fit into the political and legal arrangements in English-speaking Africa? Each of the countries, unlike Britain, has a written Constitution which is regarded as the basic law and therefore supreme. Even with Parliament's power to amend or alter the Constitution, certain specific procedures laid down by the very Constitution have to be followed, otherwise an act becomes unconstitutional and illegal. Also, certain aspects of the Constitution are entrenched, never to be changed, as, for example, the fundamental rights. All these are limitations on the powers of the Parliament, the only symbol in the political and legal framework in English-speaking Africa that can be said to be analogous to Austin's sovereign or political superior.

If one looks above Parliament for an unlimited source of power and of the validity of law, one sees the Constitution and the people—the masses or the voters. The Constitution is the people's *basic law* which must be obeyed, but in the Austinian sense the Constitution contains merely principles upon which the sovereign should act. To him it is really nothing but positive morality,[51] for sovereign power cannot be limited. Also, the Constitution cannot be the source of power and legality, and therefore sovereign, because it is not a determinable human being that can issue commands.

Can the masses and the electorates, who make and unmake the Parliament and give the required initial approval to the Constitution, be sovereign? By definition we may accept that the electorates or the people are identifiable bodies of persons who in their "corporate" existence could constitute the political superior. If, however, we accept this postulate, we are left with the other question: who then are the political inferiors who give habitual obedience to the masses or the people? Certainly, it cannot be the members of Parliament, since they too are part and parcel of the people, nor do they habitually obey the electorates. So one may end up with absurd conclusion that there is no political superior and consequently that the new States do not constitute political societies in the Austinian sense, and therefore have no laws.

The only way out, if we are to adopt the Austinian method, is to give absolute power to the Parliament. Thus, the African positivist of the Austinian type cannot afford not to be a dictator or a tyrant, where as a dictator he is not benevolent.

Where there are not political superior and docile subjects, law cannot exist in the Austinian sense. International law, like the rules of honor and fashion, is merely positive morality. There is no sovereign, i. e., no common determinate superior who is habitually obeyed by the bulk of nations and their human population. To Austin, international law "consists of opinion or sentiments current among nations generally" and is devoid of any legal sanction compelling obedience.[52]

Among rules included as being erroneously called law is customary law. In the Austinian sense, a rule of customary law is no law at all until it is made the basis of a judicial decision. Then it becomes an indirect command of the sovereign, since the judges act in pursuance of the legal rights conferred on them by the political superior. In English-speaking Africa, therefore, only those rules of customary law which the courts have accepted and pronounced upon since the introduction of courts of the British type are law. With the indigenous African, whether customary law is law in the Austinian sense would depend on how far a particular indigenous society qualifies as a political society.[53]

Case law, another important source of law in English-speaking Africa, is indirectly a command of the sovereign. This is, as in the case of customary law, because the courts derive their power from the Parliament, the sovereign, and the supreme authority. With the operation of the doctrine of binding precedent, the judge in English-speaking Africa who is an analytical positivist, taking law as it stands and not as it ought to be, ceases to be a social reformer. He will be interpreting and applying the law in its rigid form, thus impeding if not halting social reform and progress through the law.

The Pure Theory of Law

The pure theory of law which was later advanced by Hans Kelsen (1881-1975) refines Austin's general notion of law as a command of the sovereign. With his concept of *die Grundnorm* Kelsen removes the absurd position into which Austin placed Constitutional Law. In his pure theory of law, Kelsen postulates that:

(1) Law consists of a hierarchy of norms with a basic norm known as die grundnorm, i. e., the apex from which all other legal norms derive their validity. Jurisprudence is a knowledge of these "norms."
(2) A theory of law must deal with law as it is, not as it ought to be.
(3) A theory of law must be distinguished from the law itself.
(4) A theory of law must remain "pure," allowing no admixture of ethics, political, sociological and historical considerations.
(5) A theory of law should be uniform, applying at all times in all places.
(6) Law and the State are one and the same thing seen from different angles.

Though an analyst and a positivist, Kelsen denies the Austinian concept of sovereignty as a source of legal validity. Sovereignty is not a power that is innate in an individual or body of persons known as the political superior. Even legal norm derives its validity from the other legal norm above it until the stage of the ultimate norm (die grundnorm), which Kelsen refers to as the "initial hypothesis"[54] is reached.

Kelsen's basic norm is in conformity with Sir John Salmond's postulate of *ultimate principles* from which other legal principles are derived. More than three-quarters of a century before Kelsen, Salmond postulated that "certain ultimate principles from which all others are derived" must be found in every legal system. Such ultimate principles, he went on to say, "are themselves *self-existent*. Before there can be any talk of legal sources there must be in existence some law which establishes them and gives them their authority."[55]

The initial hypothesis cannot find its definition within the law itself. "The basic norm is not created in a legal procedure by a law-creating organ. It is not—as a positive legal norm is—valid because it is created in a certain way by a legal act, but it is valid because it is presupposed to be valid; and it is presupposed to be valid because without this presupposition no human act could be interpreted as a legal, especially as a norm-creating act."[56] Thus, the basic norm of any legal order is a postulated ultimate rule from which other norms of a legal order are established. They derive their validity from it and can also lose the same from it.

The hierarchy of norms must terminate at one point beyond which Kelsen thinks it is not necessary to probe. "The quest for the reason of validity of a norm," he said, "is not—like the quest for the cause of an effect—a regressus ad infinitum; it is terminated by a highest norm which is the last ground of validity within the normative system."[57]

This basis of the validity of *die Grundnorm* to Kelsen is just a fact to be presupposed and accepted. He tries to explain this with the phenomenon of revolution. A successful revolution creates a new legal order which derives merely from the fact of its success, the success having established a new *Grundnorm* which replaces the old. "Suppose," he said, "that a group of individuals attempt to seize power by force in order to remove the legitimate government in a hitherto monarchic State and to introduce a republican form of government. If they succeed, if the old order ceases, and the new order begins to be efficacious, because the individuals whose behaviour the new order regulates actually behave, by and large, in conformity with the new order, then this order is considered as a valid order. It is now according to this new order that the actual behaviour of individuals is interpreted as legal or illegal. *But this means that a new basic* norm is presupposed. It is no longer the norm according to which the new republican constitution is valid, a norm endowing the revolutionary government with legal authority.[58] If the revolutionaries fail, if the order they have tried to establish remains inefficacious, then, on the other hand, their undertaking is interpreted, not as a legal, a law-creating act, as the establishment of a constitution, but as an illegal act, as the crime of treason, and this according to the old monarchic constitution and its specific basic norm.[59]

It is at this point that Kelsen's theory ceases to be pure. He admits that force and efficacy are essential factors in the establishment of *die Grundnorm* and efficacy is the assent or support of the people. Thus, the ultimate validity of a legal norm derives from factors and considerations which lie outside the law itself. These are some of the "foreign elements" which his pure theory seeks to exclude from law, but which cannot be profitably excluded, and are in fact not excluded by his theory.

Consequently we find it rather difficult to accept Kelsen's view of a general jurisprudence. To hold that a theory of law should be uniform, that it should apply at all times in all places, is to presuppose, first, that society is static, and second, that social values and social needs are the same at all times and in all places. Humanity is one thing, and man's problems another. Man as a social animal has his needs and wants conditioned by his particular social environment and social values. Law, as an instrument for satisfying those needs and wants, and for social change, can only be adequate if it is shaped in a way that is suitable toward its solution of those very problems. For example, the reasonable man in England is reasonable only in the light of the acceptable social values in England. His act may be unreasonable in an entirely different society with different social values and culture. Besides being relative to society, reasonableness is also relative to time, and what is reasonable in one society at a particular time may cease to be so at other times.

The problems presented by received laws in English-speaking Africa should be viewed from this angle. A philosophy of law, to be adequate for a people, should be guided by the past and present experiences of the people and their future outlook to life. To advance a theory of general jurisprudence is to think of law *in vacuo*. The law as it concerns us is something secular. As Hegel has said, "The great thing is to apprehend in the show of the temporal and transient, the substance which is immanent and the eternal which is present."[60] By adopting this method we can solve our particular temporal problems, while retaining the one thing that is general—our humanity.

Unlike Austin, however, Kelsen advanced a relative theory of law which seems to offer a more accurate explanation of modern law in English-speaking Africa. The Constitution as the basic law is Kelsen's Grundnorm. It is postulated to be the ultimate rule according to which other legal norms in the State are established, receive, or lose their validity.

All these are acceptable to us, but we do not subscribe to the Sacrosanctity of the Constitution. The Constitution is functional and not ordained, as contemporary events in the political history of some African countries have shown, particularly in Nigeria and Ghana. It cannot find its own definition within the legal order itself. Its efficacy and retention are subject to the common will of the people, or the acts of their acclaimed and popular leadership.

We agree with Kelsen that the ultimate basis for the validity of the law is the assent of the people. Thus, a legal order is a formalized expression of a peoples' will. The sovereign or the political leader cannot be superior to the order that made him what he is. He is or should be a mere servant of the people within the order. Consequently, law cannot and should not be a command of the political leader, but that of the people through the order they have created. The condition presented by the people and the legal order they created is the State. Here we would disagree with Kelsen that the law, together with the institutions by which they are put into effect, constitute the legal system—the order. It is this, plus the people, that become a State. The legal order is only an aspect of the State, and a part cannot be equal to a whole. There can be no State without a people.

Another aspect of Kelsen's postulate which can be used quite favorably to explain the African legal situation consists of his view of international law. Firstly, Kelsen regards international law as a legal order, though it lacks the essential elements of Austin's "law properly so-called," namely, an effective machinery for legal sanction. Kelsen regards war and reprisal as the sanctions of international law in much the same way as "self help" in primitive societies is a sanction of primitive law. Thus far we need not look for Austin's political superior in an indigenous African society before accepting that a rule of customary law is law. The principles of effectiveness and assent are all we need to look for, for it is through these that both the sphere of validity and the reason of validity of any legal order is determined.

Secondly, in Kelsen's view legal pluralism presents no problem, for two different and mutually independent legal orders can form one normative system. Thus, the received law and customary laws in any English-speaking African State, though regulating separately the lives and transactions of those in the colonial enclave and the indigenous African of the subsistence level, respectively, can form one harmonious legal order. This reasoning emerges from an analogy that could be drawn from Kelsen's views on the reasons of the validity of municipal and international law. Kelsen says that:

> In order to answer the question whether international and national law are different and mutually independent legal order, or form one universal normative system, in order to reach a decision between pluralism and monism, we have to consider the general problem of what makes a norm belong to a definite legal order, what is the reason that several norms form one and the same normative system.... If the national legal order is considered without reference to international law, then its ultimate reason of validity is the hypothetical norm qualifying the "Fathers of the Constitution" as a law creating authority. If, however, we take into account international law, we find that this hypothetical norm can be derived from a positive norm of this legal order; *the principle of effectiveness.* It is according to this principle that international law empowers the "Fathers of the Constitution" to function as the first legislators of a State. The historically first Constitution is valid because the coercive order erected on its basis is

efficacious as a whole. Thus, the international legal order, by means of the principle of effectiveness, determines not only the sphere of validity, but also the reason of validity of the national legal order. Since the basic norms of national legal orders are determined by a norm of international law, they are basic norms only in a relative sense. It is the basic norm of the international legal order which is the ultimate reason of validity of the national legal orders, too.

A higher norm can either determine in detail the procedure in which lower norms are to be created, or empower an authority to create lower norms at its own discretion. It is in the latter manner that international law forms the basis of national legal order. By stipulating that an individual or a group of individuals who are able to obtain permanent obedience for the coercive order they establish are to be considered as a legal and legitimate authority, international law "delegates" the national legal orders whose spheres of validity it thereby determines.[61]

The analogy may be quite tenuous, particularly as we do not subscribe to Kelsen's method of argument, which gives supremacy to international law over national law.[62] But the point we are making is that if we accept the postulate that there can be two *Grundnormen* within a legal order with the principle of effectiveness or consensus as the connecting link, then the source and validity of customary law should be quite clear as resting on the consensus of the indigenous people. It need not rest on the act of a British established legal institution. The tests of reasonableness, public policy, and "repugnance to natural justice, equity and good conscience" now applied to rules of customary law in order to make them valid, would be contradictory to a system such as ours, where legal pluralism and not monism is the avowed practice.

Notes to Chapter 4

1. Aristotle, *The Politics I*, (transl.) Benjamin Jowett, (Oxford: Oxford University Press) Bk I, published with the permission of the Oxford University Press in *The Great Legal Philosophers* (Philadelphia: University of Pennsylvania Press, 1957 p. 27).
2. Grotius, Hugo, *On The Rights of War and Peace,* Bk. I, Chap. II (transl.) William Whewell (London: John and Parker, 1853) (Emphasis added) cited in *The Great Legal Philosphers* (Philadelphia: University of Pennsylvania Press, 1957), at p. 88.
3. *Ibid.,* at p. 88.
4. See, Trasymachus in Plato's *Republic, op. cit.,* Bk. I, p. 21.
5. Hobbes, Thomas, Leviathan (1651), p. 84.
6. Machiavelli, Niccolo, *The Prince,* Chap. 18.
7. Jolowicz, H. F. *Lectures on Jurisprudence* (London: University of London: The Athlone Press, 1963), p. 73.
8. Pollock, *Politics,* pp. 47–48.
9. *Ibid.,* (Emphasis added.)

10. Bodin, J., *Six Books of the Republic* (Transl.) M. J. Tooley, pp. 28–29 (Emphasis added.)
11. *Ibid.*
12. *Ibid.*, p. 35.
13. Smith, Thomas, *De Republica Anglorum* (Alstons, 1906) Bk 2, Chap. I, p. 49.
14. Bodin, *op. cit.*, p. 43.
15. See Jolowiczs, *op. cit.*, pp. 77–78.
16. This period saw the findings of Galileo (1564–1642).
17. Grotius, *De Jure Belli ac Pacis,* Book I, 10.1.
18. It is even said that Thomas Hobbes was born prematurely as a result of war, when his mother panicked at the rumors of the impending attack of the Spanish Armada.
19. Hobbes, Thomas, *Leviathan* (1651) Part I, Chap. XIII, p. 84.
20. *Ibid.*
21. *Ibid.*, Chap. XIV, p. 87. It is to be noted here that Hobbes "first and fundamental law of Nature," i. e., the ending of the state of war, differs from Cicero's First Principle of Nature, which is individual self-preservation. To Hobbes, Cicero's first principles are nothing other than natural right. "The summe of the Right of Nature." From Hobbes' postulate, only the pursuit of the Natural Right admits of war.
22. Hobbes, *op. cit.*, Part II, Chap. XVIII, see pp. 121–124.
23. *Ibid.*, Chap. XXI, p. 153.
24. *Ibid.*
25. Hobbes, *op. cit.*, p. 127.
26. Locke, John, *Two Treatises of Civil Government,* Chap. V, p. 26.
27. *Ibid.*, Chap. VII, ("Of Political or Civil Society"), p. 87.
28. *Ibid.*
29. *Op. cit.*, Chap. XI, p. 135.
30. *Ibid.*, pp. 135–141.
31. Locke, *op. cit.*, Chap. XVIII, p. 202.
32. *Op. cit.*, Chap. XIX, p. 230. In his view, however, if power is given in perpetuity to the Legislative and its successors, it can never revert to the people. This statement, which undoubtedly results from his idea that the the social pact is binding in perpetuity, contradicts his views on tyranny and the use of force to correct it.
33. *Loc. cit.*, p. 243.
34. Rousseau, Jean Jacques, *The Social Contract,* 1762 Book I, Chap. I. Translated by G. D. H. Cole, London: Everyman's Library E. P. Dutton & Co Inc. Reprinted in The Great Legal Philosophers (Philadelphia: University of Pensylvania Press 1957.) p. 215 et seq.
35. Rousseau, *Social Contract,* Bk. I, Chap. VI, p. 218.
36. Rousseau's critics argue on this point that, as the community was constituted by the pact, it is difficult to see how it could be a party to the very instrument to which it owes its very existence.
37. Rousseau, *op. cit.*, Chap. VIII, See *The Great Legal Philosophers* p. 219.
38. Rousseau, *op. cit.*, Bk. IV, Chap. II. See *The Great Legal Philosophers* p. 234.
39. Bentham, Jeremy, *The Limits of Jurisprudence Defined,* Chap. 3.
40. Bentham, Jeremy, *A Fragment of Government,* Chap. I, s. X.
41. *Ibid.*
42. *Ibid.*, Chap. IV, s. XXIII.
43. Bentham, *An Introduction to the Principles of Moral and Legislation* Chap. 1, p. 1.
44. Bentham, *A Fragment of Government,* Chap. IV.
45. Bentham, *An Introduction to the Principles of Morals and Legislation,* Chap. I, p. 2.
46. Bentham, *op. cit.*, Chap. III, pp. 34–35.

47. Austin, J. *The Province of Jurisprudence Determined,* Lecture 1 (Emphasis added.) (London: John Murray Ltd, 1832).
48. Austin, *loc. cit.*
49. Austin, *op. cit.,* p. 221.
50. *Ibid.,* p. 263.
51. *Ibid.,* p. 267.
52. *Ibid.,* p. 184.
53. It would seem that in acephelous societies, i. e., societies without chiefs, customary law would be regarded as no law, whereas in centralized societies a different view would be held. For a detailed analysis on the position of the rules of customary law in this connection, see Elias T. O. *The Nature of African Customary Law* (Manchester University Press 1962), particularly pp. 25-55.
54. Kelsen, Hans, *General Theory of Law and State* (1946), pp. 115-116.
55. Salmond: Sir John *Jurisprudence* (London and Reading: the Eastern Press Ltd, 1902 1st Ed) p. 110.
56. Kelsen, *loc. cit.*
57. *Ibid.*
58. In contemporary African politics and law, the theory of the *Grundnorm* which hitherto has been held to be the traditional foundation of judicial and constitutional supremacy, is proving to be unreal in the face of military coup d'etat. In Nigeria in *Lakanmi v. A. G. (West),* S. C. 58/69, the Supreme Court confirmed the Constitution as the basic law by holding that the Military Government as a *Constitutional interim government* came into existence by the wishes of the representatives of the people and therefore has to uphold the Constitution, only derogating from it under the "doctrine of necessity." The Military Government quickly countered this decision by passing the "Federal Military Government (Supremacy and Enforcement of Powers)" Decree No. 28 of 1970, asserting its unfettered and unlimited powers both to legislate and to exclude the jurisdiction of the courts in regard to certain acts of legislation, as it thinks fit. A similar issue had come up in Ghana in the case of *Sallah v. The Att-General for and on behalf of the Government of Ghana,* S. C. 8/70, April 20, 1970. For details of the respective issues involved and other opinions, see Abiola Ojo "The Search For Grundnorm In Nigeria"—The Lakanmi Case *(International & Comparative Law Quarterly),* Jan. 1971, p. 117; Date-Bah S. K. "Jurisprudence Day in Court in Ghana" April 1971, 1 C. L. Q., p. 315.
59. Kelsen, *op. cit.,* pp. 118-119. (Emphasis added.)
60. Hegel, *Philosophy of Right,* Preface and Addition 1.
61. Kelsen, *General Theory of Law and State* (1946), pp. 366-368 (Emphasis added.)
62. Especially as it would appear that Kelsen presupposed international law came into existence before national law, and that as a higher law the former determines and authorizes the procedure in which lower norms of municipal law, including its Grundnorm, are to be created.

Chapter 5

Popular Consciousness as the Generating Force of Law

The 18th Century, during which legal notion was developed to its climax as a sovereign act, was also the period when a new legal philosophy of the historical school produced an antithesis of the legal doctrines of both that century and the earlier natural law period. For the historical school, led by Friedrich Carl Von Savigny (1779–1861), a German legal philosopher, law is to be considered in direct relationship to the people and their life within the community where the law operates.

The boundary of jurisprudence can only be delimited by the understanding of the law, and this understanding is not possible without an appreciation of the social milieu from which the law has developed. For Von Savigny, the nature of any particular system of law is a reflection of the people concerned. It is their common consciousness, otherwise known as *der volksgeist,* in German.

Von Savigny maintains that in "the earliest times to which authentic history extends, the law will be found to have already attained a fixed character, peculiar to the people, like their language, manners and constitution. Nay, these phenomena have no separate existence, they are but the particular faculties and tendencies of an individual people, inseparably united in nature, and only weaving the semblance of distinct attributes to our view. That which binds them into one whole is the common conviction of the people, the kindred consciousness of an inward necessity, excluding all notion of an accidental and arbitrary origin. . . ."[1]

The historical school subscribes only to an unconscious and evolutionary growth of the law and not to revolutionary changes. For this school, law develops "by internal silently-operating powers, not by the arbitrary will of a law-giver." The organic growth and "connection of law with the being and character of the people, is also manifested in the progress of the times; and here, again, it may be compared with language. For law, as for language, there is no moment of absolute cessation; it is subject to the same movement and development as every other popular tendency;

and this very development remains under the same law of inward necessity, as in its earliest stages. *"Law grows with the growth, and strengthens with the strength of the people, and finally dies away as the nation loses its nationality."*[2]

Von Savigny expatiates on the complexities of the law as the people progress in civilization. He maintains that with civilization a people's national tendencies become more and more distinct. Their feeling of unity becomes incorporated in a visible form known as the State. Law, which before this time existed only in the consciousness of the community, becomes more artificial and complex. It takes a scientific direction, perfecting its language through its appropriation to particular classes of the community. The jurists, as a particular class of the kind representing the community, accept this arduous task and become the custodians of the common consciousness.

Notwithstanding that at this juncture law has become more artificial and complex because of its "two-fold life," (viz., that of remaining "part of the aggregate existence of the community, which it does not cease to be"; and "a distinct branch of knowledge in the hands of the jurists") its growth remains unconscious, which is kept alive by a continuous tradition which survives the gradual changing generation. We discern from Von Savigny's writings that it is this hard core, the "continuous tradition," that makes the law at any state of a people's development continue to be part of their common consciousness. "At different times, therefore, amongst the same people, law will be natural law (in a different sense from our law of nature), or learned law, as the one or the other principles prevails, between which a precise line of demarcation is obviously impossible."[3]

The legal theory of the historical school is negative to the notion of law as being of any universal application or as being governed by immutable universal principles, since law varies not only with people but also with ages. In this pragmatic approach to the study of law we see the cornerstone not only of the sociological school, but also of most modern law thinking. In most modern States today, law is no longer viewed, as Professor Lloyd has very aptly stated, as "an abstract set of rules simply imposed on society, but is an integral part of that society, having deep roots in the social and economic habits and attitudes of its past and present members."[4]

Perhaps, it is because English-speaking Africa has not quite grasped this conception of law, which would change the *corpus juris*, that legal efficacy presents a problem in most of the new States. "Law to be effective" said President Nkrumah, "must represent the will of the people and be so designed and administered as to forward the social purpose of the

State.... Law is converted into a reactionary force once it is regarded as an abstract concept, which is in some mysterious way universally applicable without regard to the economic and social conditions of the country in which it is being applied.... The law should be the expression of the political, economic and social conditions of the people and of their aims of progress...."[5]

Undoubtedly, Von Savigny did not have the African community in mind when he was propounding his theory. Nor can we say for certain that he had any particular community in mind when he wrote. However, his statement that any law which does not conform to the common consciousness of the people is pernicious and doomed to failure seems not just a prophecy of today, but a reality in Africa.

For Savigny, the State is a by-product of the common consciousness of a people as an entity. Hence, law precedes the State. It follows therefore that, impliedly, the creation of an artificial State with a people not linked up by a continuous tradition is a reverse process, in the Savignyan sense. There will be no law which truly reflects *der volksgeist*, for the broad principles of any legal system which represents the common consciousness receive their first concrete manifestation in early customary law. It is true that civilization with its legal complexities invokes the assistance of the jurists and the legislator for legal development, but the evolutionary development of the law should not be, and is not, for Savigny, interrupted by them.

The Savignyan theory sees legislation as giving only definiteness to law. "Particular rules, indeed, may be doubtful, or from their very nature may have varying and ill-defined limits, as, for example, all prescription; whilst the administration of the law requires limits defined with the greatest possible precision. Here a kind of legislation may be introduced, which comes to the aid of custom, removes these doubts and uncertainties, and thus brings to the light, and keeps pure, the real law, the proper will of the people."[6] Savigny agrees that "high reasons of State" may influence the legislator in altering the existing law, but such a method, he says, should be adopted with caution and should be most sparingly employed for, "enactments of this kind easily become a baneful corruption of the law."

In one of his works *(System of Modern Roman Law)* Savigny, apparently trying to balance his thesis on the original formation of law with the function of law as an instrument of social change, admits the great part that legislation plays. He says that:

The influence of legislation upon the progress of law is more important than upon its original formation. If through changed manners, views, needs, a change in the existing law becomes necessary or if in the process of time entirely new legal institutions are necessary, these new elements may indeed be introduced into the existing law by the same innate invisible power which originally generated the law. It is however precisely here that the influence of legislation may become most obviously beneficial, nay indispensable. Since those operative principles only enter gradually, there of necessity arises an interval of uncertain law and this uncertainty is brought to an end by the expression of the law.[7]

Nevertheless, he holds fast to the idea that legislation should not be used to stultify the evolutionary development of the law. He would undoubtedly subscribe to the orthodox idea that the law reform of today should follow the public opinion of yesterday.

Savigny acknowledges the fact that a people in their historical development may enter a stage with "conditions which are no longer propitious to the creation of law by the general consciousness" of the people. At this stage it becomes indispensable that legal development should devolve upon legislation. Nevertheless, even at this stage the people's law, as is evidenced by their custom, remains supreme, and a custom can change a rule laid down by statute. For Savigny it appears quite clear that "the natural developing power of popular law cannot be invalidated by the fortuitous fact that a previous formation has been clothed in the form of legislation."[8]

It is not at all surprising that Von Savigny's theory seems to bring to light more than the theories of other writers the problems of legal conception in Africa today. Germany in the time of Savigny was confronted with the problem of receiving an alien law in the nature of Roman law just in the same way (though perhaps not in the same manner) as English-speaking Africa is facing the problem of legal pluralism brought about by the reception of English law. He was, in other words, advocating legal autochthony in Germany, a problem which is confronting the new African States today. His pragmatic approach recognizes the complexities brought about by civilization and the need for development. He does not reject change; in fact, he admits it is necessary. The problem, as we see it, is how best new ideas can be adopted without doing violence to the old. The new has to be blended with the old in such a way that the core of continuous tradition which identifies a people with their law at any stage of their development can still be identified.[9]

The problem becomes more complex when one looks at the artificial nature of most African States brought about by colonialism. The central core of tradition, that everlasting link of a people's common consciousness with its varying ages, is difficult to identify in an artificial and non-homogeneous State. If we accept Von Savingny's theory, perhaps the only way out is not to go in for the particular tradition which identifies each ethnic group, but for a general tradition which is wider than the particular and which embraces peoples of African origin, in fact, that tradition which makes the African an African, irrespective of his ethnicism. If we adopt this method, we may not only be able to reduce the horizon of the centrifugal forces which are operative in the political and legal spheres of our nationhood, but we shall also be helping to consolidate the centripetal forces to build up a people which will correspond to Savigny's *ein Volk,* and thence a nation.

Another aspect of Von Savigny's work, which the African jurist should concern himself about, concerns his views on the codification of the law. Von Savigny was strongly opposed to codification. While he held that legislation might give definiteness to law without changing its nature and source of validity, he believed that codification would have an opposite effect. He based his argument on the following grounds:[10]

(1) That the substance of a Code becomes an exposition of the aggregate existing law embodying political elements, with exclusive validity conferred by the State itself. This would give the law such a technicality that it would make it a monopoly of the jurists;

(2) Since a code would look for the highest degree of precision and the highest degree of uniformity in the application, it becomes a general national law which replaces a varying customary law;[11]

(3) The code, as it is intended to be the only law-authority, is actually to contain by anticipation a decision for every case that may arise. This is unrealistic, because there are positively no limits to the varieties of actual combination of circumstances;

(4) The code, by its novelty, its connection with the prevailing notions of the age, and its external influence, will infallibly attract all attention to itself, away from the real law-authority; so that the latter, left in darkness and obscurity, will derive no assistance from the moral energies of the nation by which alone it can attain to a satisfactory state.

Besides the substance of the code itself, Von Savigny is of the view that only very few ages will qualify for a code. Young nations, he maintains, may have the clearest perception of their law which could be compiled into a code, but they are lacking in language and logical skill, which make their codes defective. With declining ages on the other hand, almost everything is wanting. They lack both knowledge of the matter (the contents of the code) as well as language for a code. With regard to the "middle period," that is, ages which are neither young nor decadent, he holds that there is no need for a code. These, as regards the law, have reached a summit of civilization, or in other words, such perfection, so that a code would be superfluous.[12]

A code composed by a nation which has reached a climax in civilization, Von Savigny says, is a code composed for the nations succeeding and less fortunate generations, for the authors of the code have no need for it for themselves. They will be laying up the code for the succeeding age "as we lay up provision for winter. But an age is seldom disposed to be so provident for posterity."[13]

Looking at Von Savingny's postulate, one sees in it not only the disadvantages of codification to legal development, but also, by analogy, the problems presented by a rigid adoption and application of the doctrine of binding precedent. The orthodox and conservative judge, who tenaciously sticks to old and outmoded court decisions, is undoubtedly confining his generation to values and precepts that are not of their time and age and thereby, as it were, fastening them to the apron strings of their predecessors. The same would go for the several criminal codes operating in most States of the English-speaking Africa. Both as to their origin and time, they are quite alien to the present generation of Africans, and in all respects, they cannot be apposite and cannot reflect the peoples common consciousness.

One obvious advantage of a historical approach to legal development is that at every stage of a people's development and progress the law is closely identified with their common aspirations and reflects their ethos. This reduces to a minimum the amount of friction and social dissatisfaction which a radical or a revolutionary legal change, that takes no cognizance of the social milieu, brings. On the other hand, a people in a hurry to catch up with modern economic and scientific developments may find the historical approach rather too slow for the achievement of those goals, even though it is the best way to achieve legal autochthony and be assured of social harmony, which a people's true law brings and sustains.

Sir Henry Maine (1822–1888), in his comparative approach to the study of law, depicts clearly the problems of legal development through a simple historical evolution. From his postulates emerges the fact that social necessities and utility call for devised methods for legal development. Without devised methods for developing its laws, a society remains static, or cannot be progressive.

Maine postulates that there are four stages in the early development of the law in any society. First, he regards the law as a personal command, or what we may call proclamation believed to be of divine inspiration, such as the *themistes* of ancient Greece and the *dooms* of the Anglo-Saxon Kings. The command, at the second stage, crystallizes into custom. Then comes the third stage, when the ruler is surpassed by a minority who takes over the control of the law, like the pontiffs in ancient Rome. The fourth stage, Maine postulates, is reached when the majority revolts against the oligarchic monopoly of the minority, and the consequent publication of the law in the form of a code.[14] Beyond this stage Maine holds that static societies do not progress further, while progressive societies go on to develop their laws further through three agencies, namely, legal *fiction, equity,* and *legislation* in that order.[15]

Like Savigny, Maine's postulate is in favor of social opinion being in advance of law. But unlike Savigny he accepts codification and legislation as methods of legal development which do not stultify the sound growth of the law but are rather among some of the instrumentalities by which law is brought into harmony with society as the society progresses. It is true that Maine did not, like Savingny, postulate a theory of the *volksgeist,* but he did identify the origin of the law with the people concerned, and its development with the compelling forces and the needs in society.

What we regard as essential in the whole exercise of the historical approach to the science of law is that the people, the masses in an African State, ought to be conscious of their law and its development. Since law is a mere superstructure, its base must be clearly defined by the people. Primarily, the definition of this base involves an economic and political ideology which is clearly defined and delimited. Until this is done, there can be no systematic legal development that will reflect the common consciousness of the people.

Notes to Chapter 5

1. Von Savigny, F. C., *Of The Vocation of Our Age For Legislation And Jurisprudence.* (London: Littlewood & Co., 1831) (Transl.) Abraham Hayward, II.
2. Von Savigny, *loc. cit.,* (Emphasis added).
3. Von Savigny, *loc. cit.*
4. Lloyd, Dennis, *Introduction to Jurisprudence* (London: Stevens and Sons 1959), p. 333.
5. Nkrumah, Kwame, *Journal of African Law* (1962) Vol. 6 No. 2, pp. 103–104, 107–108.
6. Von Savigny, *op. cit.,* III.
7. Von Savigny, *System of Modern Roman Law* (1840), (transl.) W. Holloway (1867).
8. Von Savigny, *System of Modern Roman Law,* p. 43.
9. Those who criticize Savigny on the reception of Roman Law in Germany during his time in spite of his thesis seem to underrate the flexibility in his theory, and the implication in his theory that law like language may draw on what is foreign to enrich itself as a people advances in civilization and make greater contacts, provided that the inception of new ideas does not unbalance the base, which is the continuous tradition.
10. See Savigny, *Of The Vacation of Our Age For Legislation And Jurisprudence, III.* (London) Littlewood & Co. Transl. Abraham Hayward.
11. This view would stand against the assimilation of customary law, since assimilation would arrest its flexibility and adaptability to changing circumstances and values in the community.

12. Von Savigny, *loc. cit.*
13. *Ibid.*
14. Maine cites the Roman *XII Tables* as the "most famous specimen" of these early codes. See Maine, Sir Henry, *Ancient Law* (London: John Murray 1916), p. 12.
15. *Ibid.,* p. 29.

Chapter 6

The Sociology of Law

The awareness of the essential connection between law and the society in which it develops reached a climax in the 19th Century and has since become the dominant feature of modern jurisprudence. Following the clue left by the historical school, legal philosophers of both the 19th and the 20th centuries departed from the world of metaphysics in legal thinking and adopted the line of Comte (1798–1857), that the advancement of human knowledge can only be enjoyed by application of the empirical method of observation and experiment. They began asking, not so much what law is, as what purpose it serves and is meant to serve in society.

Among the factors which tilted the balance of legal thought at this time were the quick social changes and developments of the time and the increased speed with which the States in the 19th and 20th centuries accepted social welfare, health, education, and economic development as functions of the State which should be regulated by legal means. It was also realized during these periods that the analytical approach had failed to provide an adequate explanation of the concern of law with social requirements. The Industrial Revolutions and other social crises of the 19th Century showed that social solidarity was insecure, and what is more, that it could not be achieved along with social mobility through the old approaches to law.

Some writers of the period took jurisprudence to include the study of the factors that shaped and influenced the law, such as economic conditions and moral ideas. Law ceased to be an end in itself and began to be viewed as a superstructure superimposed on the economic base, and other social needs and wants of man, for his well being as well as for the ordering of the community in which he lives.

Writers of the sociology of law or sociological jurisprudence can be classified into two broad groups. First is the *purely sociological* school, and second, the *functional* school. The latter could further be reclassified into the purely functional school, that is, those whose main interest in jurisprudence is the function that the law is supposed to perform in society. The next group, better referred to as the teleological school, does not stop at the function of law in society, but goes further to examine the values that should underlie the law. This last group seems to have taken its clue from the earliest pioneers of the thought (like Bentham's) that insist the aim of the law-maker should be utilitarian, i.e., the achievement of the "greatest happiness of the greatest number."

Sociological Jurisprudence

For our purpose here, the main protagonists of this School are:

Ihering (1818–1892)
Duguit (1859–1928)
Ehrlich (1862–1922)

Rudolf Von Ihering defines law as *"the sum of the conditions of social life in the widest sense of the term, as secured by the power of the state through the means of external compulsion."*[1] He arrives at this definition after careful study and analysis of man's problem of competing interests in society and the part that law plays or should play therein. The main theme of Ihering's thesis is that law is a tool for balancing these competing interests.

Ihering sees as "the grave problem of society" the reconciliation of selfish purpose with social purpose, or what amounts to the same thing, the suppression of selfish purposes when they clash dangerously with social purpose. To encourage the social purpose, which he gives precedence over selfish purpose, Ihering advocates the employment of a mechanism which encourages the social purpose while still accommodating selfish interest. One of the chief methods he advocates is the identification of man's selfish interest with some larger social interest.

The identification of man's selfish interest with some larger social interest is obviously a relic of the motivation of the social contract. Unlike the social contract theorist, however, Ihering does not advocate a surrender of man's interest to a selected sovereign for the common good. Rather, he postulates a practical and persuasive method which diverts man from his egoistic interests and directs him toward a required social goal. He sees two principal levers; namely, *reward* and *coercion*, as essential in making man less egoistic and more philanthropic. For the reward lever he chooses as an example commerce. "Commerce is the organization of the assured satisfaction of human wants which is based upon the lever of reward...."[2] A social purpose of satisfying the economic wants of man is achieved through trade, which holds out to the individual the satisfaction of his egoistic profit motive.

Where the reward lever cannot apply, society uses coercion, a social mechanism that is characteristic of law. For him, organized coercion makes the State and the law. The other part of coercion, which he identifies as unorganized, is analogous to Austin's positive morality and is in the nature of social etiquette and conventions.

Opposed to both the two lower and egoistic levers of reward and coercion are two other impulses, which have no egoism as their motive and presupposition. These he classifies as the *higher*, or the *moral* or ethical levers of social motion; they are the *Feelings of Duty* and of *Love*. These, together with the other two, constitute the *principles of the levers of social motion* which divert man's egoistic interests toward the achievement of social ends.

Notwithstanding *the principle of the levers of social motion*, for Ihering, law is coercion organized by the State. He recognizes force as an essential ingredient of law. "Law without force is an empty name, a thing without reality, for it is force, in realizing the norms of law, that makes law what it is and ought to be."[3] The difference between *force* and *law* is that the latter is organized in a set form which, unlike naked force, accommodates individual interests and selfish motives as a means of achieving desired social ends.

Another writer whose postulates removes the notion of law further from metaphysical speculations is Leon Duguit. He uses social solidarity as the basis of his thesis. Since man is born in society and cannot exist outside it, Duguit takes to the view that no individual right can exist quite independent of society. Therefore, law can serve no end and no useful purpose, unless it be a social one.

Duguit argues further that even the so-called individual needs of man are incapable of satisfaction without social cohesion. No matter what man's needs are, they fall into two categories. Man's need may be one which he shares in common with others, which can therefore only be satisfied by collective effort. Or, if the need is peculiar to man, it cannot be such that a lone man can satisfy it alone without exchange or division of labor with other men. Consequently, a rule of conduct known as law is imposed on man by the nature of his living in society, that he must so act that he does nothing which may be prejudicial to the social solidarity upon which he depends. More positively, he must do all that which lies within his power and which naturally tends to promote social solidarity, for his own ultimate good.[4]

One of Duguit's main theses is that the duties imposed by the principle of social solidarity are binding on every member of society, including the corporate body known as the State. Both the governor and the governed as well as the State are subject to law and are bound by it. No special position or privileges should be accorded to the State or to the sovereign. The State is only one form of human organization. Inasmuch as the command of the State is issued in furtherance of social solidarity, there is a duty to obey, uphold, and encourage it. Once the State deviates from the main function of achieving and promoting social solidarity, the citizen is bound to suppress it; that is, he is not only justified if he disobeys the law, he has a duty also to revolt against the State.

It follows from Duguit's thesis that neither the State nor sovereignty is sacrosanct and indispensable. As a social organization of human beings, the State is functional and all State powers are limited by the principle of social solidarity. The leaders of the State have to conform to this principle, as well as those they lead. The State and its leaders must be prevented from acting in a way that will jeopardize social solidarity. Where Constitutional checks and balances and other legal means, such as the judges' power to quash legislation, fail to keep the State powers in check, revolution is left as the only means available to the subjects to correct the tyranny of the rulers and steer society back to a normal course to attain its main goal.

The corollary is, therefore, that those who revolt against the State are not necessarily breaking the law. So long as their course is justifiable within the principle of social solidarity, they are the true champions of the social order. It is the ruler who acts in a way that is detrimental to social solidarity who is anti-society. That he possesses the State powers and force does not alter the position. Once he deviates from the goal of the society he is analogous to the individual criminal who ought to be punished or corrected by the use of any effective force.

The abstraction of the State, it appears, would not be in conformity with the principle of social solidarity. For Duguit, the State does not exist as a collective person distinct from the individuals making up a given society and from those individuals who are in power in the society. The individuals constituting a State may be united to one another by the very strongest sociological ties, they may desire the same thing, believe in the same future, have identical recollections of the past, hope for the same things, pursue the same ends, and be conscious of the same ideal—but they remain individual human beings. They suffer individually and trust in the future individually. "Because a million, ten million, forty million individuals will and do the same thing, think and believe the same thing, we cannot conclude that for this reason there exists a person one and collective, a national person organized as a State, having a conscience and a will distinct from those of the individuals." Phrases such as *national spirit* or common consciousness, *the personality of the nation* or of the State, though convenient and expressive, are to Duguit not expressions of reality scientifically established by observation.[5]

Political power, for Duguit, is a mere fact. The power to govern is vested in men who govern because they, in fact, are in possession of it. Their control of power is never legitimate by origin, and as a result it does not constitute a right in them as against the governed. Equally so, the individual has no right against those who govern. The only way the governor can impose his power legitimately is by exercising it in conformity to the jural principle (la règle de droit) founded on social solidarity.

Duguit has been criticized as postulating "a theory of justice, a value judgement on social ends."[6] His critics, however, ought to concede him the fact that if man's life in society is purposeful, that social purpose must present a guide to human conduct. Since law is not an end in itself, but a means to an end, that end must provide a maxim by which law must be judged. The main problem, as we see it, is how best to determine the social purpose, or what may amount to the same thing, to state the ends which law should serve.

Here Duguit's three formative laws, which he holds out as the criteria for legal validity, may present useful guide. Respect for property, freedom of contract, and no liability without fault, he says, are formative laws to which all positive law must comply. To these we may add: respect for human life. A purported law achieves validity only by approval of the major public opinion. Public opinion is distinctly expressive of the principle of social solidarity, which in itself is the legal matrix. Legal development should be centered around the mass of public opinion. Only in this way can the gap between what Ehrlich terms the living law and the formal law be narrowed down.

Eugene Ehrlich is another subscriber to the sociological approach to law. He sees "the centre of gravity" of legal development in nothing other than society itself. Summarizing his work, *die Grundlegung der soziologie des Rechts,* Ehrlich says: "At present as well as at any other time, the centre of gravity of legal development lies not in legislation, nor in juristic science, nor in judicial decision, but in society itself."[7] Like his other colleagues of the Sociological School, he rejects any *a priori* notion of law.

For Ehrlich, the formally stated rules of law are inadequate to govern the life of a people in society. What matters most is the actual behavior of man in society. It is this behavior that determines the norms which govern the life of a people. Thus, in a given society two categories of normative rules exist: the norms of the *formal law* and those of the *living law.* The formal law lags behind the living law, and in some cases its norms contradict the latter. In other words, he emphasizes, by implication, the need for major public opinion in law reform if the formal law has to catch up with the living law.

Ehrlich sees no difference between the sources of efficacy of formal legal norms and norms of customs and morality. Both derive efficacy from social pressure. One could not agree with him more, especially when one thinks of laws which formally remain valid only on statute books, whereas in practice the people act in breach of them, regardless of the statutory sanctions. Examples in Nigeria are the *Limitation of Dowry Law*[8] and *The Abolition of the Osu System Law*. Both laws, though valid to this day, have not been efficacious. In the former, for instance, there is an utter neglect of the express provisions of the law by all parties engaged in a marriage under the customary law. Suitors still pay, and parents or guardians of the bride receive by far more than the statutory amount fixed as dowry.

Lawrence records that among the Iteso of Uganda the maximum limit for marriage payment fixed by law is being evaded "wholesale." The men, he says, find it profitable to pay the legal penalty of one hundred and fifty shillings in the unlikely event of being detected.[10] On the other hand, a chief's edict prohibiting bride-price among the Ngwato of Bechuanaland has been seen to be effective,[11] presumably on the basis that the edict is expressive of the peoples' wish.

Some of the examples to be found in English law, where English practice differs from the formal law, are mainly in the field of commerce. These include *Leaman's Act of Stock Exchange*, the *Marine Insurance Act, 1906, Sec. 4*, and the Money Lender's Act, 1900. In all these cases the people persistently neglect the provisions of the Act in question. The most curious thing about the practice is that even individuals who are adversely affected by the breach fail to bring cases to court to avail themselves of the relief offered by the Act.[12] Other examples abound where people's practices deviated from the formalized legal norms, thus rendering the latter inefficacious. To be binding and efficacious law must be dictated by the social order, which is an expression of the collective purpose and power of society.

As the structure of human relationships in society, any law which does not reflect the social sentiment may be enforceable as a valid formal law, nevertheless, it is generally regarded by the people as not naturally binding. For example, an Act of Parliament may conform with all legislative procedure and receive the Royal Assent (i.e. assent of the Head of State) which makes it valid, but inasmuch as it goes against the social sentiment which is the soul of legal efficacy, it is regarded as not binding. Such an Act can, of course, be enforced (unless in the meantime the people have successfully rebelled against it). For just as the Lion pounces upon its prey for no just cause except that it has the power and wants to assuage its hunger, so does the upholder of a law that is devoid of the social purpose lay hold of the so-called violator, because those promulgating it possess the sheer brute force necessary for its enforcement.

We would agree with Ehrlich that analytical positivism which limits the scope of jurisprudence to a study of the formal law is not only narrow but unrealistic. It confines jurisprudence to what we may call the arena of *legal mechanics*, and denies law its dynamism, which stems from society itself. Since the formal legal system of a society is only a fraction of the law, no true study can be made of law without an understanding of the social milieu.

The Functional Approach

As we have stated earlier, the main problem of legal conception in Africa, particularly in English-speaking Africa, is how to marry both the *directing and* the *compelling elements* of law for a dynamic legal system that will satisfy the relics of the old and at the same time meet the modern requirements of a new society. Here we may not go all the way with Ehrlich, whose theory, by implication, does not stand much in favor of the teleological approach. Sufficient weight should be given to the formal law to influence and reform the practices of the old society for a society that is modern and forward-looking. The main task is determination of the right values and how best to get the masses, the possessors of the majority opinion, involved in the creation and acceptance of the new values that will form the basis of the formal law.

Apart from maintaining the established social order, law has as well a major task in effecting social change. It is from this angle that Roscoe Pound (1870–1964), views law. Pound, the Dean of the Harvard Law School from 1916 to 1936 and one of the most well-informed American jurists, with a very wide knowledge of all forms of law, maintains that the chief end of law is social control. He defines jurisprudence as "a science of social engineering having to do with that part of the whole field which may be achieved by the ordering of human relations through the action of politically organised society."[13]

Developing Ihering's doctrine, Pound is of the view that a legal system attains the ends of the legal order by "social engineering," in other words, by balancing the competing interests in society. It does this by identifying the interest in the first place, then the limits within which the interests shall be recognized and given effect are determined and further secured within those limits. Pound asserts that these interests exist independent of the law and are part of the phenomena of man's life in society. The goods of existence, the scope for free activity, and the objects on which to exert free activity, are limited in our world, while the demands upon those goods and those objects are infinite. The object of law is therefore to adjust relations and order conduct and activities of men in their endeavor to satisfy their demands, so as to enable satisfaction of as much of the whole scheme of demands with the least friction and waste.[14]

For Pound, law has a triple meaning. It may be used in reference to the *legal order*, the *rule for conduct*, or the *judicial process* itself—that is, the process of deciding disputes. As a legal order, law is the "regime of adjusting relations and ordering conduct by the systematic and orderly applications of the force of a politically organized society."[15] It is the fact of the existence of a regulation, rather than the nature of the regulation, that Pound gives the meaning of law. Thus, respect for law is respect for the regulation, the legal order itself, rather than its nature. As a rule for conduct, law refers to the whole body of legal precepts existing in a political society. Law in this sense is a body of precepts, techniques, and ideals. It is a body of authoritative precepts, developed and applied by an authoritative technique in the light or on the background of authoritative traditional ideals.[16] To Pound this is the oldest and longest continued use of the term *Law* in juristic writing.[17]

Pound puts interests which are the concern of the law into three categories as follows:

(a) Individual interests
(b) Public interests, and
(c) Social interests.

Individual Interests would include matters such as a man's personal liberty, reputation, freedom of will, and freedom of opinion; marital and family interests; interests in property, such as freedom of contract, security in employment. *Public Interests* include the interest of the State as a legal entity and the interest of the State as a custodian of social interests. The former interest, that of the State as a juristic person, embraces such matters as the territorial integrity of the State and of its sovereignty, State security, and its freedom to act as a sovereign independent State.

The *Social Interests* are more elaborate. These include social interest in the general security, the security of social institutions, general morals, conservation of social resources, general progress, and individual life. General security embraces security against those forms of action and conduct which are prejudicial to or threaten the existence of the society itself. Social interest in general morals is to the security of social life against acts or courses of conduct offensive to the moral sentiments of the general body of individuals therein for the time being.[18] As to the interest in general progress, it is that the development of human powers and of human control over nature for the satisfaction of human wants go forward; the demand that social engineering be increasingly and continuously improved, as it were, the self-assertion of the social group toward higher and more complete development of human powers.[19]

Pound regards the social interest in individual life as the most important of all, in some ways. It is "the claim, or want or demand of society that each individual be able to live a human life...according to the standards of the society...that, if all individual wants may not be satisfied, they be satisfied at least so far as is reasonably possible and to the extent of a human minimum."[20]

After reviewing the interests which are the concern of law in society, Pound sums up his thesis with the following words:

> Looked at functionally, the law is an attempt to satisfy, to reconcile, to harmonize, to adjust these overlapping and often conflicting claims and demands, either through securing them directly and immediately, or through securing certain individual interests, so as to give effect to the greatest total of interests, or through delimitations or compromises of individual interests, so as to give effect to the greatest total of interests or to the interests that weigh most in our civilization, with the least sacrifice of the scheme of interests as a whole.[21]

It is Pound's *jural postulates* which he propounded in 1919[22] that puts his work in the special category we refer to as the *teleological approach* to jurisprudence. In adducing the values that ought to govern law he puts forward the following jural postulates which law ought to pursue in a civilized modern society:

1. In civilized society, men must be able to assume that others will commit no intentional aggression upon them.

2. In civilized society, men must be able to assume that they may control for beneficial purposes what they have discovered and appropriated to their own use, what they have created by their own labor, and what they acquired under the existing social and economic order.

3. In civilized society, men must be able to assume that those with whom they deal in the general intercourse of society will act in good faith, and hence

   (a) will make good reasonable expectations which their promises or other conduct reasonably create;

   (b) will carry out their undertakings according to the expectations which the moral sentiment of the community attaches thereto;

(c) will restore specifically or by equivalent what comes to them by mistake or unanticipated or through not fully intended situations whereby they receive at another's expense what they could not reasonably have expected to receive in the circumstances.

4. In civilized society, men must be able to assume that those who engage in some course of conduct will act with due care not to cast an unreasonable risk of injury on others.

5. In civilized society, men must be able to assume that others who maintain things likely to get out of hand or to escape and do damage will restrain them or keep them within their proper bounds.

In his *Social Contract Through Law,* Pound envisages new emergent postulates. These include the right of the employee to security of employment, the imposition of a burden on enterprises in industrial society to compensate for the necessary human wear and tear, and the postulate that the risk of misfortune to individuals be borne by society as a whole. These postulates will provide the values that ought to govern the law in a good contemporary society.

There are areas of conflicts between Pound's emergent new postulates and his earlier jural postulates propunded in 1919,[23] but we do not see these as minimizing the value of his thesis. Rather when the conflicts are considered, bearing in mind the time factor, that is, the period between his two relevant works, they go to prove the non-static nature of values in society. They also go to show that while old values may change yielding place to new values, there is always a period when the old and the new overlap, thus creating additional conflicts of interest which the law must take care of. We therefore see within Pound's work a positive proof of his postulate on the function of law as that of balancing competing and conflicting interests in society.

Unlike analytical positivism, sociological jurisprudence teaches us a fundamental principle that law is made for man and not man for law. What is made for man is for his comfort and progress, and law ought to meet these ends. Since man's life and values in society are not static, law, which controls that life and those values, must not be made to stand still. It must encourage and advance movement and progress. The task of the law-giver is to balance the evolutionary process of society with revolutionary concepts for rapid development. In this way social mobility and progress can be achieved without unbalancing social solidarity.

The predicament of a new African State today is that it is a country in a hurry without a really defined goal. Enmeshed in the quagmire of nationalism versus neo-colonialism, it struggles with its colonial tools against the colonial psychological mechanism to fully emancipate itself and build up a modern and progressive society. Because of the complexities of its creation, there is a general clash of interests. Individual interests conflict with other personal interests, while foreign interest and national interests oppose each other. There are also group interests, which may be tribal or class interests, and which align themselves with foreign interests or conflict with national interests in such a way as to create favorable conditions for the furtherance of the foreign interests.

If we take Pound's postulates as a guideline we soon see in a new African State group of interests which are always in conflict. Those in the subsistence sector of the economy, viz, the native peasants and the petty traders, represent a group with interests which conflict with the interests of those in the colonial enclave, that is, the elite and the petty bourgeoisie. To the most conservative and the right-wing forces in the latter group, power was transfered by the colonial masters who strove hard to bring them out on top before Independence was conceded. These frequently adopt policies which, more often than not, feature law as an instrument to protect their individual and class interests. There are also the national or State interests which, though at variance with the class interests of the petty bourgeoise, are often misrepresented by the ruling elite. They try to equate their class interests with the national interests.

During the struggle for Independence the nationalist movement, which aimed at overthrowing the colonial ruling class, was not a movement only of the masses, who are in the subsistence economy, but a movement of all who were oppressed or restricted by the colonial overlords, including the conservative and right-wing sector of the elite and the petty bourgeoise. The alliance formed by wide sections of the people against the main enemy—the colonial masters—and the fact that leadership and the financing of the movement generally came from those in the colonial enclave, gave advantages to the present rulers. They posed as the custodians of the peoples' will and the protectors of their common interests. The national or State interest was therefore thought of by the people as what Parliament decrees or enacts, or equal to the government's interest.

With a further growth of education and political and national consciousness it has become obvious to the people that most of the rulers had been groomed and maneuvered into positions both to protect their own personal or class interests, and certain foreign interests. The Parliamentarian is no more what he was looked upon to be, and the State interest has become the class interest of the parliamentarians. The State with its machinery is in most cases taken as something through which the will of the ruling class is imposed on the rest of the people. This attitude has affected the law and its efficacy, and represents the ultimate background to that political instability which gives rise to coups and counter-coups.

The people have begun to view law from a set of facts which are different from the facts which obtained and prevailed during the colonial era. They now ask a different set of questions, have a different set of values, and are confronted with problems not too similar to the past.

If they are still enchanted by the present system of laws it is because no adequate alternative has been produced in the realm of legal philosophy which will provide an adequate explanation of the past and offer suitable guidelines to their modern problems and aspirations.

Most of the conflicts could be seen in the fields of education, economic planning, social welfare, and social institutions. For example, in Nigeria in the case of *Olawoyin v. A. G. for Northern Nigeria,*[24] the right of a father to educate his children the way he thinks fit conflicted with the State interest of protecting children under 15 from engaging in political activities as stipulated in Part VIII of the Northern Region Children and Young Persons Law of 1958. The case is also illustrative of State interest conflicting with the wider national interest provided for in the Constitution, which guarantees private and family life, freedom of conscience, and freedom of expression.

In the sphere of economic planning, one sees State interest in rapid industrialization through State-owned corporations and industry conflicting with foreign monopoly interests and the interest of the conservative and the ruling minority who gain from the economic arrangements with the foreign capitalist firms. Even in this sphere, the interest of the peasantry sometimes conflicts with a wider national interest. To mechanize agriculture, for instance, the indigenous system of landholding needs reorganization in a way that will promote large collective farming but which will detract from the individual interest of small family landholding. To change the entire structure will call for formal laws with values, not of the old, but for a modern society that is ready for scientific advancement and willing.

Other outstanding examples are seen in social institutions, domestic, religious or political institutions. Taking religious institution, for example, there have been instances where the interest of some religious sects have been seen to conflict with political interests of the State resulting in the banning of some of the sects by the governing body[25] and thus detracting from the members' fundamental right of freedom of worship. The clash is not necessarily between the individual's freedom of religion and the State interest in preserving the dominance of the established churches. It is between the freedom of religion and the State interest in preserving social solidarity, such as was the case of the Lumpa Sect in East Africa.

Another example is the marriage institution. The laws of divorce, particularly the received aspects, aim solely at the preservation of marriage as a social institution. These try to balance the constant conflicts between the social interests in the security of the institution and the individual interests of unhappy couples. The other aspects of the law, which are more receptive to local conditions, seek not only to balance the interest of the spouses with the interest of society in the security of marriage institution, but also to balance the former interest with the interest of a larger unit—the extended family. Thus, while the law in European countries goes so far as to attach legal disabilities to the children of adulterous unions as a punitive measure to discourage procreation outside wedlock, the law of illegitimacy is a misnomer in most indigenous African laws of marriage. The principle of legitimacy is based on the acknowledgement of a child by either the putative father or the natural father. Once either of the two acknowledges the child as his, the fact that the child is the result of an adulterous union becomes immaterial and the child is accepted as a legitimate child of the acknowledging father, having equal privileges with his children born in wedlock.[26] The position of the unmarried mother is more precarious, and her interest is not taken care of by the law within the institution of marriage. Unless by a subsequent marriage under customary law, or marriage under the Ordinance where appropriate, she becomes a wife to the father of her child, she has no right of inheritance to the man's property on his death.

There is much that we can draw from the postulates of the writers of sociological jurisprudence. The first is that law must have a function, and that that function must be for the interest and security of the society. Secondly, that since society is made of individuals with varied interests, social harmony demands that these interests be not suppressed or submerged, but rather balanced in such a way that social solidarity can be achieved and maintained. Thirdly, since society is always forward-looking, law as an instrument of social change should be progressive. New values ought to be infused into the law for social advancement and progress, but these values, to be effective and not hamper the efficacy of the law, must be expressive of the peoples' general will, and be such as will enhance the achievement of the new aspirations.

We have seen that analytical positivism is inadequate to explain contemporary facts in modern States in Africa, nor can it act as a future guide to legal development. A justification for the exercises of legal power is required. This justification is to be found in society itself, not in the character of the person in power. This is the theme of sociological jurisprudence. As Duguit would have it stated: there is no end which justifies law, except a social end.

Notes to Chapter 6

1. Ihering, Rudolf Von, *Law as a Means to an End* transl. Isaac Husik (Boston: Boston Book Co., 1913). Reprinted in *The Great Legal Philosophers* p. 398, Part I, Chap. VIII, s. 12.

2. Ihering, *ibid.*, Chap. VII, s.3.

3. Ihering, *ibid.*,Chap. VIII, s.2.

4. Duguit, *Manuel,* transl. Allen in *Legal Duties* London: Oxford University Press (1931) at p. 159. p. 10. See further, Laski, "M. Duguit's Conception of the State," in *Modern Theories of Law* (1933), p. 52.

5. See, Duguit, L. *"The Law and the State,"* in 31 Harvard Law Review (1917) pp. 1-185, especially pp. 162-178.

6. See, Dias and Hughes, *Jurisprudence,* 1st ed. (London: Butterworth & Co. (Publishers) Ltd. 1957) p. 416; Allen, C. K., *Law in the Making* 4th ed. (Oxford: Clarendon Press, 1946) p. 489.

7. Ehrlich, Eugene, *Die Grundlegung der Soziologie des Rechts* (1913) (foreward). Translated by Moll, W. L. in *Fundamental Principles of the Sociology of Law* Cambridge, Mass., Harvard University Press (1936).

8. Eastern Nigeria, No. 23 of 1956.

9. Eastern Nigeria, No. 13 of 1956.

10. Lawrence, J. C. D., *The Iteso,* (1957) pp. 202-203.

11. See, Schapera, I., *A Handbook of Tswana Law and Custom* (London: International Institute for African Languages and Culture, 1955) 2nd ed., pp. 145-146.

12. See, Allen, C. K., *Law In the Making* (Oxford: Clarendon Press 1946, 4th ed.) p. 126.

13. Pound, Roscoe, *Jurisprudence* (1959) Vol. 3, p. 152.

14. Pound, Roscoe, *My Philosophy of Law,* (West Publishing Co., 1941). See also, *Jurisprudence,* Vol. 3, p. 324.

15. *Ibid.,* Vol. 2, p. 104.

16. *Ibid.,* p. 107.

17. *Ibid,* pp. 25-32.

18. *Ibid.,* p. 303.

19. *Ibid.,* p. 311.

20. *Ibid.,* p. 316. See also p. 315.

21. *Ibid.,* p. 324.

22. See his *Introduction to American Law* (1919) which was slightly modified in *Outlines of Jurisprudence* (1943).

23. On this, see Dias and Hughes, *op. cit.,* pp. 430-431.

24. (1961) 1 All N. L. R. 269.

25. In Zambia, a religious sect led by one Alice Lenchina, was banned for allegedly spreading dangerous doctrines prejudicial to the security of the State, and the leader was for sometime detained. Similarly, religious sect in Kenya was banned by the Government.

26. See, for example, per Ademola, C. J. N., in *Lawal v. Younan* (1961) 1 *All N.L.R.* 245, p. 250. (1961) WNLR 197; *Jirigho v. Chief Anamali* (1958) W. R. N. L. R. 195. In the latter case, Duffus, J., held legitimation by acknowledgment to be a principle of the customary law of the Kwale tribe in Mid-Western Nigeria. The principle does not apply in marriage contracted under the marriage act, which is therefore a monogamous marriage. A husband cannot, in the circumstances, make a child born out of wedlock legitimate by acknowledgement during the duration of the marriage. Such a child is and remains illegitimate, unless legitimised under the Legitimacy Act. See *Cole v. Akinyele* (1960) 5 F. S. C. 84; as per Brett, F. J., p. 88.

Chapter 7

The Court and the Law

We have thus far considered legal notions which view law from either the metaphysical view, or else, adopting purely an analytical approach, attribute law to the commands of a political superior. Also, we have been concerned with views which maintain that law and the State are mere arrangements of men in society for social ordering and the balancing of competing interests for social harmony. We shall now consider another general intellectual movement which seems to have been much influenced by the characteristic tendencies of the Sociological School and which adopted the line of legal realism rather than formalism in law.

One group of such jurists from America view law as what the courts do. Their approach to law is epitomized in the famous definition of Justice Holmes that "the prophecies of what the court will do in fact, and nothing more pretentious, are what I mean by law."[1] Oliver Wendell Holmes, Jr. (1841–1935), was Chief Justice of the Supreme Court of Massachusetts from 1899–1902. (From 1902 to 1932 he was an Associate Justice of the U.S. Supreme Court.) Until then he had practised law. As a practising lawyer, Holmes knew very well that the concern of his clients was to know what decision the court would give in any case which concerned them.

In addition to any personal experience acquired from legal practice or teaching of this group of the realist movement, the root of their realist approach is attributable to the Common Law system of the Anglo-American order, where the judges have always played a great role in developing the law through the doctrine of binding precedent. However, unlike in Britain where Austinism has been a dominant theme in legal thinking until recently, legal realism has been for more than a generation the dominant legal theme in the United States. In Britain, while Parliament as the supreme authority can always have the last word, statutes in the United States of America are subject to the Constitution. The courts, whose duty it is to interpret the statute function as if coordinate with and not subordinate to the Congress. Since the legislature (Congress) cannot have the last word, in the view of some American jurists, law is only what the court accepts as binding.

The second group is of Continental Europe. It includes Petrazhitsky, Hagastrome, and Olivecrona, with Lundstedt[2] and Ross.[3] These had not been exposed to a system like that of the Anglo-Americans. Unlike their Anglo-American counterparts, their legal notion is not an approximation of legal theory to legal practice as a result of any practical experience. Nevertheless they had one thing in common: both are quite skeptical about traditional notions of law. While the Anglo-American realists adopt a more practical approach, with the courts as their main focus, the realists of Continental Europe take a philosophical line which concerns itself with the psychological character of law. Both groups, however, agree on a central note that law is not primarily composed of normative rules which the States' legal machinery is obliged to enforce.

The Anglo-American Realism

The Anglo-American jurists of the realist movement define law in terms of what the courts do. Salmond defines law as "the body of principles recognised and applied by the State in the administration of justice. In other words, the law consists of the rules recognised and acted on by courts of justice."[4] For him the State has two essential functions; namely, defense against any external enemy through the waging and execution of war, and the administration of justice, i. e., the maintenance of peace and order in the community itself. The latter function, he says, the State assigns to the courts, hence law becomes or consists of the rules recognized and acted on by the courts of justice.

Salmond, however, takes the view that in administering justice the courts do not necessarily have to follow the rules of law which the State sets up to guide them in the duty assigned to them. It may be desirable that the courts should follow the rules, but he says "the administration of justice is perfectly possible without law at all." The duty of the courts is to settle disputes and thus prevent a disorderly settlement of the disputes. Nevertheless, whether or not the court applies the rules in performing its duty of the settlement of disputes, the appropriate State force is evoked to uphold the decision of the court.

To arrive at his conclusion, Salmond was influenced by the discretion left to the judges in the settlement of disputes. Maintaining that a judge's duty to apply the rules is a moral duty arising from his oath of office, he insists that a judge does not necessarily have to apply the law for his decision to be supported by the State force. He goes on to state that the possibility of the removal of a judge for failure to apply the law does not disprove this fact. The removal of a judge for failure to apply the law may, he argues, require some sort of judicial procedure, which in itself demands that some person or body of persons be entrusted with the duty to determine what the law was and whether the judge has broken it in their judgment. Such a body would be tantamount to a court of justice, and there is no guarantee in Salmond's view that it would, in exercising this function, also apply the law.

Furthermore, Salmond argues, that where a court of first or second instance has its decision or judgment reversed on appeal, there is no guarantee that the highest court of appeal did, in doing so, apply the law. Since there is no other body or person that can correct the decision, the judgment of the highest court of appeal remains the law. Thus, law cannot be defined correctly without reference to the courts.

Obviously, Salmond's thesis seems to have grossly minimized the effect of political forces and political considerations on a judge's exercise of discretion not to apply the rules, or even to apply the law strictly. In countries with long-established constitutional and legal tradition, a stage of such political stability has been reached (as under the Anglo-American system) that even in the absence of a written constitution which guarantees security of tenure to the judge, his position is quite firmly secured by convention. In a country with such an established system Salmond's thesis has much to be said in its favor, but not in a country with political instability. In the new States of Africa, particularly English-speaking Africa, the effect of political instability on the judges and court decisions, (notwithstanding the fact of a written constitution which guarantees security of tenure to judges) is such that it will not be quite realistic to define law correctly with reference to the court only.

In Ghana, for instance, Sir Arku Korsah was removed in 1963 from the post of Chief Justice of that country as a result of the decision his (special) court gave in the treason trial involving Messrs. Adamafio, Adjei, and Cofie-Crabbe. Subsequent to the decision of Sir Korsah's special court, an Act was passed empowering the President to retrospectively annul any decision of any special court not acceptable to the government. This power was used immediately against Sir Arku Korsah. Following up this further, there was a constitutional amendment (then proposed) to empower the President to remove at will from office any judge of the Supreme Court or the High Court. In Nigeria we have an example of similar interference by the legislature with the decision of the Court. In *Adegbenro v. Akintola,*[5] the decision of the Judicial Committee of the Privy Council was found unacceptable by the politicians then in power and steps were taken by the legislature to pass a law with retroactive effect, which enabled the government to bypass both the legal and the obvious political effects of the Board's decision.[6] There are other examples[7] which highlight the struggle between the Courts and the government of the day as to who has the final say in judicial decisions.

Another interesting aspect of Salmond's thesis which concerns us derives from his inclination to the imperative theory. Like Austin, the State to him is a necessary prerequisite to the existence of law. Consequently, he rejects the historical school's idea as to the nature and basis of law. To him, normative rules prior to and independent of the State may resemble law, but these may be the primeval substitute for law, or the historical source from which law proceeds and is developed, and are never themselves law. The analogy which he drew between these prestate rules and law was summed up in the following words:

> There may have been a time in the far past when a man was not distinguishable from the anthropoid ape, but that is no reason for now defining a man in such manner as to include an ape.[8]

The obvious implication of Salmond's view on pre-State rules is to deny rules of customary law the name law. They may qualify as law only after they have been processed and acted upon by the courts. In fact Salmond sneers at the historical argument of eminent writers like Bryce, Pollock, and Maine. These state that law can exist before any state, and that the imperative theory is plausible and is at first sight sufficient only as applied to developed political societies of modern times, and not to less advanced societies. Primitive societies may have no adequate means of compelling legal observance or some regular process of legal enforcement, but they do have laws, even with a good deal of formality.[9]

The American realists have taken an extreme view of the wide discretion of the courts to interpret the law to deny any rule not sanctioned by the courts the definition of law. Gray, like Salmond, was much impressed by the uncontrolled power of the Courts (especially the Supreme Court of Appeal) to interpret statutes. He therefore maintains, in the words of Bishop Hoadly, that "whoever hath an absolute authority to interpret any written or spoken law, it is he who is truly the law-giver to all intents and purposes, and not the person who first wrote or spoke them."[10] He concludes *a fortiori* that "whoever hath an absolute authority not only to interpret the law but to say what the law is, is truly the law-giver."[11]

Implied in Gray, therefore, is not only a rule of customary law, but the idea that a statute is no law until it has been pronounced on by the Court and approved as a basis for decision. Yet he sees and admits a seeming absurdity inherent in his view, to the effect that the law of a great nation would mean "the opinion of half-a-dozen old gentlemen, some of them conceivably, of very limited intelligence." Nevertheless he maintains that "if those half-a-dozen old gentlemen form the highest judicial tribunal of a country then no rule or principle which they refuse to follow is law in that country."[12] In his view, therefore, "the law of the State or of any organised body of men is composed of the rules which the courts, that is, the judicial organs of that body, lay down for the determination of legal rights and duties."[13]

We agree that where a judge of the highest tribunal who has unfettered discretion to interpret the law does so inductively, he is more of a law-giver. However, inasmuch as he can be removed for political reasons for misinterpreting, or even for correctly applying the law, his power to make law is not absolute. To define law, therefore, only in terms of what the courts do, is to underrate the effects of political and social pressure on the judge in the exercise of his duty to administer the law.

Judge-made law is an existing reality. Its scope is confined to an area where other sources of law, like the statute or rules of customary law, do not provide a clear and unambiguous answer to the issue at hand. It is here that the judge must look elsewhere, using his hunches, if need be, to provide an answer. We have also seen, above, that precedent as a source of law, a legal armory of judge-made law which is strongly guarded by the doctrine of binding precedent, is not an ultimate and sole source of law. It may be disregarded where necessary in a subsequent decision, when distinguished or overruled. What is more, even though precedents are based on basic "juridical conception which are the postulates of judicial reasoning," they ultimately rest on "the habits of life, the institutions of society in which those conceptions had their origin."[14] Thus we come back to society, and cannot define law adequately without proper reference to it.

Like Gray, other best-known and recent writers of the American realist movement have an ardent belief in the uncertainty of the law which has greatly influenced their legal thinking. These would include Jerome Frank, and Llewellyn, K.

For Frank, Law is "actual specific past decisions, and guesses as to actual specific decisions."[15] It follows, therefore, that only precedent and good forecasts based on them as to future specific *decisions*[16] are law. He maintains that, because circumstances of life are constantly changing, it is both impossible and undesirable to have any law other than decisions. Commending legal fluidity, he says, "much of the uncertainty of law is not an unfortunate accident. It is of immense social value."[17] Those desiring certainty in the law, he thinks, are suffering from an Oedipus complex. They have still surviving in them the child's craving for security which makes him ascribe to his father omnipotent and omniscient powers.

Llewellyn, in his *The Bramble Bush,* expanded the realist view almost to the point of absurdity. In his definition, law is what officials of the law do about disputes. "This doing of something about disputes, this doing of it reasonably, is the business of law. And the people who have the doing in charge, whether they be judges or sheriffs or clerks or jailers or lawyers, are officials of the law. *What these officials do about disputes is to my mind the law itself.*"[18]

The skepticism of the American realists as to legal fixity leads them to a rejection of legal rules as providing legal uniformity, and points to the uncertainty of establishing facts themselves. They hold that a judge does not apply mere logic to arrive at a decision, but that his personal psychology comes into play. His prejudices against a litigant, or against his counsel, his conception of ethics and values therein, are necessary factors in his decision. Thus, a judge may first take a decision or a stand in a given case, only to find reason for it afterward.

The legal anarchy which the realists introduced into the study of jurisprudence cannot be better summarized than in Cardozo's words, for if we accept the realists' view, "Law never is, but is always about to be. It is realized only when embodied in a judgment, and in being realized expires. There are no such things as rules or principles: there are only isolated dooms."[19] Because of the role of law as an instrument of social change, legal fluidity is a necessity. Fixity in law may be undescribable due to constantly changing circumstances of life in society, but this should not lead to denial of the existence of a body of legal rules. Aside from a situation where social change results in anarchy, that is, a state of lawlessness, all other social changes are desired and organized either by a group of persons or the people as a whole. To bring about orderly change, and to sustain it, guiding rules and principles are necessary, and law serves the purpose as a superstructure to the desired goal, with principles and rules at its base.

The Continental Realism

The continental realists—Petrazhitsky (1867–1931), and a group of Scandinavian realists led by Hagerstrom (1868–1939), and Olivecrona have a common platform with the American realists in that both groups believe that law is not primarily made up of rules or norms and principles that are enforceable by the State. Unlike their Anglo-American colleagues, however, the realists of Continental Europe are no victims of practical experience at the bar. They do not confine the definition of law within the scope of what the courts do, but take philosophical and psychological approaches.

Petrazhitsky views law as the consciousness of rights and duties which exist in the minds of men. Law, he says, "is essentially a psychological reality, a part of our mental process," and "the chief end of law is to educate men in the spirit of active love for their neighbours."[20] He categorizes law into two main divisions, namely, *positive law,* and *intuitive law.* Positive law covers cases of judgements determining the ideal pattern of behavior and made with reference to established normative facts, such as statutes and judicial decisions. Intuitive law, on the other hand, covers judgments formed without reference to the normative facts.

Further, he classifies positive and intuitive laws under two heads; namely, *official,* and *unofficial* law. Thus, law may be either:

1. (a) Positive and official law
   (b) Positive and unofficial law; or
2. (a) Intuitive and official law
   (b) Intuitive and unofficial law.

Positive-official law, according to Petrazhitsky, is the law which corresponds to the usual "lawyer's meaning" of law. For example, when a court renders a decision and refers to article "X" of the civil code, or to a precedent, this is positive law because of the reference to the normative fact and, simultaneously, official law because of the character of the agency enforcing the law. Law, on the other hand, becomes *positive-unofficial* law when, for instance, a *freely-chosen arbitrator* solves, say, an industrial conflict by reference to a well-established practice. At this juncture the law remains positive because of the reference to a normative fact but, at the same time, unofficial law because of the character of the agency. Law is intuitive-unofficial law when, for example, in a frontier dispute men take the law into their hands and hang a "bad man" because "he deserves it." This is intuitive law because of the lack of reference to a normative fact, and unofficial because of the absence of an official agency.[21]

With Petrazhitsky's analysis, therefore, we see that the decision of the court and that of any officially-appointed tribunal or arbitrator is either positive law or intuitive law, depending on whether or not the judgment is reached with reference to an existing legal rule or principle, or otherwise. On the other hand, any decision of a non-official agency is positive or intuitive law, also depending on the same principle; but while the former is official law, the latter is unofficial. This law is not limited to what court officials do, or to what any other duly-established law enforcement agency does, but includes what even the bandit does, so long as he is in a position to take a decision and carry it out.

Hagerstrom (1868–1939), as founder of the Swedish realist movement, postulates that all legal notions and concepts are purely psychological and subjective mental factors. There are no objective values, and the notion of right duty relations and legal obligations are quite subjective. "Goodness" and "badness" exist subjectively in the minds of men. They represent expressions of subjective emotional or psychological feeling.

For Hagerstrom, both the value that is, or the value that ought to be, have no objective reality. The notion of justice and legal reality are matters of opinion or personal evaluation and cannot be proved or processed scientifically. He applied his technique to classical Roman Law and saw the concepts as purely psychological realities based on metaphysical beliefs. If we extend his technique to indigenous laws in Africa, we see that rules of customary law will stand at par with statute law or precedent. All will come within a legal definition that gives precedence to none.

Another effect of Hagerstrom's thesis is that implicitly it seems to supply the answer to the perennial questions of the binding force of law. The compelling factors for obedience to law would, by implication in his thesis, be rooted in the individual himself, his beliefs, and his accepted values. We need not therefore ask further why X obeys a particular law which Y has pleasure in disobeying. Or why a primitive society with no centralized machinery for law enforcement, like the Nuers of Southern Sudan, are nevertheless able to maintain an orderly and law-abiding society. It would also seem to explain why, in modern societies with formidable legal sanctions, the question of legal efficacy is still a recurrent problem.

Olivecrona, following Hagerstrom's thesis, has gone further into the psychological element in law. He begins his legal postulates with a detailed analysis and examination of the burning issue of the *binding force of law*. He shows no particular interest in the definition of law. Rather, he believes that by description and analysis of the facts of law its true nature will be seen.[22]

He starts his quest for the source of the binding force of law with a review and a reappraisal of the schools of jurisprudence, from the natural law theory to analytical positivism. He finally comes to the conclusion that the binding force of law does not exist, that it is a mere mirage.

Olivecrona sees the binding force of law not definitely the same as the fact that unpleasant consequences will follow consequent to a breach; that naturally it is in our own interest to avoid doing an act which will result into unpleasant consequences, but we are not in any way obligated to avoid any such act. The avoidance is simply in our own interest. With law, on the other hand, the obligation is thought to be mandatory, regardless of our own interest. The "binding force" cannot be equated to sanction, for legal sanction is inflicted because a binding rule has been broken, i. e., it is inflicted when the binding force has failed to compel obedience to law.

Furthermore, he does not see the "binding force" of law in the natural law idea, which is sustained by mere metaphysical belief. Nor does it lie in the feeling of being bound, or in personal inhibitions, for law is thought to be binding on all and sundry, whether or not they possess such feelings. For him the answer is to be found neither in Kelsen's *Grundnorm* nor in his "world of ought." Law is not the will of the State and cannot be binding because it is such. "The will of the State" is pure imagination.[23] Only human beings have a will, and each has a will of his own. It is therefore unrealistic and impossible to define law as an expression of a common will of individual persons. Olivecrona states that even members of Parliament, who unlike other members of the public are in a position to legislate, do not and cannot will the law. Olivecrona therefore concludes that law is a system of rules about force. Law as applied in a community is an organized force used according to definite terms. What happens is that the law-giver through the basic law, the Constitution, acquires a psychological mechanism which gives him the monopoly over legislation and commands obedience to laws promulgated by him.[24]

We agree with Olivecrona that a kind of psychological mechanism is necessary to command obedience to law and may, in fact, be the *sine qua non* for legal obedience. His postulate, however, that the psychological mechanism is acquired through the Constitution, is another way of reverting to the Kelsenian postulate of the Grundnorm which he rejects. Furthermore, his assertion that only the law-giver acquires the mechanism to the utter exclusion of everybody else who is debarred from using it or building up another of its kind, underrates the effects of social needs on legal efficacy.

For the Constitution to be the source of the psychological mechanism which commands obedience to law, it must by itself command obedience to itself. Where then lies the source of its efficacy as the basic law? "Political power," said Mao Tse Tung, "springs from the barrel of the gun." Law, including the Constitution, is only one of the civil instruments for sustaining that power. If we go this far it becomes obvious that the psychological mechanism owes its origin to extra-legal factors. Both the law and the Constitution may, in the Austinian sense, be commanded by the political superior. This possibility is not in doubt. What the political superior cannot command or guarantee is legal efficacy. It is at this juncture that we part company with analytical positivism, for the fear of sanction is not enough to command obedience to law.

A psychological mechanism is essential for legal obedience. We do not see the source of this psychological factor in a Constitution, written or otherwise. It emanates from the peoples' needs, beliefs, and aspirations in relation to the law-giver and the law that he gives. Olivecrona sees organized force as still necessary, in spite of the attitude of mind in the general public which is the product of the acquired psychological mechanism of the law-giver. Thus, he agrees that force steps into law to command obedience at the point that the psychological mechanism of the law-giver fails. In other words, if a law is popular it is obeyed mechanically by the people. Their minds are shut off to other directions, and nobody else can secure attention or obedience in the field where the law-giver promulgates a popular law. But if the law is unpopular, one of two things will happen, viz., either the people disobey the law, or they are compelled to obey it for fear of sanctions. With this last possibility we come back to the Austinian theory of Sanction as the binding force of law, which Olivecrona also rejects.

In trying to disprove traditional legal philosophy as having provided the answer to the binding force of law, Olivecrona gives an example of a successful revolution which in its origin is illegal. The Revolutionaries, having succeeded, may take over the existing machinery with its psychological mechanism already associated with it, to make laws which the people accept as binding. Or they may strike a new path, creating new machinery with a new psychological mechanism. In both cases force and propaganda, he says, are necessary to maintain the new order, and in the case of the latter to crystallize the newly-acquired psychological mechanism, for obedience to the laws of the new regime.[25] This is a tacit admission of the fact that the psychological mechanism does not inhere from the Constitution.

One sees two kinds of force in a state relevant to legal obedience. First is the orthodox state force, which is equal to the organized force to which Olivecrona refers, and, second, a counter force, i. e., the force mustered by the people in rebellion against a system when it becomes retrograde and therefore unpopular. Both forces have identical aims, for while the state force is trying to restore the enchantment of the discredited psychological mechanism, the counter force aims at building up a new psychological mechanism which will command obedience to new laws for the new ideology of those in revolt. Whichever force succeeds depends on which of the opposites presents a program that is more acceptable to the people as in line with their economic needs, social aspirations, and political ideology, and not necessarily on the established Constitution.

The Constitution may be retained, suspended, or replaced by a new one, depending on which of the forces wins, and the force and power of the Constitution will depend on how far it goes on behalf of the needs and social ends of the people, and to what extent it remains a good instrument for achieving those needs and social ends. Once we believe that a new psychological mechanism can be achieved by ousting a regime which previously has acquired a psychological mechanism "through the Constitution," and that those ousting the regime can rule successfully by suspending, altering, or entirely rejecting the established Constitution, then we concede the fact that the psychological mechanism for legal obedience has its source, not necessarily in any immemorial tradition; it is a variable, varying with time and a people's outlook on life at any given period. It is something that normally emanates from the people's feelings of satisfaction with a regime, taking into consideration the problems of their time and the conditions of their existence. When a people possess such a feeling, they accept the law as of their own making, and the government as the people's government. In other words, the psycholgical mechanism emanates more from a people's general will than from a Constitution, whether written or unwritten.

There could be cases, however, when a regime may acquire a monopoly of the psychological mechanism of law enforcement, not because it is a popular regime, but because of the "tendency of most people to submit to actual power and even to the normative tendency of the factual."[26] The reasons for the submission to or acceptance of the authority of the law-giver in such a case may be several. They may include one or a combination of the following factors: indolence, apathy, and fear. Thus, in Ian Smith's Southern Rhodesia we observe that public knowledge that breach of the illegal regime's laws, or any violent attempt to overthrow, it will be punished, has reduced incentive to openly disobey the laws of the regime. What is more, as Claire Palley aptly observed, the judges in Rhodesia have, by refusing to see themselves as a focus for resistance, helped the regime acquire a seeming monopoly of the psychological mechanism of law enforcement.[27] A psychological mechanism so acquired is merely transitory. It is inferior to the psychological mechanism which emanates from the general will, and which is the bedrock of law and order in a truly democratic society.

Contemporary events in Africa, which show military rule in that Continent as something now both fashionable and endemic, present a factual analysis of Olivecrona's thesis. For example, events in Nigeria since the Revolution in January 1966 apparently show the military rulers as striking a new path, creating new machinery with a new psychological mechanism. It cannot be rightly maintained that the people's obedience to laws of the military regime derives from any respect for the Constitution. The Constitution was suspended, and the Parliament and Council of Ministers gave way to the Supreme Military Council and the Federal Executive Council. Legislation by Parliament and Houses of Assembly was replaced by promulgation by Decrees and Edicts. At least for the initial stage of the revolution, force and propaganda were apparently used to turn the people's minds in favor of the new regime. Some force was used to suppress the old regime, and political parties were banned to prevent the coming back of the old rulers.

To wipe out the existing psychological enchantment of the old regime, the excesses of the past were highlighted, propaganda was mounted to discredit the old regime, and a commission of inquiry was set up to probe the assets and activities of those holding responsible posts in the ousted government. On the other hand, to help the creation of a new psychological mechanism in favor of the new regime, a more just and egalitarian society was promised to the people.

The Supreme Court has since, in the *Lakanmi* case, ruled that there was no revolution in January 1966 but a mere handing over of power by the Council of Ministers of the old regime to the Army. Implicit in this decision is the reasoning that it is the old psychological mechanism which was acquired through the Constitution that still commands obedience to laws in Nigeria today. Both the civilians and the Armed forces, therefore, will be subject to the Constitution. A similar issue emerged in Ghana in the case of *E. K. Sallah v Att. Gen.*[28] The case centered on whether or not, as a result of the *coup d'etat* of February 24, 1966, the National Liberation Council which formed the military government of Ghana reestablished or created anew all the laws of Ghana. The Supreme Court of Ghana took a view similar to that taken in the *Lakanmi* case. In the views of Apaloo and Sowah JJ.A., there is continuity of the legal system, and *coups d'etat* do not affect this continuity. To permit an existing law to continue after a coup d'etat was to acknowledge its previous existence, not to create it anew. The obvious conclusion would again be that in Ghana the preexisting laws functioned after the coup d'etat on the old psychological mechanism.

However, in view of the Nigerian Decree No. 28 of 1970,[29] in which the Federal Military Council restated that it has a right to an unfettered and unlimited legislative competence above the Constitution, the above assumption can no longer be sustained in Nigeria. The military rulers seem to have succeeded in demolishing the charm of the psychological mechanism of the old regime and the reverence for the Constitution, replacing these with a new psychological mechanism of their own which commends obedience to the Decrees and Edicts, as well as the unabrogated preexisting laws.

Before the above stage was reached in Nigeria, there was a tripartite struggle in the country for control of the psychological mechanism which commands obedience to laws in the country. First, there was the contest between the civilian regime or what was left of it after January 1966, and the Army. Secondly, within the Army itself there was the contest between the Biafran revolutionists and the Federal Forces. The civilian government, the Federal Forces, and the Biafran revolutionists were all vying for control of the legal order and the psychological mechanism of law enforcement. Until Decree No. 28 of 1970, it was not clear that the Federal Military Government did not rely on the old psychological mechanism for its successes and obedience to the laws. As between the Federal Forces and the Biafran revolutionists, however, it was certain during the three years of the civil war that each maintained obedience to its laws as a result of the respective psychological mechanisms that each built around men in its area of control. The Federal Military Government was unable to successfully extend its laws to areas occupied by the Biafrans until the defeat of Biafra in 1970. Thus, for the whole country during the three years of the civil war the *binding force* of law in Nigeria remained quite nebulous and unpredictable, until the end of the war.

Ghana, after the overthrow of Dr. Nkrumah and the suspension of the 1960 Republican Constitution of that country, under which Dr. Nkrumah ruled, by a combined body of the Army and the Police known as the National Liberation Council, is another apt example. The psychological mechanism of the Nkrumah regime (the Sallah case notwithstanding) was destroyed by the National Liberation Council through force and propaganda. Subsequent events in Ghana after the first military rule, where Busia's civilian Government was ousted and Nkrumah's image seemed to be gaining ground before his death in 1972, go a long way toward proving again that psychological mechanism is a variable and emanates from a people's general will and aspirations, rather than from an established Constitution or force. Being apprehensive that the psychological mechanism of the new regime was waning, the Busia Government resorted to laws calculated to legislate Nkrumah and Nkrumaism out of the constitutional and the political history of Ghana.[30] The fall of the government came about mainly as a result of its failure, through its economic and political programs, to satisfy the general will, and the economic and political aspirations of the Ghanaian people, as compared with what they enjoyed under the Nkrumah regime.

The succeeding military government originally headed by Colonel Ignatious Acheampong may have acquired for itself an adequate new psychological mechanism to rule Ghana. It is, however, doubtful from developments now in Ghana whether or not the regime will successfully retain this psychological mechanism to remain in power for long.

A more recent topical example is Uganda, under General Idi Amin. The former President, Milton Obote, was ousted in January 1971 by a military coup. Events in that country present an example of yet another transitional stage where the new psychological mechanism grapples with the old. It is not the Constitution, but the impact that both the two contending leaders through their political and economic programs have on the people of Uganda that will be the deciding factor.

To conclude, we may state that a legal order must not be confused with the source of its validity. A successful revolution does not necessarily bring about the end of a preexisting legal order, but it does certainly shift or alter the basis of its validity. As Kelsen has postulated:

> From a juristic point of view, the decisive criterion of a revolution is that the order in force is overthrown and replaced by a new order in a way which the former had not itself anticipated. Usually, the new men whom a revolution brings to power annul only the Constitution and certain laws of paramount political significance, putting other norms in their place. A great part of the old legal order "remains" valid also within the frame of the new order. But the phrase "they remain valid" does not give an adequate description of the phenomenon. It is only the contents of these norms that remain the same, not the reason of their validity. They are no longer valid by virtue of having been created in the way the old Constitution prescribed. That Constitution is no longer in force; it is replaced by a new Constitution which is not the result of a constitutional alteration of the former. If laws which were introduced under the old Constitution "continue to be valid" under the new Constitution, this is possible only because validity has expressly or "tacitly" been vested in them by the new Constitution.[31]

The new Constitution, which here includes an old Constitution that is retained by the revolutionary regime, derives its binding force from the new psychological mechanism of the revolutionists.[32]

Notes to Chapter 7

1. Holmes, *Collected Papers* New York (1920), p. 173.
2. See, Lundstedt, A. V., *Legal Thinking Revised* (1956).
3. See, Ross, A., *Law and Justice* (1958).
4. Salmond, *Jurisprudence,* 11th ed. by Glanville Williams, (London: Sweet & Maxwell, 1957) p. 41.
5. (1963) 3 All E. R. 544. See also *Akintola v. Adegbenro,* F. S. C. 187/1962 where it seemed the Federal Supreme Court based its decision on a canon of interpretation which was more acceptable to the then-government.
6. The Constitution of Western Nigeria (Amendment) Law 1963 was passed as a result of the Privy Council's adverse decision. It was given a retroactive effect, making it impossible for the Regional Governor to remove a Premier from office except in consequence of events in the legislative House, such as a vote of no confidence passed by the House. This was in line with the canon of interpretation adopted by the Federal Supreme Court, which decided the case in the first instance in favor of the government.

Subsequently, the Republican Constitution put the matter to rest by abolishing the power completely.

7. See, The Federal Military Government (Supremacy and Enforcement of Powers) Decree No. 28 of 1970 Nigeria, which had an overriding effect on the Supreme Court's decision in the case of *E. O. Lakanmi and Kikelomo Ola v. The Attorney-General (West) and The Secretary, and the Counsel, to the Tribunal S. C.* 58/69.

8. Salmond, *op. cit.* p. 55.

9. See Bryce, Lord James *Studies in History and Jurisprudence* (London: Oxford University Press 1901), Vol. 11, 44 249; Pollock, Sir F., *First Book of Jurisprudence* (London: Macmillan, 1929) 6th ed., p. 24; Maine, *Early History of Institutions,* Lectures 12 and 13 (London: John Murray 3rd Ed. (1880) pp. 364 and 380 respectively.

10. Gray, John Chipman, *The Nature and Sources of Law* (New York: Columbia University Press, 1948), p. 102.

11. *Loc. cit.*

12. *Ibid.,* p. 82.

13. *Ibid.,* For comments and criticisms on Gray's views see Goodhart, *Modern Theories of Law* (1933) p. 5, also, Cross, *Precedent in English Law,* (1961) pp. 154–155.

14. Cardozo, Benjamin Nathan, *The Nature of The Judicial Process* (New Haven and London: Yale University Press 1922). See introduction.

15. Frank, Jerome, *Law And The Modern Mind* (New York: Coward-McCann. London: Stevens 1930), p. 47.

16. Frank originally classifies law into two groups: (a) *actual law,* i. e., law in a given situation where there is a specific past decision on the point at issue, and (b) *probable law,* i. e., a guess as to a specific future decision.

17. *Ibid.,* p. 7.

18. Llewellyn, Karl, *The Bramble Bush* (New York: Oceana Publications, 1960) p. 9.

19. Cardozo, *op. cit.,* p. 126.

20. Petrazhitsky, *Law and Morality* (transl. by Babb, in *20th Century Legal Philosophy Series, vii).*

21. *Ibid.*

22. See, Olivecrona, K. *Law As Fact,* p. 25 et seq.

23. *Ibid.,* p. 24.

24. *Ibid.,* pp. 54, 60.

25. *Ibid.,* pp. 66–69.

26. See Stone, *Human Law And Human Justice,* 1964 London: Stevens & Sons Ltd. p. 255.

27. See Falley, Claire, "The Judicial Process: U.D.I. And the Southern Rhodesian Judiciary" *Modern Law Review* (1967) Vol. 30 No. 3, pp. 263, 287.

28. Const. S. C. 8/70, April 20, 1970. In this case the Court of Appeal sat as the Supreme Court by virtue of s.8 of the Transitional Provisions of the 1969 Constitution. The relevant section of the Constitution considered was s.9(1).

29. Titled "Federal Military Government (Supremacy And Enforcement of Powers) Decree No. 28 of 1970." The Decree was promulgated as a sequel to the decision of the Supreme Court in the *Lakanmi* case which challenged the supremacy of the Federal Military Government's power to legislate above the Constitution.

30. A bill was passed through Parliament making it a criminal offense for any person or organisation to display the photographs of the ex-President, or to try to resuscitate the C.P.P., which was the governing party under ex-President Nkrumah's Government. The Bill was rushed through Parliament because some 2,000 copies of the ex-President's photographs were sold during a political rally of the People's Progressive Party, Kumasi, a stronghold of Dr. Busia's party, which was then in Government.

31. Kelsen, Hans, *General Theory of Law And State* (1961), p. 117.
32. *Cf.,* The Ghanaian Court of Appeal's decision in *E. K. Sallah v The Attorney-General,* Const. S. C. 8/70. Judgment given on 20/4/70. The Court was of the opinion that to allow preexisting laws to continue after a military revolution was not to create them anew.

Chapter 8

Economic Facts and the Law

Underlying the whole conception of law in society at any given time is the desire for peace, stability, and orderliness. It is a desire to pull man out of his natural self as a selfish animal and to integrate him in society where his wants and desires are to be identified and satisfied in consonance with the wants and desire of others who are sharing the same environment with him. If man were to live with no interests at all, or with interests which in no way conflict or could conflict with those of his neighbors in society, there would be no need for law. Law becomes necessary where man's interests conflict with those of others. In other words, the notion of law starts with conflicting interests in society.

What are these interests? They are many, but each may be broadly classified as a religious or economic interest. We are concerned here with economic interests, or all interests that are rooted in economic facts. Law, as an instrument for balancing those interests, is a superstructure on the economic facts.

All past history of mankind has been consistent with struggles. In its primitive stages, the struggle is between individuals, but as mankind advances and states emerge the struggle, though retaining some of its individualistic facets, assumes the character of group or class struggle. The social antagonisms are the product of economic conditions. The wars of the classes, which are of a later development in man's history, are always, as Engels put it, "the products of modes of production and exchange—in a word, of the *economic* conditions of their time; the economic structure of society always furnishes the real basis, starting from which we can alone work out the ultimate explanation of the whole superstructure of juridical and political institutions as well as of religious, philosophical and other ideas of a given historical period."[1]

The argument of those who favor the economic approach is that economic facts exist before the law and are independent of it. Law is only a superstructure of an economic system.[2] A closer examination and analysis of most of the various schools of thought we have earlier considered would support this view. Such analysis would reveal, in one form or the other, the fact that it is man's materialistic tendency, a product of his selfish motive for self-preservation that complicates society and makes law inevitable. This reasoning is quite a plausible deduction from the writings of the legal philosophers of the sociological school. It is consonant with the cornerstone upon which the social contract theory was built. Bentham's principle of utility is in agreement with it, and even natural law theorists cannot effectively disassociate themselves from it. What makes their approach different is that in their theory of justice they apply universal ethical principles and metaphysical notions to balance secular conflicts, which ultimately are economic facts in society.

Karl Marx (1818–1883), and his friend Frederick Engels (1820–1895), are the most outstanding socialist writers to contribute to legal theory through the examination of economic facts in society. They concern themselves mainly with the evolution of law, then, the social function of law, and not necessarily the nature of law. Unlike the positivists, however, they are not indifferent to the just or unjust nature of law. They championed the cause of the workers—the majority—against the injustices of the employers—the minority. Their view is that, inasmuch as the physical world is governed by a universal principle of causation, social phenomena are likewise governed by a universal principle; namely, the economic principle.

Marx and Engels were influenced by the methodology of Hegel, who deviated from 18th Century rationalist individualism to propound a new kind of philosophy. Hegel embodied the principle governing the course of human history in a mystical world-spirit, setting up the ideal as an abstract toward which reality must lend. He devised a new logical dialectic by which two contradictory propositions do not eliminate each other, but rather produce a third and higher element in the form of a synthesis. Thus, thesis and *antithesis* together find a solution in the form of synthesis. Marx accepted Hegel's dialectic approach, but set it as he put it; 'right side up,' on a material base. He reflected Hegel's idea that spirit rather than matter represents the true reality and governs the universe. For Marx, ideas could only be reflections of reality, not the other way round. Thus, spurning the Hegelian spiritual principle as governing the world and history, Marx developed his own dialectics, based on materialism: nothing exists in actuality but the material world, and the dialectic method, as applied to human affairs, had to be interpreted in material terms.

He saw class conflicts as the inevitable product of private property interests. The institution of individual ownership of property and the consequent conflict of interests gave rise to the State which the (few) property owners use as an instrument to protect their interest against the less privileged class, i. e., the non-owners. Law becomes one of the state tools in the hands of the property owners to dominate the non-property owners in furtherance of the former's property interests.

For Marx and Engels law is therefore the first result of thesis *cum* antithesis, that is, the first result of social conflict between capital and labor. They see no antithesis in primitive society, due to the existence of equal distribution of commodities under conditions of scarcity. In their view, it is subsequent inequalities in appropriation and distribution of commodities that give rise to class struggle between capital and labor. The result of the struggle is the emergence of the State, which now displaces tribal and local social structure and becomes the instrument of the stronger against the weaker class.

In the capitalist state the stronger class is the minority, controllers of capital and all the chief economic resources of the State. When the majority, the working class, succeed in overpowering the minority and gaining control of the economic resources, they will seek to eliminate the minority through the medium of a proletarian dictatorship. Nevertheless, even at this stage, the class struggle continues.

> After the proleteriat has grasped power, the class struggle does not cease. It continues in new forms, and with ever greater frenzy and ferocity, for the reason that the resistance of the exploiters to the fact of socialism is more savage than before.[3]

The government of the proletariat represents "the highest form of democracy possible in a class society."[4] Notwithstanding this, law remains an instrument of domination, now in the hands of the proletariat, who use it to eliminate the power of the capitalist minority. Though a dictatorship, the government of the proleteriat is a democracy in that the distribution of commodities at this stage follows the maxim: "from each according to his ability to each according to his work."

The ultimate result of the class struggle which follows the dictatorship of the proletariat is a synthesis, which is seen as communism, or classless society. This would be a perfected democracy where the distribution of commodities would be governed by the principle epitomized by the maxim: "from each according to his ability, to each according to his need." At this stage domination and inequalities will cease and both the State and law will "wither away" to be replaced by "an administration of things."[5]

Paschukanis (1891–1937), another writer adopting the economic approach rejected the view that production, i. e., capital and labor, form the legal basis of society. Rather, he saw law as a reflection of economic conditions consisting of the *exchange of commodities*, and not *produc-*

tion.[6] Law, in his view, is an instrument for the peaceful settlement of conflicting interests of persons. All law is built upon individual relationship and presupposes theoretical equality, not subjection. Like his colleagues, however, he advocated that in the ultimate perfect society there would be unity of purpose. Law would then be superfluous and no longer necessary.

Critics of the economic approach accuse Marx of divesting law of its moral and spiritual values and making it a mere economic adjunct. Also, they focus their attention on legal practice in the Socialist world, particularly the Soviet Union. They see the withering away of the State and the law and the advocated replacement by an administration of things as a source of conflicts and contradictions. They look at the practice in the Soviet Union and see, not a withering away, not even a decline of the law, but rather a tightening up of the legal rules and principles, and a fortification of the legal machinery very much in favor of the State.[7]

Our interest in the economic approach to law does not however rest on the successes or failures of those who have tried it or are still trying it, as, for example, the Soviet Union, China, or the rest of the Socialist world. The failure of a theory may depend on two fundamental factors. A theory may be based on a wrong premise, in which case it is *ab initio* incapable of attainment. On the other hand, a theory may be sound in principle, but men make errors in its practical application and interpretation. In this instance the fault is not with the theory itself but with its interpreters. Our interest is in the rationale of law. Without the economic principle we find it hard if not impossible to justify man's illogical existence in this meaningless world. The whole idea of justice is based on what is fair and equitable to man and his existence here on earth. Outside the sphere of religion, economics is the matrix of man's existence on earth, and any moral and humanistic evaluation of law must deal with it. Thus far we agree with the notion that economics is the base and that law is its superstructure. The economic approach presents a more realistic base for the evaluation of law.

On the question of the synthesis, the emergence of communism, and the withering away of the State and the law, we can only see a possible vicious circle with the economic approach. On the assumption that communism is possible of attainment[8] and that Marx's and Engel's theory of the evolution of law is correct, communism will usher in a period in legal development which will be analogous to that of a primitive society. This last being the starting point, then a vicious circle must have been completed. Unless, in accordance with the speculations of Marxism, by that time—by virtue of an abundance of social wealth and a very high level of social consciousness—man has had a complete change in his nature from selfish animal with self-preservation as a first and guiding principle, the conflicts between man and man or classes will start all over again, and consequently the law and the State will reappear. The process will continue; but this by no means belies the veracity of the economic principle.

In the new African States there is a class conflict which is rather three-dimensional. There, is on the one hand, a conflict of interest between those in the subsistent sector of the economy, i. e., the peasants, and those in the colonial enclave (now the African elite) whose position is analogous comparatively to that of the controllers of capital and economic resources in a capitalist society. From the latter, we have the ruling class. On the other hand, there is a conflict between the working class who, strictly speaking, cannot be classified as belonging to the subsistent sector of the economy, and the elite. Lastly, the interest of the workers who have become urban dwellers are not always in harmony with the interests of the peasants.

Before the arrival of the imperial masters at the second half of the 19th Century, the economic structure was subsistence economy. The respective trades and skill of individuals were geared to producing for themselves and their families their daily needs. There was no wage labor, and where it became necessary for a family to seek labor assistance outside the family circle, the general principle was that of mutual assistance. No class antagonism resulting from economic facts existed. The social structure of the economy was one that responded favorably to the indigenous legal norms. Customary law provided answers without exception to problems arising in that society of subsistence economy and the then-existing social values. As the colonial masters began their extensive exploitation and imposed new political rule, a second economic enclave of relatively modern technology was imposed upon the society. State force had to be monopolized in order to protect the economic interests of the ruling overlords. Therefore, pursuant to the requirement for the monopolization of force in society, English Criminal Law was introduced, along with that other body of English law which we now know as *received law.*

Customary law, the indigenous law, was left to serve mainly the needs of those within the enclave of the subsistence economy. It was left to operate more for administrative convenience in civil matters, and was subject nevertheless to the test of "natural justice, equity and good conscience," in the European, rather than the African sense.[9] With its diversified rules and principles, customary law met the legal problems of the "natives" of the subsistence economy. It governed the hereditary lives and succession of the new, growing working class, products of the imperial technology, and of the elite, the new class, provided that the latter in their general mode of living approximated more to that of the ordinary "native."

The English drafted their own law upon the pattern of customary law. On granting Independence they entrenched the colonial heritage firmly in the hands of a selected group of the new class, with the duty to protect both their own economic and political interests and those of their erstwhile colonial masters, as against the general and particular interests of the working class and the peasants. Such was the motivating factor for the complex nature of our legal system. From this analysis one can understand generally the function of law in English-speaking Africa today.

From an economic approach, we thus see that the desires which are met by the enactment of laws in English-speaking Africa are the desires of those groups which prevail in the struggles brought about by conflicting interests in society. More often, force, as a legal ingredient, is exercised arbitrarily. This accounts for much of the unrest we now experience. Unless force is exercised within a social order to give effect to the wishes of the masses, its operation has no structure, and it can hardly command effective obedience to law.

In the words of Thompson, "within a social order, force does not control action; its existence and the willingness to use it may help to maintain a social order, but force is not the foundation upon which society exists."[10] As a structure of human relationships within a society, law must transcend force and bring force into submission to itself. This can be achieved, not by the arbitrary action of the ruling few, but by the wishes of the majority of the people.

We see from a study of law in primitive societies that the function of law is to maintain the basic structure of a classless society by providing and regulating the conditions under which the immediate affairs of the society are carried on. At this stage the problem of obedience to law is not an issue. Every man is his brother's keeper and a champion of social harmony and social solidarity. In a contemporary African State the problem is different. Law has assumed the function of bringing about the achievement of new goals and lay out new paths of social action in response to the impact of modern developments and scientific technology. Law at this stage is understood to concern itself with what is desirable, in the sense of fulfilling human desires generally, and in particular, man's economic wants. The problem, therefore, is to find a yardstick to justify the law. That yardstick is the end that law serves. For the end to be desirable, and for law to have maximum support and efficacy, law must function for the greatest happiness of the majority, i. e., the peasants and the workers.

Notes to Chapter 8

1. Engels, Frederick, *Socialism: Utopian and Scientific* (1892) Transl. Edward Aveling (New York: International Publishers) p. 51.
2. Marx, Karl, *Introduction to A Critique of Political Economy,* p. 11.
3. Vyshinsky, Audrei, *The Law of the Soviet State,* p. 39. See also p. 3.
4. *Ibid.,* p. 41, pp. 77, 204, *et seq.*
5. Modern Soviet writers envisage this stage as the period when capitalism disappears entirely in the world, for without such disappearance capitalist encirclement from other parts of the world continues to constitute a threat to communism. See Vyshinsky, A. *op. cit.* pp. 59–62, 65–70; Golunsky, S. A. and Strogovitch, M. S. "The Theory of the State and Law," in Babb and Hazard *Soviet Legal Philosophy,* 1951, pp. 353, 400.
6. Paschukanis, E. B. "General Theory of Law and Marxism," in *Soviet Legal Philosophy,* p. 111. Compare Paschukanis' exchange commodity theory with Seagles views on law, and his denial of the existence of law in a society where trade is by barter. See Dr. Schlesinger's criticism of Paschukanis in *Soviet Legal Philosophy,* p. 157, where he challenges Paschukanis' theory as historically unsound.
7. For example, The Civil Code (1922) Art. 5 of the U.S.S.R. calls for the infliction of heavier penalties on criminals who are enemies of the regime, than persons who, for purely personal motives, interfere with their fellow citizens. Originally, the judge had to determine when an act was prejudicial to the regime, or purely personal in character.
8. In our view that what obtains so far in the so-called Communist world is Socialism, a step *toward* communism, if not the final stage to communism.
9. See above, Chapter 1.
10. Thompson, S. "The Authority of Law," *Ethics,* Vol. LXXV October 1964, p. 19.

PART IV
LAW AND SOCIETY

Chapter 9

Social Facts and Legal Theories

From our survey of the various theories of law we see that if the notion of law has changed from society to society, and from generation to generation within the same society, it is not simply because new facts have been brought to light within each era. It is not even necessarily because each generation views law from a different set of prejudices. It is largely because each generation asks a different set of questions, has a different set of values, and is confronted with problems not too similar to the past. Each generation wants a transformed and a better society than that of its predecessor. The province of law, the instrument of social transformation, is therefore reviewed constantly. That law means different things to different generations.

If, on the other hand, man is still bewildered and rather bemused by the "ideal law," it is because, society apart, men have inherited a lot in common from humanity. Man's practical problems may vary, depending on his time and social environment. His idea of what is fair and equitable is a particular product of his environment, based on social facts and his experience, yet his notion of justice has an ultimate base which stems from his humanity. It is this ultimate base that we find to be the central core of the ideal law. It is this that links the various legal notions of every generation and which has influenced most legal philosophers.

Social Facts and Legal Change

A seeming consensus among leading jurists is that law does not exist *in vacuo*, that it is the result of life in society. Law exists to serve certain social interests, but becomes sterile when divorced from its milieu and conceptualized as Austin and his school have done.[1] In a ruder society law exists to maintain the established social order. It functions to compel as well as prevent certain acts, depending on prevalent social values and beliefs. In a developed State the sphere of the function of law is more extensive, as can be seen in its various branches, most of which are non-existent in primitive law. Among other things, law regulates existing property rights and duties between persons and fixes labor relations. It determines the constitutional system and fixes the forms of administration of State machineries. Furthermore, it determines the legal status of the individual and his relationship with the State, his mode of education and its standard, and the general welfare. Finally, as in early law, it lays down rules to compel certain acts in furtherance of the State's objectives and to prevent other acts, regarded as inimical to those objectives or capable of disrupting the established order.

In a developing society law assumes the above functions, with something much more. Apart from maintaining and regulating already achieved social ends, law has the major task of making possible the achievement of new goals. New paths of social action have to be established and maintained, and the basic structure of society changed, if necessary, in order to catch up with new and modern developments. It is at this juncture that legal development runs into great difficulties. Without a government of the people that understands the people and the society, the tendency is for the lawmaker to try to use law to create a society of his own choice, one which offers him and his class great privileges and advantages in the name of modern development. With a government of the people which understands the people, the position is different. Only a government of the people can use the law to advance society's economic and political life to reflect the peoples' wishes and desires. A regular and permanent feature of law, as seen by our study of the schools, is that law must respond to the desired social change. It is a flexible instrument of social order deriving its strength and efficacy from the socioeconomic system and the political and moral values of the society that it is to serve.

The existence of superior and inferior as prerequisites to the existence of law is an inadequate feature of law. As a pattern of legal experience it is more of a conventional than a universal feature. Austin and Kelsen failed to provide us with an acceptable general and universal theory of law. Analytical positivism offers no adequate explanation of law everywhere, and in particular in English-speaking Africa where legal pluralism exists, with customary law forming part of the dual system. Kelsen's pure theory gives no proof for the efficacy of the *grundnorm* which is the basis of his legal thesis and which we regard as forming a yardstick for distinguishing formal law from living law in English-speaking Africa.

The theory of the social contract is a sound theory as to the origin of sovereignty. It may provide a clue to the evolution of States, but it offers no adequate answer to the binding force of law. The core of orthodox legal notions lies in the general idea that law must go back to an ultimate power which posits and sanctions it. The holder of that power is regarded as the fountain of law.

Legal experience shows that the ultimate power varies in societies and in accordance with changes in every society. The changes are in turn determined by the common desires and aspirations of the people. If all law must go back to the ultimate power, and the ultimate power owes its existence to extra-legal factors, the obvious conclusion is that the mainstay of law lies *beyond* the ultimate power.

Legal change is a sequel to change in society. A sound legal philosophy should therefore not gloss over the factors that command social change. Law in primitive society, where there is a lack of governmental organs, developed leadership, and legal institutions, fits the facts of social and economic life in such a society. It functions to maintain the existing order and its authority gains strength from superstition, social ostracism, and fear. These last factors give force to tribal devices for the maintenance of public order and the settlement of disputes. Thus, the nature of law in a tribal setting is reflective of the social milieu.[2]

Law in a developed State is a result of changed socioeconomic and political life in society. High reasons of State may demand regimentation of the law, which is generally lacking in primitive society. The existence of a superior or predominant class may be necessary at this stage to sustain force and give directives to law. All along, legal rules express the interest of the ruling class and the socially privileged sections of the society. The politically and economically dominant section of society relies on its strength and wealth to hold the reins of power. It lays down norms of behavior designed to safeguard its interests. These are made to be binding on all, and force is used to command obedience.

As Marx and Engels point out, "the individuals who rule in these conditions, besides having to constitute their power in the form of the *State*, have to give their will, which is determined by these definite conditions, a universal expression as the will of the State, as law.[3] Thus, by doing so, their general and particular interest as fixed in the law are camouflaged as they enforce their will through the law. The individual will, which may not be in accord with conditions necessary for the development of the State for the general interest of all its citizens, is given definiteness in State acts. Acts which otherwise would be individual arbitrary acts, and seen openly as inimical to the general progress and stability of the people, receive State sanction and are buttressed by State force.

The tactics of the privileged ruling class are not so easily discernible with a progressive or a benevolent (not a Socialist) government. By acting for the society as a whole, it tries to keep faith with the people. Moreover, since it is progressive, society seems to be able to identify its interests to some extent with the interests of the ruling class, and the latter, through the law, give definiteness to some of the general rules of behavior which the society approves. Sometimes the class assumes a patronizing attitude, granting some concessions to the ruled, which go a long way to pacify the people or make them more indolent and apathetic to revolutionary measures. These subtle tactics notwithstanding, coercion remains a necessary ingredient of the law, because by and large the interests of the ruling minority represented by law often clash with the interests of the ruled majority.

In a developing State, where the urge is to achieve new goals, law is expected to establish new paths of social action to hasten the achievement of the new goals. From the beginning, therefore, the ruling minority have a task to perform in which the majority have much interest. The latter become more vigilant, thus making it less easy for the former to camouflage their particular and general interests in the law with great impunity. Because a developing State is in an experimental stage, and because of the greater disparity in economic, educational, and social achievements, and differences in ideological orientation, the clashes between competing interests are greater. Class conflict is more vigorous and political authority much more vulnerable and transient. Coercion, therefore, is not enough to sustain law that is not in conformity with the common, fundamental desires of the people.

Because of the absence of a common ideology, which should influence the law and direct social action toward a popular end, the position of the law as an instrument of oppression becomes too obvious in a developing English-speaking African State. The ruling minority creates law in accordance with the ideology of its class, which hitherto is involved with budding capitalism and which is not strictly in harmony with the socioeconomic facts and the desires of the masses. In the circumstances law fails, even with all the coercive forces it can muster to exercise a salutary influence on social and individual consciousness, as it does in a developed State. By failing to exercise sufficient great influence on the consciousness and behavior of men, its ideological or educational role fails to be fulfilled. The definite principles and normative rules of behavior, which are laid down and made mandatory to encourage obedience, are looked upon with great dissatisfaction and suspicion. The prospects of sanction and punishment, held out in the absence of non-compliance with the law, fail to encourage observance of it. What we have, in consequence, is dissatisfaction and social unrest, leading to military coups and countercoups.

During a period of great social change the ideological and educational role of law cannot be minimized. With a common ideology, legal acts give definiteness and expression to principles and ideals of the new social system. As the legal rules are made mandatory for all, and with the goal accepted by the people as a reflection of their general will, law becomes an acceptable and important means of social transformation. An ideology that is popular amongst a people is therefore the sole base of law. It is a prerequisite to socioeconomic transformation in a developing country. Legal notions should revolve around it, and legislation give definiteness to its demands through enacted laws.

Legal Notions and Ideology

Gray once said, "...suppose Chief Justice Marshall had been an ardent Democrat (or Republican as it was then called) as he was a Federalist. Suppose instead of hating Thomas Jefferson and loving the United States Bank, he had hated the United States Bank and loved Thomas Jefferson—how different would be the law under which we are living today."[4] This statement was made while Gray was trying to advance the realist idea on the function of the Court as the law-making organ. On closer analysis we find that the statement is far-reaching. Putting it another way to show the ideological implications, one would say: "...supposing Chief Justice Marshall had been as ardent a Socialist as he was a Capitalist," then the United States during his time and under his influence would have lived under a different law and perhaps built up a different socioeconomic system from the present.

What we are trying to say is that ideology exercises a formidable influence on law. Law is made by man and therefore it cannot help being an expression of definite ideological motives of the lawmaker. Just as, according to the realists, a judge's prejudices, and even the state of his digestive organs influence his decision, which is held to be the law, legal rules laid down by State authorities reflect the ideology of the class wielding the political power. The success or failure of law in the circumstances would depend on the ideological orientation of the generality of the people and the extent to which their common desire is in harmony with the ideology of the ruling class.

While ideology exerts great influence on law, law in turn exercises an influence on social as well as individual consciousness. Thus, the ruling minority may successfully impose the ideology of its class on the masses through law. Such success can be achieved with ease in an indolent and less-educated society. The educational role of law here takes the form of ideological indoctrination, which may yield good results for the rulers by crystallizing the ideology of their own class before society in the mass is mature enough and well enough informed to ask questions. It is only in a society with educated and well-informed men and women, whose common ideological belief is quite different from that of the ruling few, but in keeping with the yearnings of the masses, that the process of ideological indoctrination of the people through laws made by the minority ruling class meets with a very formidable opposition, and more often fails to achieve the desired goal.

The effect of ideology on law is also discernible in legal philosophy. Legal philosophers are the products of their time and their society. The problems of their time, the facts of their society, the content of the law in force, the way people react to it, and the method which the government adopts to compel obedience to law—all these together leave impressions on the minds of legal writers. Their personal reaction to the happenings around them are ingrained in their analysis of the situation and their philosophy of law. They may try to be objective in seeking for an ideal law, but their objectivity is sometimes affected by their personal and local experience. In the circumstances, their postulates cannot form an indisputable basis for postulating a general theory of law that holds true at all times and in all places.

For example, the natural law theorists lived in a world of metaphysical beliefs and social inequilibrium. They sought to resolve their problem of social stability by an appeal to moral and ethical values and principles. They sought universal neutral and immutable principles to guide man in his social actions. This they found in natural law. The social contract theorists, like Thomas Hobbes and John Locke were all products of their time and experience. The analytical positivists could not reconcile the practical life of law in their society with metaphysical beliefs. The result was the propounding of a theory of law which tried to expunge those beliefs from the practical realities of law and life in society. The writers of the historical school, incensed by the tyranny inherent in legal positivism, took to an evolutionary theory of law which identified the ideal law with the people, their ways of life, and their common consciousness. The Benthamites, the writers of the sociological school, and even the Marxists, in their approaches to law were all influenced by the shortcomings and the injustices inherent in orthodox legal notions which they experienced. Their legal theories sought to harmonize law with society as a way of ending injustices and inequalities, to which the orthodox legal notions gave no adequate solution.

The experience and methods of indigenous Africa are not different from those of other societies whose stages of social, economic and political advancement were similar. It is true that in the African case the absence of writing leaves us with no authentic records from which we can discern the legal philosophy of the earliest period, but later works by anthropologists reveal the existence of courts of law and discernible sets of legal rules which, when analyzed, are seen to be patterned to reflect the socioeconomic, political, and moral values of the time.

Most writers, for example, find the division between criminal and civil laws in indigenous Africa (or the so-called primitive society) either non-existent or too subtle to form a real distinction.[5] This is so because the general notion of law was based on social harmony, in which not only the living, but also the dead ancestors had a stake. Both criminal law and civil law were, therefore, administered with this requirement in view, and the pervading principle in judicial decisions was the principle of reconciliation and the maintenance of social equilibrium. The wronged had not only to be compensated for the wrong done but the offender had to reconcile with him. In case of public offense, after the offender had paid the due penalty, he had, in more serious offenses to propitiate the ancestors by offering an appropriate sacrifice.

The clan had the duty of settling disputes within the clan, or judging criminal offenses committed in the clan by its members in a way that would promote rather than disrupt social harmony within the clan. Offenses outside the clan, or disputes between clans or members of different clans, were also punished or settled in the same spirit between members of the clans concerned. Collective responsibility became an attribute of legal responsibility, to compel the clan to educate its members within the spirit of the law and the common consciousness of the tribe as a whole.

Contemporary Africa has become much more complex. The new States have been exposed to modern economy and politics. The old order, with orthodox and received law, is no longer adequate to meet the demands of modernization. The new economic, political, and social life has not been stabilized. Everything is in flux, and so is the law. The big problem is to find a philosophy of law adequate to solve present problems and act as a guide to the future achievement of popular new goals.

A more adequate theory of law for a developing country wanting to transform its socioeconomic and political system must combine legal positivism with some aspects of the Savignian theory of the *Volksgeist*. With the latter, the emphasis should be on the general weal and the common aspirations of the people, rather than on common consciousness as a mere revolutionary process.

The period of transformation in the history of any society is a period where the orthodox and the unorthodox grapple for survival and hegemony, respectively. While a break with the old law and the old legal notions, and the establishment of new laws based on a popular ideology to achieve the desired ends of society is the only way out, common rules which are acceptable in any civilized society can form a link between the old and the new. Coercion will remain as a necessary ingredient of law to command the obedience of the conservative minority which is too orthodox and not easily susceptible to change.

The circumstances of life in a developing State demand, *inter alia*, social ordering, change, and development through law. A sound legal theory in a developing modern State ought, therefore, to adopt a teleological approach, but the values to underlie the law must derive from an ideology that is popular among the people. To meet the exigencies of social stability, class conflicts and the struggle for authority must be taken care of through legal coercion that is backed up by a psychological mechanism which derives from the general will and the common aspirations of the people, and not from the sheer power of the political superior.

Notes to Chapter 9

1. Elias, T. O., *Law in A Developing Society*, Lagos: 1969 Ibadan University Press p. 5, citing Pound's *Interpretations of Legal History*, London: Cambridge University Press (1923), Chap. 6.
2. Most of the work in this field is by anthropologists. See Malinowski, B., *Crime and Custom in Savage Society* (London: Kegan Paul 1926); Meek, C. K., *A Sudanese Kingdom* (London: Kegan Paul 1931), especially p. 347; Hartland, E. S., *Primitive Law* (London: Methuen 1924). Consider also the Hobbesian system, and Von Savigny's theory of the Volksgeist. See also, Driberg, J. H., "Primitive Law in East Africa," in *Africa*, Vol. 1 1928, pp. 63–72, especially p. 65. A more recent work, which gives an apt and legal analysis of law in native Africa, is Elias, T. O., *The Nature of African Customary Law* (Manchester University Press 1956), Chapter 3, in particular, pp. 27–34, also, Chapters 4 and 5, pp. 37–75.
3. Marx and Engels, *The German Ideology*, (Moscow: 1964) 1964 edition, p. 357.
4. Gray, J. C., *The Nature and Sources of the Law* (New York: Columbia University Press 1921), p. 226.
5. See, for example, Seagle, W. A., "Primitive Law and Professor Malinowski," in the *American Anthropologist*, Vol. 39, Part II, 1937. Hone, H. R., "The Native of Uganda and the Criminal Law," *Uganda Journal*, Vol. VI, No. 1, July 1938; *cf.* Malinowski, B., *Crime and Custom in Savage Society* (London: 1926). Also, Elias, T. O., *The Nature of African Customary Law*, Chap. 7, pp. 110–129.

Chapter 10

Evaluating Laws in English-speaking Africa

The Received Law and Legal Conceptions

There are three main conceptions of law which we deem more relevant for an analysis of the reception and function of received English laws in Africa. These may be summarized as follows:

1. The conception of law by the analytical positivists as a body of commands of the political superior in a politically organized society regulating the social conduct of the subject.
2. The economic conceptions of law as a body or system of rules imposed on men in society by the dominant ruling class in furtherance of its own class interests;
3. The idea that law embodies the dictates of economic or social necessities which seek to regulate man's conduct in society. Such laws are discoverable by observation and are worked out through human experience.

There are other conceptions of law which are not entirely irrelevant to an objective analysis of the function of the received English Laws. These, however, unlike the three mentioned above, do not provide an adequate basis for a sound positive analysis. For example, the notion that law is a tradition of the old customs which stems from the people and which grows with them, having as its ultimate goal the achievement of their common aspirations, may present a good basis for a positive analysis of customary law and maybe local legislation, but not for the received laws. Also, the conception that law embodies the agreement of men in politically organized society, which regulates their relationship with one another, if applied to the received laws, will present no real convincing argument. As we have noted above, the received laws grew out of social, economic, and political backgrounds which are quite distinct from those of the African countries into which they were imported.

The relationship between the Africans and their chiefs on the one hand, and the English who conquered them or caused them to cede their territories to the British Crown on the other, was such that the new community they formed could not be described as purely democratic. Therefore, laws imported or allowed to operate in the colonies could not be rightly said to reflect the general will of the people.

On the other hand, the Africans could not have by any form of agreement have allowed such laws. The concept of contract implies an agreement between equal parties with each of the parties knowing his rights and liabilities under the contract; or at least with each party realizing the common intention of the agreement otherwise there can be no *consensus ad idem,* and therefore no binding contract. The relationship between the indigenous Africans or their representative heads or chiefs and their colonial masters at the time was such that no equality of the type necessary for a valid contract existed. Any notion, therefore, that the received laws resulted from any agreement between the Africans and the Europeans who conquered them, is untenable.

Nothing much can therefore be achieved by examining the received laws and the act of reception on such grounds. It is for this reason that we shall confine our analysis only to the conceptions which are more relevant to their manner of importation, the objectives of their importation, which may provide a good basis for an examination of their function and their adequacy to solve the problems of the receiving countries, both at the initial period of reception and after the attainment of nationhood.

If analysis is the accepted tool of jurisprudence, then certainly it is not necessary that the received laws should fulfill any beneficial function to the receiving country. Equally so, it would not be worthwhile to examine to what extent they helped the economic and political motives of the Imperial masters at the expense of the Africans. What would be important is, in the Austinian sense, to identify the receiving colony as a society political, and to determine the political superior who was in the habit of receiving habitual obedience from the subjects without giving any loyalty or obedience in return. Or, in accordance with Kelsen's theory, the hierarchy of the normative rules plus their concretization are all we need to determine the existence of the legal order or the State, since both are one and the same thing.

Undoubtedly the received laws were imposed on the African colonies by the imperial administrative officers acting under the directives of the British Crown. Initially the main objective was economic. If the colonialists' economic interests were to be expanded and maintained in the colonies, then it was imperative to introduce laws that would take care of the new venture and simplify the operation of the colonialist. English law, which was the law they knew at home, formed a suitable base. The traditional customary law was unsuitable. In any case it operated to regulate modes of conduct and transactions which were quite alien to the colonial masters, and sometimes inimical to their interests.

It was, however, realized that the advent of the British introduced complexities into a society that until then could be termed a simple society. Class conflicts could arise which would disturb the legal order. Such conflicts might be greater if the European aliens and the indigenous Africans were to be equally subject to the same laws. Consequently, a perverted legal pluralism was introduced. Those in the colonial enclave became subject to the imported laws, while the Africans who represented the subsistent sector remained subject to customary law, the law which had always taken care of their transactions before the advent of the British, and which is part of their history and culture.

Having adopted this strategy, the received law had a comfortable basis to operate from. Then it made its inroad, crystallizing as the accepted law of the colony. It operated as a superior law, which prevailed over customary law in cases of conflict. Even within the areas of no possible conflict,[1] customary law might be made subject to English standards or values before it could be enforced, or the subject matter of the transaction (if alien) could invoke the application of English law in preference to traditional law. In the area of public law the aim was complete domination by the imported law to enhance the British monopoly of force in the colony.

While we may maintain that the received law is a body of rules imposed on English-speaking Africans by the dominant British ruling class, it is equally true to say that they were dictated by social necessities. The complexity which arose in the socioeconomic life in the colonies as a result of the presence and the commercial activities of the British called for laws that would be adequate to meet the social and economic exigencies of the time. Since the inhabitants of each colony could belong to one of the two classes (the colonialist enclave and the subsistent-economy sector) whose social backgrounds, culture, tradition, and economic and political orientation were different, it was impossible to discover any law by observations worked out by experience to regulate the people's conduct. Such a law, if it were possible at all, was not available to satisfy the immediate needs and solve the immediate problems.

The particular question, therefore, is whether the received laws, from their time of reception through the period of their crystallization unto this day, have undergone any stage or stages of metamorphosis which would justify their realistic and strict identification with the receiving countries. From our previous analysis, the answer is: No. What has happened so far is that the African elites have either taken the place of the aliens who were in the colonialist enclave, or have, on changing their mode of living, gone to swell the number of that class. They, with the senior and intermediate workers who depend on employment by government and corporations for their livelihood (broadly speaking), form a class in themselves, while the junior workers, the peasants, and village dwellers remain within the subsistent sector. The received laws operate as before, and the attainment of nationhood has not altered the pattern established by the British. The Bench and the Bar are manned mainly by persons who received their legal education in England and who are still deeply steeped in the British legal tradition. The result is that the received laws operate quite comfortably in English-speaking Africa, still in the spirit of their makers.

Law and Social Order

The American sociologist Ross, in his book *Social Control,* sees obedience as the cementing factor of social order. "It is *obedience* that articulates the solid bony framework of social order." He felt rather disappointed that in an industrialized modern State the forces of sympathy, love for justice, sociability, and a sense of resentment are so weak as not to bring about and sustain "natural social order" without legal imposition. Consequently, he inclined toward a "wise minority" or "organization of distinct elements of the population" to exert social control through legal coercion.[2] Thus, where those directing the country's affairs are not happy with the existing state of the society, they can use changes in the law as a means of altering the society to their taste and use force to achieve their objective.

By accepting the government of the "wise minority" or the "organized distinct elements" in society, Ross abandons the task of determining those phenomena in society which command spontaneous obedience. Obedience is the mainstay of social order. As we have seen (in Chapter 7), coercion steps in at a point where law has failed to command obedience to itself. In evaluating laws, therefore, one cannot afford to ignore those factors that, in the words of Ross, "articulate the solid bony framework of social order" with spontaneity, *nec vi.*

The factors which strengthen those forces that ought to bring and maintain "natural social order" without legal coercion are very relevant to the binding force of law. In other words, to be able to identify and eradicate those elements in society that weaken the forces that command spontaneous obedience to law is to solve the problem of legal coercion.

From our analysis (in Chapter 8), we see that the function of law in society is very relevant to the degree of *obedience* that it can command. Where the function is to maintain the basic structure of a classless society and lay down conditions under which present and future programs of the society are to be carried on within an accepted social philosophy or political ideology, obedience becomes spontaneous and poses no problem. On the other hand, where the function of law is to bring about the achievement of new goals and establish new paths of action in a society with *divergent* social and political philosophy, obedience becomes an issue. Its spontaneity would rest on both the reasonableness of the function and the adequacy of the method laid down for the achievement of the goal. In other words, the popularity of the end and the ways and means of achieving it command obedience.

The problem becomes even greater in a complex and developing society where, due to class and the absence of an ideology; or due to fluidity of ideas, no overall goal has been accepted or allowed to crystallize. Breaches of law, in spite of very formidable State forces to coerce obedience, prove to us that there are primary social factors, whose primacy are quite independent of law. They can generate forces to oppose any law that is not in harmony with the social tenets which they dictate. It is these factors that prove the substratum of any social order.

To evaluate law in any society, one should consider the substratum. The adequacy of law and its suitability to any given society lie in its harmonious effect and the tranquillity it brings to the order it serves. Thus, the law must command obedience to itself not by reliance on State forces to coerce obedience to it, but by the fact of its being the accepted popular venue for ushering in the popular goal and bringing fulfillment and satisfaction to the wants and desires of the people.

The Economic and Political Matrix

Economics and politics together provide the basis for legal development in English-speaking Africa. The existing legal pluralism is a sequel to Africa's political history and the dual economic pattern which emerged from colonialism. As we have seen (in Chapter 8) the legal machinery in English-speaking Africa is patterned on the English legal system. A pluralistic legal system provides the norms which govern the society and, in the main, protect the commercial interests and demands of British imperialism and neocolonialism.

The legal pluralism which exists was imposed on the new States by the colonial overloads. It is concomitant to the social facts which emerged with colonialism. Before the imperialists began their extensive exploitation of the continent in the second half of the 19th Century the economic structure was subsistence economy. The culture of the economy, though medieval in point of time and character, was rich and varied. Individuals learned the skills for their respective trade and callings in order to produce for themselves and their family their daily needs. Wage labor was nonexistent, and where it became necessary for a family to seek labor assistance outside the family, the general guiding principle was that of mutual assistance.

No class antagonism existed in the pre-colonial days. Journeymen and apprentices worked more for their own education, to acquire the skill necessary for their own vocation, than for board and lodging. Even in the very few instances where it could be said that a master-servant relationship existed, as in cases of self-pledge or pawn, the relationship was not based on wage labor but on mutual assistance in the traditional way. The social structure of the economy was one that could respond quite adequately to its problems. *Customary* law provided the legal norms which gave answers aptly to problems brought upon the society by the subsistence economy and the prevailing social values.

With the coming of the imperial masters a second economic enclave was imposed upon the society. The economic enclave, which had relatively modern technology, was quite exploitative and based on extractive industry. It was organized to achieve the profitable exploitation of Africa, never to serve the pre-existing subsistent economy. The extractive industry was impelled by purely profit motives. On its heels came the big trading firms: Unilever which, through the United African Company still dominates the trade of English-speaking Africa, G. B. Ollivant, John Holt Batholomew, and several others.

The imperialist enclave of the economy provided channels through which the rich raw materials of the country were sent to the English metropolis to feed home industries, such as the soap factories of Unilever, the smelters of Birmingham, and the chocolate factories of Cadbury and Fry. The roads, railways and ports built in the African countries were designed solely to meet the primary demands of the interest of the colonial overlords.

Having introduced a plural economy, a legal superstructure was imposed to stabilize the complex economy and political activities. Pursuant to the requirement for the monopolization of force in society, English Criminal Law was introduced to regulate the activities of all within the country. It operated along with that other body of English laws, all of which we now know as the *received law*. This body of law was to serve primarily the economic and other interests of the non-natives who made up the colonial enclave. The indigenous law, which is customary law, was left to meet the needs of the natives who remained in the subsistence economy. It was left to thrive, not out of respect, but more for administrative convenience in civil matters, subject to the imperial test of "natural justice, equity and good conscience."

Customary law, with its varied rules and principles, was accepted as good enough to meet the legal problems of the natives of the subsistence economy. It governed the hereditary lives and succession of the growing working and urban class—the product of imperial technology. The elite, the new class, were at this stage very few, and customary law governed their heredity and succession lives, provided their mode of living approximated to that of the ordinary native. Otherwise they moved up to the group to whom the received law of inheritance and succession applied.

The customary rules governing land accommodated the twin facts of communal land ownership and individual landholding (short of ownership) which afforded the individual an opportunity to bring a particular alloted piece of land to fruition by his efforts and that of his family. The general principle was that land belongs to the community and is incapable of alienation by the individual. The nominal "owner" of land, however, could allocate portions of unoccupied land directly to individual members of the relevant group or family who, in turn, could sub-allocate on demand, and according to need, to their individual members. Generally, an individual's interest in land was usufructuary. It did not go beyond mere possession. The exclusive possession of a piece of land by the individual or his family was generally subject to effective use of the plot.

Customary law provided no detailed rules governing general contracts. With the exception of marriage contract, which was governed by locally varied rules, most of the transactions, as in early Europe involving exchange of goods and services between persons, were not specific. Exchange of property, goods and services were made in the spirit of comradeship, as between members of leaders of political groups, or as kinsfolk or affines. The link between people in transactions generally gave little or no room for a master-servant relationship. Therefore there was no class consciousness and no class antagonism within the enclave or the subsistence economy, and customary law was adequate to meet the demands of the time.

The English grafted their own law upon the pattern of customary law, as we have described above. The form of reception of the English law made customary law the "exceptional" law, with English law as the "basic" law. For example, establishing the English law in Nigeria in 1876, when Nigeria was part of the West African Administration of the British, the Supreme Court of the Gold Coast of that year stated as follows:

> The common law, the doctrine of equity, and the statutes of general application which were in force in England on the date when the colony ob-

tained a local legislature, that is to say, 24th July 1874, shall be in force within the jurisdiction of this court.[3]

The same statute went on to provide that

> Nothing in this Ordinance shall deprive the Supreme Court of the right to reserve and enforce the observance, or shall deprive any person of the benefit, of any law or custom existing in the said colony and territories subject to its jurisdiction, *such law or custom not being repugnant to natural justice, equity or good conscience, nor incompatible either directly or by necessary implication with any enactment of the Colonial Legislature....*[4]

The position was the same in all English-speaking Africa and has continued to be so, even after Independence. *The Gambian Protectorate Order in Council*, Cap. 7 s.30, for example, enjoins the High Court as follows:

> All native laws and customs existing in the Protectorate whether relating to *matters of succession, marriage, divorce, dowry, the rights and authorities of parents, the tenure of land or any other, shall where not repugnant to natural justice, nor incompatible with the principles of the law of England* or with any law or Ordinance of the colony applying to the Protectorate ...continue and remain in full force and effect and shall be taken cognizance of and enforced in all courts of law, whether in the colony or the Protectorate in all cases and matters whatsoever arising in or relating to the Protectorate.[5]

From the various dates of reception we see that the received English law (the common law and the statutes of general application), which was made the superior law, was the law of 19th Century England. At that time England had already developed her tendency to separate ownership of property and individualism in the sphere of work.[6] This presented a sharp contrast to the customary law position of communal ownership of property, in which the right to use land was intimately connected to the actual user. Real property in England at that stage, like any other property, was treated as a necessary factor of production, a capitalist commodity which was liable to the demands of the market. This trend was transported to English-speaking Africa.

Furthermore, customary law, which was relegated to the second place of an exceptional law, governed the lives of a vast majority of the people. Its application was subject to the tests of "repugnancy" and "incompatibility" with received English law. Thus, received law was to operate with no disadvantages or obstacles from the indigenous law. It was necessary that it should so operate, since it was designed to accommodate the interests and demands of the British masters whose activities were organized around the central notion of economic exploitation of the countries.

Problems from the Colonial Heritage

The pattern of law upon Independence in the new States of English-speaking Africa remains the same, and has persisted thus far with the countries enjoying political independence. A plural legal system provides, to this day, the norms of social conduct in the now complex and developing States. There is great yearning everywhere for rapid changes in the economic sphere. Rapid industrialization, modernization of the economy, political stability are the things desired most. These and the need for universal education form the focus of political development. Undoubtedly the goal cannot be achieved without the law playing an important role. The problem is to determine the kind of law that adequately meets the present demands of the people, commands obedience, and acts as a well-accepted guide to future development and more modernization of the States.

The problems posed by the historical data are the definition and the function of law. Looking at the legal pattern left by colonialism, law in English-speaking Africa is not necessarily a set of rules acceptable to members of the community as binding. *Acceptance* of bindingness connotes the exercise of free will of those obligated. This is not strictly the case in English-speaking Africa. Even customary law as we know it, is now losing its authority and bindingness, which originally stemmed from the mere fact of the consensus of the indigenous. All along in the colonial era the guiding legal philosophy was positivistic as well as analytical. The trend continued after political independence, and there has been little or no sign of a legal revolution. Rather, it is legal evolution that is being practised, with the date of reception of English law as the starting point. Inherited legal concepts are being maneuvered so as to serve the rapidly-growing socioeconomic demands of the developing States.

Customary law, as the law of the subsistent sector, remains a personal law. The rules of customary law of an ethnic group attach to the members of the group, wherever they go to govern, their marital status, heredity, and succession lives. Like law in primitive society, it still functions to compel certain acts and to prevent others. It does not direct lines of actions for the achievement of new goals. The judicial technique in dealing with rules of customary law has shown certain trends toward modernization of the law. This, however, has failed to keep pace with the rapid economic and political developments. Much that has been achieved by the courts so far is in the area of gradual alteration of the nature and authority of customary law, as law par excellence.

The received law, with the great impact it has made, remains the dominant law. It is alien to the people and has no roots whatsoever in the States in which it operates. However, by force of history, it now provides the basis of our legal development. The problem posed is that, in the absence of legal revolution, how far and in what ways can the inherited legal concepts be adopted to achieve popular social, economic, and political ends in the States?

If we take the case of *property law,* for example, the present position, due to the colonial heritage in our system, is that land is generally vested in the urban areas in the Crown (now the State). Community (or family ownership) remains a feature of land tenure in the rural areas. What is more, there is a growing trend toward individual ownership of land, also due to the imported British idea of land being regarded as a commodity, strictly liable to the demands of the market.

Land law under the traditional system was designed to ensure a rational and equitable use of land and its resources by all members of the community. It avoided the ownership of large landed estates by any member of the community, including the chief or the clan head, thus eliminating any possible exploitation of the peasants based on land ownership.

The concept of Crown land, though now referred to as State land, is not the same as communal ownership of land. Land designated as Crown land has the following characteristic features which are unknown to communal land under the indigenous system:

(a) Crown ownership is based on treaties either of cession[7] or otherwise between the representatives of the British Crown on the one hand, and a local king, chief or chiefs on the other hand, when in fact under customary law, native land is inalienable and no king or chief had ownership in land to transfer to the British Crown.[8]

(b) Crown (State) rights over land may be absolute, overriding any traditional title of the owners at the time of acquisition.[9]

(c) The Crown can make grants of parcels of land to individuals, giving the grantees *absolute* rights of ownership in the parcels of land concerned.[10]

(d) Generally, the Crown leases land under its control to individuals for fixed periods, collecting rents, land rates or taxes. Land is not made available free to citizens to satisfy their personal requirements, such as putting up a dwelling house or farming as under the traditional land tenure without these charges.

Thus, while land relations arising on the basis of communal ownership under indigenous land tenure has a socialist characteristic as a feature, land relations arising from the concepts of the received law are purely capitalistic and exploitative.

The big English firms, such as the Royal Niger Company, like the British Crown, acquired absolute title of ownership to lands from local chiefs by means of treaties and other legal devices.[11] The lands so acquired and their harbors were turned into trading posts and prospecting fields where the natives, the original and the real owners of the land, were made to work for wages.

When some of the big firms left their posts, the principle of reversion, which is a well-known principle of landholding in England, which favors the holder of the fee simple, was not allowed to apply. The land did not revert to the natives. Instead, through several laws, ownership of these lands passed to the British Crown, while the trading posts and minerals remained revested for a time in the company concerned.[12]

Under the received land law, the use of land ceased to be free for the native peoples. Legal devices purporting to preserve their right to the land negated freedom of tenure under the indigenous law. For example, again in Nigeria, the *Land and Native Rights Ordinance No. 1 of 1916* removed the right of trusteeship of land from the Emirs and vested it in the governor in a way that changed the relations of the natives to the land that was once their communal property. Section 4 of the Ordinance provided that: "All native lands, and all rights over the same, are hereby declared to be *under the control and subject to the disposition of the Governor*, and shall be held and administered for the use and common benefit of the natives of Northern Nigeria; and no title to the occupation and use of any such lands shall be valid without the consent of the Governor."

Under the indigenous land tenure no absolute proprietary title is possible of acquisition under the law by anybody. But unlike provisions of the indigenous rules, rights of occupation were to be secured by a "certificate of occupancy," revocable at the will of the Governor. Furthermore, occupancy was subject to the payment of rents by the grantees of the certificate.[13]

The overriding principle in customary land tenure is that land is allotted to the individual and his family to satisfy their personal needs. In some countries of east and central Africa the individual is prohibited from using wage labor in cultivating a piece of farm land given to him and his family. In other words, he is not allowed to turn any portion of communal land given to him into a capitalist commodity for the enrichment of himself and family by the exploitation of others. In cases where portions of land are tilled and cultivated by communal effort for the chief or clan head, the principle behind it is compensation for his work as the custodian of the community land. The fruits of communal labor are utilized by the chief for the benefit of himself and his family, not as a capitalist commodity. The surplus is, in fact, used mostly by the chief for the entertainment of his subjects and assistance to those less privileged.

In the field of *domestic relations,* the dual system of law introduced by the colonial administration, notwithstanding, the received law introduced in complex situations. Indigenous family law lays down conditions and procedure governing the contract of and dissolution of marriage within each ethnic group. It regulates the rights and duties of the spouses, the relations between them in the first place, as the individuals physically concerned with the marriage, and in the second place, the relations between their two families. The interests of the children of the spouses concerned are protected in accordance with their birth within wedlock or outside it. Generally, the rule is that no child is illegitimate who is acknowledged either by the husband of the mother or the natural father.

The received law, with its concept of monogamy, gives a definition of marriage as "the voluntary union for life of one man and one woman, to the exclusion of all others."[14] This, in African society, tends to destroy the traditional second feature of marriage as a union of the two families concerned. It has also brought in the notion of illegitimacy, which disinherits any child born out of wedlock, though by adaptation the principle of acknowledgment is now acceptable, giving the child the rights of legitimate issue. The loosening of the families' involvement now makes it less possible for the families of spouses to play a very active role in saving a marriage from breaking down.

Another feature of the received law of marriage is its refusal to mix with the traditional form of marriage, which is potentially polygamous. Once married under the Marriage Act, (or Ordinance, as is the case still in some of the countries), one cannot take up another wife, and a wife cannot remarry while the other spouse is living, and the marriage is not dissolved. Nor can a man marry another woman, under customary law, when his previous statutory marriage subsists. It follows also that where a man is married to several women under customary law of marriage, he cannot during the lifetime of all or any of the other wives, try to elevate the status of one of them by purporting to marry her under the Act or Ordinance. Such an attempt would be a mere matter of superfluity in marriage ceremony.

The dualism of marriage law poses various legal problems, most of which remain in the realm of speculative law, since they have not found their way to the courts. For instance, how far can a woman married under customary law pledge the credit of the husband? The right to pledge the credit of the husband is a right which her counterpart, married under English law (which is the equivalent of statutory marriage), enjoys as of legal right, but which may be denied her under her local customary law. To hold the husband liable, the principle of cohabitation may be resorted to, or the doctrine of holding out. These two are characteristic features of the received common law of England. Their application, while practicing legal pluralism, would in effect mean having one's cake and eating it.

Examining some of the specific problems posed by the dualism of marriage law, we see that in most cases double standards apply. Take, for example, *rules of evidence and liability for criminal offenses* as they affect spouses in both forms of marriages. Under the received English criminal law, a spouse is not normally a competent and compellable witness against another spouse, except for offenses which relate to acts of personal violence against the spouse. The same principle has not been applied systematically in the case of polygamous unions in English-speaking Africa.

In Nigeria, for example, section 161 of the Evidence Act provides as follows:

> When a person charged with an offence is married to another person by *a marriage other than a monogamous marriage*[15] such last named person shall be a competent and compellable witness on behalf of either the prosecution or the defence: Provided that in the case of a marriage of Mohammedan Law neither party to such marriage shall be compellable to disclose any communication made to him or her by the other party during such marriage.

A similar provision is found in the Ugandan Evidence Act (as Amended) 1955. Section 119 provides that where a person charged with an offense is married to another person *other than by a monogamous marriage,* the other spouse is a competent and compellable witness. Where the marriage is monogamous, the spouse is a competent but not compellable witness.

Such provisions create disparities between spouses of statutory marriage and those of customary law marriage. What is more, the exclusion by the Nigerian provision of Marriage by Mohammedan Law, which is in itself at least potentially polygamous, leaves traditional customary law marriage as the only marriage in Nigeria where a spouse may be regarded as competent and compellable to give evidence against the other spouse. Thus it creates another double standard within customary law marriage itself, since customary law includes Islamic Law.

The courts have also displayed a strong tendency toward favoring marriage under English law (often known as marriage by Christian rites) as against customary law marriage. Thus, in the Zanzibar case of *Abdulrahman bin Mohammed and anor. v R*[16] the witness and the accused were married by Makonde Custom, by which a man may have only one wife at a time. The court held that the wife was a competent witness against her husband. This was so though, under the Zanzibar law, the wife of a monogamous marriage would not in such circumstances be a competent witness. The same principle was applied much earlier in Uganda in the case of *Petero Sebaggala v R*, where the High Court took the view that in the British courts of the Protectorate,

> the evidence of *a wife, that is to say, a wife married by Christian rites*, cannot be given in evidence against her husband without his consent. This is founded on public policy which should prevail as much in the native courts of the Protectorate as in the British Courts.[17]

In *Robin v R*,[18] the Court of Appeal for Eastern Africa held that the English rule of non-admissibility of a wife as a witness against her husband never applied to a native polygamous marriage. On the same principle, communications made by a husband to his wife by native custom have been held not privileged.[19] Similarly in Nyasaland, where section 78 of the Courts Ordinance 1921 provided that the wife of a person charged shall not be called as a witness except upon the application of her husband; Johnson, J., notwithstanding the provision held in *R v Ziyaya*[20] that "wife" in the context is wife by Christian rites only. Also, in *R v Sikisi*,[21] a husband killed his sister-in-law while he was quarrelling with his wife, whom he had married under customary law. It was held that the wife was a competent witness for the prosecution. Thus we see that all along the rule as to the privilege applies only to wives of monogamous marriages, thereby, in this connection, reducing the status of spouses married under customary law to that of unmarried persons under English law.

The divergent standards applied in rules of evidence extend also to some aspects of criminal liability by spouses in some territories. In English-speaking African countries there is generally a fairly well-accepted principle that penal codes must be interpreted in accordance with English law, subject to the rule laid down in *Wallace Johnson v R*.[22] But where the terms of the local penal code are clear and unambiguous, "they must be construed free from any glosses or interpolations derived from English case based on English law."[23] Since customary law marriage is unknown to English law, "spouses" would, in effect, in the absence of any contrary provision of a local penal code, mean spouses of a Christian marriage only.

However, in a Tanganyikan case of *Laila Jhina Mawji and anor. v. R*,[24] the Privy Council, in disagreement with the Court of Appeal for

Eastern Africa, held that in the absence of a clear provision to the contrary by the local penal code the definition of "conspiracy" in the penal code must be interpreted subject to the English rule that a husband and wife alone cannot be convicted of conspiracy with each other, and that in Tanganyika this rule applied to the spouses of any marriage recognized as valid under the local law.

But in Nigeria, s.34 of the Criminal Code Law exempted only spouses of a Christian marriage from the crime of conspiracy. The section provides as follows:

> A husband and wife of a Christian marriage are not criminally responsible for a conspiracy between themselves alone.

The same Nigerian Code Law, with regard to the offenses of *accessory after the facts, compulsion of husband, and liability of husband and wife for offenses committed by either with respect to the other's property,* came out clearly in favor of Christian or statutory marriage. Section 10 provides as follows:

> A wife does not become an accessory after the fact to an offence of which her husband is guilty by receiving or assisting him in order to enable him to escape punishment; nor by receiving or assisting in her husband's presence and by his authority, another person who is guilty of an offence in the commission of which her husband has taken part, in order to enable that other person to escape punishment; nor does a husband become accessory after the fact to an offence of which his wife is guilty by receiving or assisting her in order to enable her to escape punishment.

In this section the terms "wife" and "husband" mean, respectively, the wife and husband of a Christian marriage."[25] The definition of "Christian Marriage" in section 1 of the Code completely excludes customary law marriage. It reiterated the definition in *Hyde v Hyde*[26] as follows:

> "Christian marriage" means a marriage which is recognized by the law of the place where it is contracted as the voluntary union of life of one man and one woman to the exclusion of all others.

Section 33 provides that
"A married woman is not free from criminal responsibility for doing or omitting to do an act merely because the act or omission takes place in the presence of her husband."

But a wife of a Christian marriage is not criminally responsible for doing or omitting to do an act which she is actually compelled by her husband to do or omit to do, and which is done or omitted to be done in his presence, except in the case of an act or omission which would constitute an offense punishable with death, or an offense involving grievous harm to the person of another, or an intention to cause such harm, which case the presence of her husband is immaterial. Again in this section, the express exemption of a wife of a Christian marriage would exclude a wife of a customary law marriage. Similarly, section 36 of the same Code also provides that

> When a husband and wife *of a Christian marriage*[27] are living together, neither of them incurs any criminal responsibility for doing or omitting to do any act with respect to the property of the other, except in the case of an act or omission of which an intention to injure or defraud some other person is an element, and except in the case of an act done by either of them when leaving or deserting, or when about to leave or desert, the other.

Subject to the foregoing provisions, a husband and wife are each of them criminally responsible for any act done by him or her with respect to the property of the other, which would be an offense if they were not husband and wife, and to the same extent as if they were not husband and wife.

But in the case of a Christian marriage, neither of them can institute criminal proceedings against the other while they are living together.

In this section the term "property" used with respect to a wife means her separate property.

The above examples undoubtedly show that both by case law and statute law the status of a wife of a marriage under the received English law is superior to that of a wife under customary law marriage. No true attempts have been made to unify the two systems and solve the problem of the double standards now being applied.

A fundamental aspect of the conflict and confusion of the dual system in marriage law in Africa is that every marriage, whether customary or statutory, starts off with performances under customary law. Even where a man marries only one wife, the problem posed is: Does a court's dissolution of the statutory form of marriage end the marriage entirely? Or do the customary performances and ceremonies bind him to accept the divorced woman as still as his wife, under customary law?

One could go on indefinitely to point out the anomalies of legal pluralism in English-speaking Africa, not only in the areas thus far mentioned, but in other branches of law, like inheritance, succession, and the law of contract. Both the internal and external conflicts are compounded the more as the States advance in the modernization process without a radical change in the law.

Those favoring the evolutionary process believe that through adaptation of the received law, social, economic, and political changes in Africa can be effectively achieved to suit the Africans. These seem to be impressed by the manual skill with which the jurists and the politicians of 19th Century Western Europe adapted inherited legal concepts to serve the rapid social changes and demands of their time during the Industrial Revolution. We agree that received legal concepts can be adapted to suit social change or bring about evolutionary changes in society. This is, however, possible only in a society whose culture and value systems are the same or similar to those of the country which imports the law.

The same is also possible even in a revolutionary situation, where the countries concerned have similar or identical cultural and value systems, as in the case of the Industrial Revolution of Western Europe. But it must be noted that the Industrial Revolution of 19th Century Western Europe was a revolution from a feudal to a bourgeois society. Such a revolution involved only a change in personnel, not in principle. The bourgeoisie that overthrew the feudal lords and took over power were guided by the same oligarchic principles and aims which governed those they overthrew. They aimed at the protection of private property, for free individual enterprise, a monopoly of means of production, and the accumulation of private capital at the expense of human labor.

Both classes had the same, or at least similar economic and cultural outlooks. The difference was, that while the feudal lords were satisfied with concentrating the means of production in the hands of a few lords, the bourgeoisie were concerned with broadening the ranks of those, like themselves who were to control the means of production, while the masses, in either case, remained only the tools of production—"hands."

Where a social and economic revolution is concerned mainly with turning over the means of production to the masses in order to set up a government of the prolateriat, as in the Soviet Union, alien laws not the production of the same revolutionary situation will serve no useful purpose. The existing legal system of the bourgeoisie will not help either. It is even more true when there is a great deal of difference in the cultural background and value systems of the receiving country and the country from where the law is imported.

Modernizing the Law

With the sort of legal inheritance which exists in English-speaking Africa, the legal problems which slow down or impede social economic and political advancement in the States are monumental. The new States have first to determine the political structure which is popular, and by which they will in future be governed. Generally, each of the colonial territories acquired a Constitution which determines its political future through an Independence Act passed by the United Kingdom Parliament at Westminster. The Constitutional Order in Council, made by the Queen in London, which forms the basic law, sets out a State's Constitution and the procedure for its amendment to guide and direct the State's political future.

The effect is that the Constitution, the laws, and the authority of the institutions of government are set out in an alien enactment, which very often do not reflect the wishes of the people. Few countries (Nkrumah's Ghana, Tanzania) have tried to remedy the situation, and later the state of affairs, by making new Constitutions whose authority and validity do not depend on enactments of Westminster. Several others have stuck to the old and foreign-enacted Constitutions. The changes made are few, and even those countries like Nigeria who have adopted new Constitutions by reverting to a republican system of government, have not entirely succeeded in shaking off the relics of the British political, economic, and value systems in their basic law.

To reject any alien, and particularly Anglosaxon influence on its law, the modern English-speaking African State will begin with the alteration of the Constitution to make it the basic law of the people, having its authority and validity not from an alien source, but from the society itself. As the source of legal power, the Constitution must be in accord with political and socioeconomic desires and aspirations of the people. It must provide the procedural rules and the guiding principles for the enactment and enforcement of laws that will help to achieve the desired end.

The next step will be to effect a change in the system and the hierarchy of the courts, particularly the appellate structure. Until very recently the Board of the Judicial Committee of the Privy Council was the traditional final court of appeal for both the dependent and the independent States within the African countries and territories of the British Commonwealth. Countries like Ghana, Tanzania, and Nigeria, and those other countries who have changed from monarchies to republics within the Commonwealth, have abolished the right of appeal to the Privy Council. This, however, has had no effect generally on the nature of the law itself and its administration, due to the British doctrine of binding precedent. The change was dictated more by political considerations and the national pride that followed in the wake of independence. The result is that laws in those countries are no more republican and African today than they were in monarchical, British yesterday. The old decisions of the Privy Council still remain part of the law which is binding, or have very strong persuasive effect on the courts.

The third point is the received English law. We have already noted the dates and mode of reception of the English Statutes of general application in these countries during the colonial period. The received laws, which are mostly feudal laws of England, to date form the great bulk of the law in most, if not all modern African States. There have been trends, however, seeking to replace the received statutes by local enactments, but the reasons have no bearing on a desire to revolutionize the law or to bring legal autochtony to the States concerned.

The attempt to replace the received statutes with locally enacted Acts[28] does not even show a strong trend toward modernization of the law. It has been quite negative in its approach, being concerned more with solving the problem of uncertainty. The general mode of reception does not always make clear which statutes are of "general application" in England and therefore applicable. To be perfectly sure which statute is applicable and which is not will involve the almost impossible task of courts searching through the English statute books, from the date the country got its first local legislature back to the 13th Century,[29] to find the statutes which might have been received and are still applicable today in the country concerned.

The tendency, as we have seen in the case of Western Nigeria, is to bring out a reprint of a catalogue of the statutes accepted as applicable laws through local enactments. The clarity obtained by this method does not go to state how far an accepted statute of general application would apply in the receiving country. Nor do the local statutes make it clear how to modify an applicable statute to make it suitable for application in local circumstance to reflect the spirit and desires of a nation that is looking for rapid modernization. The local statutes thus far used in this way to solve the problem of uncertainty in the applicable laws, have either repealed a statute of general application or a section of it as no longer applicable, with no further directives given. The interpretation of that which remains applicable is still a matter for the courts, which remain a pattern of the English system and follow the doctrine of binding precedent.

The position of the received common law and the doctrines of equity have remained the same. No attempt has been made, to our knowledge, to change it. What is more, the rules and principles of English common law are reflected in local statute law through the interpretation of the courts. As discussed above, the legal systems in English-speaking Africa are based on the English legal system. The latter (and this is followed by the former) is based on the "doctrine of binding precedent," with its overriding importance and binding authority placed in earlier decisions of the courts on the true meaning of the material contents of the law. With their English legal training and orientation, the African judges have clung tenaciously to this doctrine, sometimes to the point of absurdity.

For example, in English-speaking West Africa, the lawyers cite in court, and the judges to this day, consult English authorities both recent and old to determine what to them is the correct interpretation of the words, both of the received English statutes of general application, and of locally enacted Acts of Parliament. In East Africa the same method is applicable. Both the bar and the bench refer to decisions by Indian Courts, which are very much influenced by English decisions, to interpret the Contract Act adopted from India, another English-speaking country. Sometimes decisions of the courts in other Commonwealth countries, like Canada and Australia, are referred to, and decisions based on them, or their persuasive authority, utilized to interpret local statutes.

Recent attempts to break away from the old and sometimes outmoded decisions of the English courts have often ended up as mere political stunts. For example, the Ghanaian Courts Act, 1960, and other legislation associated with it, expanded the sphere of received English Common Law to include *assimilated rules of customary law.* Thus far it has not been easy to determine the assimilated rules, and English Common Law still bestrides the Ghanaian Courts' decisions. The same Act provides that no decision of foreign courts should be binding on the courts of Ghana. The modernizing effect of such enactments on Ghanaian law is yet to be seen. On becoming a republic, Ghana, like other republican States in English-speaking Africa, retained the old laws. These are products of the English legal system and English court decisions, and the principles that laid down in them are reflected in every decision of the local courts. In effect, while an attempt is being made to stop the influence of recent alien laws, linkage is still maintained through the "ghost" of the old received common law, which is very much alive in court decisions through the doctrine of binding precedent.

Local legislation is potentially powerful to revolutionize the law and to make it a superstructure on the economic base. It could be a formidable tool in the hands of African legislators to usher in a new political ideology and a rephasing of the people's socioeconomic life. But in English-speaking Africa it has not been fully utilized in a positive sense. The main contributory factors are the conservatism of the bench and the bar, due to their English legal training and background. Also, on the economic phase, the dualism of the economic base and the existing plurality of law seem to encourage complacency.

The success or failure of local legislation in English-speaking Africa to bring an adequate conception of law to socioeconomic and political advancement in tune with the yearnings of the generality of the people, would depend on two main factors. First, the final result of the power struggle now going on in the States, second, to what extent legislation is used for the general weal and the common aspirations of the people.

Hitherto there has been a dichotomy in the political arena. The more conservative elements, to whom power was handed on the retreat of imperialism, tend to maintain the *status quo ante* by retaining legal systems which continue to reflect English legal philosophy, political, and cultural value systems, and capitalist economy. One can see this tendency by looking at the negative approach to law reform which governments adopt. The more progressive elements now growing in number, on the other hand, wish to have legal systems which may accurately reflect African traditional cultures and beliefs and at the same time keep pace with the current aspirations of the people and the drive to political and socio-economic advancement and modernization of the States.

The more radical elements are averse to continuing to sustain both alien and indigenous institutions and social and economic relationships which are felt to have outlived their usefulness and positively impede rapid economic and ideological transformation of the society. The history and purposes of legal reform and unification in countries like Tanzania and Nkrumah's Ghana, where the government is or has at one stage or another been directed by radical and progressive leadership, illustrate these points very well.[30]

Where the radicals control the government, they go in for law reforms in areas where socioeconomic conditions demand radical change and immediate action. They seize the opportunity presented by the general need for rapid modern development to revolutionize the law to meet the common aspirations current among the people.

There is, however, one factor which militates against efforts of African radical governments toward social transformation through law. It is the doctrine of binding precedent. As with the governments of the less progressive and very conservative elements, the doctrine of binding precedent retains its English background, history, legal purpose, and methods with all governments in English-speaking Africa, because of the court system. Support of the notion that judges are merely there to discover and declare the law is a clog in the wheels of legal development in Africa. It offers little scope for more dynamic and progressive development of the law, even with the most radical government.[31]

A New Legal Philosophy For English-speaking Africa

A contemporary legal philosophy for Africa cannot afford to adopt too orthodox and general a notion of law. Africa's historical data, and the imperatives of modern development, call for a conception of law that is both meaningful and unique to Africa. If rapid political, economic, and social progress of the people is to go forward, the link with orthodox and too conservative notions of law must be broken.

Thus far, laws in Africa and the society are not in full harmony. The idea of obtaining obedience through coercion is failing and will continue to fail, until triumph of the goals and the social purpose of the masses over the arbitrariness of the ruling minority, which has been imposed on the people through colonial and neo-colonial laws.

With the cultural, political, and economic revolutions either going on now in some of the States, or about to begin in others, one of the main tasks is to develop a new social awareness of law in a way that will enhance its popularity, prestige, and authority. Legality must have significance to the socioeconomic life of the people. Without close interconnection between the people, their culture, their political and economic outlook and aspirations on the one hand, and law and order and legality, on the other, legal obedience will cease to be a dutiful submission to authority. Compulsion or force will continue to be a very strong and necessary feature of law, with the resultant civil commotions and political instability.

Justice would lose its ethical or moral meaning, and sink to a mere charitable treatment of the enslaved and the oppressed by those in power, without the involvement of the people in designing their legal system. The law-giver will continue to stand above the law which he manipulates to entrench himself and fortify his position. He will not be concerned with justice and legality, in their true sense except to use these as slogans for keeping faith with the people.

Law in Africa must be conceived of and evaluated in terms of its social purpose, function, and the value system. the spirit of the time, the tempo of socioeconomic and political development in the new States, and above all, the greatest happiness of the masses, should be the main guiding principles underlying legal development.

The great educational role of law should not be minimized in the process. For law in Africa to play a great educational role it must be clear to the people and be within the reach of their understanding. The present esoteric style, archaic, and sometimes obscure terminology used by the courts and other legal functionaries in the administration of law, make the law something that is remote and sometimes beyond the comprehension of the generality of the people. Expressions that are quite incomprehensible cannot serve as an adequate medium of imparting knowledge. Their use in legal administration enshrouds law with a kind of mysticism which hinders widespread legal awareness among the people. It promotes apathy to law among the citizens generally, and often results in legal maladministration due to ignorance and misinterpretation of the law, even by law enforcement agencies themselves.

No major changes can be made or sustained in political and social arrangements which will modernize Africa and promote rapid economic development within a framework answering to the yearnings of the people, if legal development remains based on the colonial and neo-colonial legal systems. It must also be admitted that to fall back on the traditional system of customary law cannot adequately cope with the tempo and the imperatives of quick social, economic, and political changes.

New laws, based on a new legal philosophy which will explain Africa's historical past, as well as act as a future guide to modern governments of the people, are needed. Much of the unrest in Africa today is due to political and socioeconomic arrangements which do not reflect the wishes and desires of a people in a hurry for modern economic and political advancement. There is a general desire by the masses to break away from the rigid capitalist economy of the West and move toward socialism. One of the major problems is definition of the content of the type of socialism to be followed. Another, involves the ways and means of arriving at this desired goal, and how soon, or how late. Thus, in the process of legal development there should be, increasingly, closer integration of laws made by the State with the social yearnings of the people, and their outlook on life.

Law in Africa should be expressive of the social purpose of the people. It follows that the system, the procedure, and the content of the law, particularly of the received law as it now stands, call for radical change that will forward that social purpose. As Dr. Kwame Nkrumah of Ghana once said: "Law to be effective must represent the will of the people and be so designed and administered as to forward the social purpose of the State."[32]

Law becomes an instrument of oppression and suppression, once it is converted into a reactionary force through abstract conceptualization. Abstract concepts cloak law with a mysterious universal application, without regard to the economic and social conditions, as well as the value system prevalent in the country in which it is being applied. "The law should be the legal expression of the political economic and social conditions of the people and of their aims of progress."[33] It is in this way that legal responsibility and respect for law by the people can be promoted, and social harmony assured.

To conclude our analysis, therefore, we would like to subscribe to the postulate that the essence of law lies outside the law itself. It is to be found in the people, their ways of life, the value system, and their common aspirations. The socioeconomic and political life and outlook of the people should provide the base for the superstructure, which is law.

Notes to Chapter 10

1. Confined to cases where only natives are parties; in mixed cases, i. e., cases between a non-native and natives, English law was preferable.
2. Ross, E. A., *Social Control*, Borgatta, and Mayer ed. (1959) pp. 8 and 20; also, pp. 28-31.
3. Section 14. Later, for Nigeria the operative date was extended to January 1900.
4. *Ibid.*, section 19. See also Chap. 1.
5. (Emphasis added.) "All native laws and customs" in the context is presumed to include Islamic law. (See Anderson, J. N. D., *Islamic Law in Africa*, p. 228, note 1.) See further, Sierra Leone, Court Ordinance Cap. 7 s.38; Ghana before July 1960, Court Ordinance Cap. 4 s.87(1); Kenya, Colony Order in Council (1921) Art. 7; Tanganyika, Order in Council (1910) Art. 24; Uganda, Order in Council (1902) Art. 20; Sudan, Civil Justice Ordinance s.5; Somali Republic, The Constitution, Art. 43; Northern Rhodesia (now Zambia) N. R. O.–inc. (1924) Art. 36; Southern Rhodesia (Ian Smith's Rhodesia) S. R. O.–in C 1898 Art. 50. There are similar provisions in the Nyasaland O in C s.12(a), in Bechuanaland (Botswana) General Administration O in C 1891 s.4, and Swaziland, Order in Council 1903, as Amended s.5, some of which go even further in subjecting customary law to the exercise of "Her Majesty's Power and Jurisdiction."
6. See Friedmann, *Law in a Changing Society* (1959), p. 72.
7. In the Colony of Lagos, Nigeria, Crown ownership is traceable to the Treaty of Cession of 1861 between the British Government and King Docemo of Lagos. Section 1 of the Treaty reads as follows: "I, Docemo, do, with the consent and advice of my council, give, transfer and by these present grant and confer unto the Queen of Great Britain, her heirs and successors for ever, the Port and Island of Lagos, with all the rights, profits, territories and appurtenances whatsoever, thereunto belonging freely, fully, entirely and absolutely." In Lagos, the four white cap chiefs who were not privy to the Treaty were looked upon as the "owners" of Lagos land, which they held in trust for their people. King Docemo had, therefore, only his political sovereignty to transfer, *not* ownership of Lagos land.
8. See *Amodu Tijani v Secretary, Southern Nigeria* (1921) A. C. 399 where the Privy Council held that both sovereignty and land passed to the Crown under the treaty. Compare, however, per Viscount Haldane, *ibid* (1921) A. C. 399, p. 407.
9. Nigeria. The Public Lands Acquisition Ordinance 1903.
10. See the Ikoyi Lands Ordinance 1908. However, compare The Crown Grants (Township of Lagos) Ordinance No. 18 of 1947, and see also Nos. 19, 20 and 21, ordinances of the same year, where attempts were made to subject such absolute ownership of land granted to individuals to all incidents of customary tenure.
11. In Northern Nigeria, for example, the Emirs and other rulers, like their counterparts in Southern Nigeria, had no proprietary right in the lands they were said to have transfered to the Royal Niger Company between 1885 and 1890. They were mere trustees of the land on behalf of their local communities.
12. See, for instance, Nigeria: Niger Lands Transfer Ordinance 1916, which on the revocation of the Charter of the Royal Niger Company and the establishment of the Protectorate of Northern Nigeria, vested all lands, rights and easements of the company with a few exceptions on the British Crown through Lugard the High Commissioner. Later, the mineral rights of the company were bought off by the then colonial government for £865,000, with a royalty of 50% in addition to the agreed cost reserved for the company and its successors. In 1951 the U. A. C., as the successor of the Royal Niger Company, was paid the lump sum of £1,000,000 in final settlement of its royalty rights.
13. So far, natives of Northern Nigeria do not hold under the certificate of occupancy, but other citizens of Nigeria of Southern origin residing in the North do.

*Now by the *Land Use Decree No. 6 of 1978* which became effective from 29th March 1978, all Land in each State of the Federation are vested in the Military Governor of that State to be held "in trust and administered for the use and Common benefit of all Nigerians" (Section 1). It is however too early to determine the effectiveness of the Decree.

14. *Hyde v Hyde* (1866), L. R. 1 P&D 130, p. 133.
15. (Emphasis added.)
16. (1963) E. A. 188.
17. (1932) 5 U. L. R. 4. (Emphasis added.)
18. (1929) 3 Nys L. R. 34.
19. *R v Amkeyo* (1917) 7 E. A. R. L. R. 14.
20. (1935) High Court (Cr.) case No. 134; 4 Nys L. R. 54.
21. (1936) 4 Nys. L. R. 73.
22. (1940) A. C. 231.
23. Per Conroy, C. J. *in R v Zulu* (1961) R and N 645 (Northern Rhodesia); also *R v Singh* (1947) 14 E. A. C. A. 111 (Kenya).
24. (1957) A. C. 126; (1956) 23 E. A. C. A. 609; also (1957) 2 W. L. R. 277.
25. (Emphasis added.)
26. (1886) L. R. 1 P. D. 130.
27. (Emphasis added.)
28. See again Western Nigeria, Law of England (Application) Law Cap. 60. In East Africa, received Indian Law is being replaced and reenacted. E. g., The Tanganyika Law of Contract Ordinance, English Law of Contract, is adopted en bloc to replace the colonially inherited Contract Act.
29. This was the period when the Bill of Rights came into existence and the British King gave up ruling by arbitrary proclamations.
30. We have already mentioned the attempt to assimilate customary law in Ghana; and the attempt to break the link between alien laws and Ghanaian law which the doctrine of binding precedent made imperative. In Tanzania, the *Tanganyikan Unification of Customary Law Project* is designed to achieve uniformity in personal customary laws; also, the restatement of customary law which has a quasi-legislative effect seeks to eliminate any feature of customary law, which is regarded as offending modern notions, e. g., the abolition of bride price and parental consent for the marriage of girls who have reached 21 years of age. See further, The Administration of Lands Act, 1962, which tried to control the use of land in Ghana, laying emphasis on the factor of public control of the socialist type. *Cf.,* Land consolidation in Kenya, which abolished the traditional tenure system and replaced it with registered individual title on the English model.
31. See again, Chap. 2, especially The Technique of the Courts in interpreting Enacted Laws.
32. *Journal of African Law* (1962) Vol. 6, No. 2, pp. 103-104. We would like to stress here that the "State" in this connection should not be a mere abstraction, but something which means the people as a collective body.
33. *Ibid.,* pp. 107-108.

Select Bibliography

1. Allen, C.K. *Law in the Making.* London: Oxford University Press, 1946.
2. Allot, A.N. *Judicial and Legal Systems in Africa.* London: Butterworths, 1962.
3. Anderson, J.N.D. *Changing Law in Developing Countries.* London: Allen and Unwin, 1963.
4. Aristotle. *Ethica Nicomachea.* (Trans. Sir D. Ross) Oxford: Oxford University Press.
5. Aristotle. *The Politics.* Book1 (Transl. Benjamin Jowett) Oxford: Oxford University Press.
6. Austin, J. *The Province of Jurisprudence Determined.* London: John Murray, Ltd., 1932.
7. Bryce, Lord James. *Studies in History and Jurisprudence.* London: Oxford University Press, 1901.
8. Cardozo, Benjamin Nathan. *The Nature of Judicial Process.* New Haven: Yale University Press, 1922.
9. d'Entreves, A.P. *Natural Law.* London: Hutchinson and Co. (Publishers), Ltd., 1963.
10. Diamond, A.S. *Primitive Law.* London: Watts and Co. Publishers, 1935.
11. Dias, R.W.N. and Hughes, G.B.J. *Jurisprudence.* London: Butterworth and Co., Ltd., 1957.
12. Dicey, A.V. *Law and Public Opinion in England During the Nineteenth Century.* London: Macmillan, 1926.
13. Duguit, M. *Manual.* (Transl. Allen in *Legal Duties*). London: Oxford University Press, 1931.
14. Duguit, M. 'The Law and the State' 31 *Harvard Law Review,* 1917.
15. Ehrlich, Eugene. *Fundamental Principles of the Sociology of Law.* (Transl. Moll, W.L.) Cambridge (Mass): Harvard University Press, 1936.
16. Elias, T.O. *Law in a Developing Society.* Ibadan: Ibadan University Press, 1969.
17. Elias, T.O. *The Nature of African Customary Law.* Manchester: Manchester University Press, 1962.
18. Engels, Frederick. *Socialism Utopian and Scientific.* (Transl. Edward Aveling) New York: International Publishers, 1892. (Reprint 1935).
19. Frank, Jerome. *Law and the Modern Mind.* New York: Coward-McCann; London: Stevens, 1930.

20. Friedmann, W. *Law in a Changing Society.* London: Stevens and Sons, Ltd., 1959.

21. Friedmann, W. *Law and Social Change in Contemporary Britain.* London: Stevens, 1951.

22. Gray, J.C. *The Nature And Source of the Law.* New York: Columbia University Press, 1921.

23. Grotius, Hugo. *On the Right of War and Peace:* Book I. (Transl. William Whewell) London: John and Parker, 1853.

24. Hartland, E.S. *Primitive Law.* London: Methuen, 1924.

25. Hobbes, Thomas. *The Leviathan.* Oxford: Oxford University Press, 1957. See also a reprint from the edition of 1651. London: Oxford University Press, 1909.

26. Holland, T.E. *Jurisprudence.* Oxford: Clarendon Press, 1916.

27. Holmes, Oliver Wendell. *The Common Law.* Boston: Little Brown and Co., 1923.

28. Holmes, Oliver Wendell. 'The Path of the Law'. 10 *Harvard Law Review,* 1897.

29. Ihering, Rudolf Von. *Law as a Means to an End.* (Transl. Isaac Husik). Boston: Boston Book, 1913.

30. Jolowicz, H.F. *Lectures on Jurisprudence.* London: The Athlone Press, 1963.

31. Kelsen, Hans. *General Theory of Law and State.* (Transl. Wedberg). London: Kegan Paul, 1946.

32. Llewellyn, K. *The Bramble Bush.* New York: Oceana Publications, 1960.

33. Lloyd, Dennis. *Introduction to Jurisprudence.* London: Stevens and Sons, 1959.

34. Main, Sir Henry. *Ancient Law.* London: John Murray, 1920.

35. Main, Sir Henry. *Early History of Institutions.* London: John Murray, 1880.

36. Marx and Engels. *The German Ideology.* Moscow: Progress Publishers, 1964.

37. Malinowski, B. *Crime and Custom in Savage Society.* London: Kegan Paul, 1926.

38. Meek, C.K. *A Sudanese Kingdom.* London: Kegan Paul, 1931.

39. Olivecrona, K. *Law as Fact.* 2nd ed. London: Stevens and Sons, 1971.

40. Paton, G.W. *A Text Book of Jurisprudence.* Oxford: Oxford University Press, 1951.

41. Pollock, Sir F. *First Book of Jurisprudence.* London: Macmillan, 1929.

42. Pound, Roscoe. *My Philosophy of Law.* West Publishing Co., 1941.

43. Rousseau, Jean Jacques. *The Social Contract.* (Transl. G.D.H. Cole N⁰ 660A, Everymans Library. Reprint by Permission of E.P. Dutton and Co. Inc.) Philadelphia: Philadelphia University Press.

44. Salmond, Sir John. *Jurisprudence.* (8th ed. by Manning C.A.W.) London: Sweet and Maxwell, Ltd.

45. Savigny, Von. F.C. *Of the Vocation of Our Age For Legislation and Jurisprudence.* (Transl. by Abraham Hayward). London: Little Wood and Co., 1831.

46. Savigny, Von F.C. *System of Modern Roman Law.* (Transl. by W. Holloway). London: Little Wood and Co., 1867.

47. Schapera, I. *A Hand Book of Tswana Law and Custom.* London: International Institute of African Language and Culture, 1955.

48. Stone, J. *The Province and Function of Law.* Sydney: Maitland Publication, 1961.

49. Stone, J. *Human Law and Human Justice.* London: Stevens and Sons, Ltd., 1964.

Index